Seven voices
One dream

Mary Ann Cahill

Betty, Vi, Mary White, Marian
Mary Ann K, Mary Ann Cahill, Edwina

La Leche League International
Schaumburg, Illinois

First Edition, August 2001

© 2001 La Leche League International, Inc.

All Rights Reserved
Printed in the United States of America

Edited by Judy Torgus
Assisted by Deirdre O'Neal

Book and Cover Design, Digital Concepts LLC
Cover photos, David Arendt and Rae Cassin

ISBN 0-912500-87-5
Library of Congress Card Number 2001091627

La Leche League International
1400 N. Meacham Road
Schaumburg, Illinois   60173-4840 USA
www.lalecheleague.org

Contents

Foreword

Eight years ago Mary Ann Cahill began a quest. Armed with an unreliable tape recorder and a collection of questions, she set off to meet with each of the Founders of La Leche League International. Though the story of LLL has been told and re-told, Mary Ann realized that each of the Founders had a unique perspective on the events that had shaped and shaken the organization over the years. She felt the time was right to get the story straight from the Founders themselves. Of course, once the Founders started talking about subjects dear to their hearts, breastfeeding, mothering, and La Leche League, Mary Ann found herself with quite a daunting collection of interview tapes. Hundreds of hours filled with recollections, stories, memories, and history.

How would these tapes ever become a book? Mary Ann felt that the only way to keep the voices of the seven Founders accurate was to transcribe the tapes herself. Once the transcribing was done, the interviews needed to be edited and compiled.

At this point, Deirdre O'Neal, a writer and journalist who was a close friend of Mary Ann's daughter, Liz, made an off-hand comment that someone should write a book about La Leche League's Founders. Liz replied that her mother was in the process of doing just that. Deirdre offered to help, and worked with Mary Ann on the project for almost two years.

Once the preliminary work was completed the manuscript was reviewed by the Founders. This led to some interesting comments as each discovered things they hadn't known before or questioned one another's recollection of an event. In the end they all agreed the book would be much better if they just had a little more time to work on it!

This book is a fascinating look into an organization that has made a difference in the lives of countless women around the world. More than 45 years after they began, these seven special women still share one dream, and continue to work together toward their goal of helping mothers enjoy breastfeeding their babies.

La Leche League has been part of my life for most of my life. I began attending LLL meetings before my oldest son was born in 1959, when LLL was just three years old. Over the years I have been involved in various aspects of the organization's development. Working with Mary Ann and Deirdre, and the other Founders, on this book brought back many memories. I, too, learned some things I hadn't known before!

This book is not only a tribute to the Founders, but to all who have contributed to the fulfillment of their dream—that mothers everywhere would be able to find the information and support they need to give their babies the best start in life by breastfeeding them!

Judy Torgus
Publications Director, La Leche League International
June, 2001

Introduction

In 1956, throughout most of the USA, the practice of bottle-feeding babies was firmly entrenched. Breastfeeding was considered a poor second, a choice that was out of step with modern lifestyles and worse yet, an invitation to trouble. The would-be nursing mother attracted an avalanche of advice, most of it critical. "Your milk is too rich." "It's not rich enough." "Nursing a baby is such a 'cow' thing!" And perhaps the most blunt of all, "The best time to stop nursing is before you start!"

New advances in science had captivated people's imagination, and the medical profession was enjoying tremendous prestige at the time. It was hardly surprising that two areas that had long been the province of women, namely childbirth and infant feeding, had been shifted under the helm of the medical profession. In the course of a generation, the hospital had become the setting for giving birth. What was lost in the shuffle and what few seemed to notice was the fact that the most important players, the mothers, fathers, and babies, were routinely separated, even isolated, from each other.

Babies were kept in the central nursery and brought to their mothers for feedings on a four-hour schedule during the day. At night, the nursery staff fed the babies, formula of course, on the assumption that the mothers needed to rest and shouldn't be disturbed. And if a baby didn't take the breast well at a particular feeding, perhaps sleeping the whole time in his adoring mother's arms, and woke up crying on his return to the nursery, the nursing staff would take pity on the hungry little tyke and give him a bottle. As it was, the first feeding had almost certainly been postponed 12 to 24 hours, with the baby handed over to the nursery nurses for "observation." It all seemed quite proper, since the mother couldn't be expected to do anything other than look at her baby following a medicated labor and delivery. First-time mothers, especially, had to cope with the usual lack of confidence in their new role as well as a sore bottom from the episiotomy that was pretty much standard hospital birthing procedure. Why would any mother want to breastfeed and be plagued with sore nipples as well?

Once home, it was common for the baby to seem hungry all the time and want to nurse continuously. For the mother, this was a sure sign that something was wrong. Babies should go four hours between feedings; all the child care books said so.

Here again, new theories had taken over the feeding and handling of the baby, with a strict schedule governing a mother and baby's day. Previously, the influential pediatrician, Dr. Emmett Holt, had recommended that babies be "trained" to a schedule from the first week of life. Of course this included breastfed infants. Kissing the baby was frowned upon, as was handling the baby in general. By the 1940s and 50s, in place of cuddling her baby, a mother was kept busy sterilizing things—bottles, rubber nipples—and mixing up a concoction of syrup and cow's milk with other ingredients that had been dutifully prescribed by the doctor to replace her milk. Newly designated authorities quickly claimed that artificial infant foods performed as well as mother's own milk, and it would take another 20 years to prove them wrong. In the meantime, the production and sale of artificial infant feeding products had become a booming business, and bottles and bottle-feeding permeated the culture. As for the health sciences, medical students received extensive training in prescribing infant formula and little or no information on breast-feeding.

But seven young mothers wanted more for their babies than science had to offer. In their hearts, they knew that breastfeeding their babies would give their little ones the very best start in life. And they shared a dream. Let me tell you their story.

Chapter 1—THE WAY WE WERE

There was scant reason to think that anything momentous was about to happen. Neither the time nor the place lent itself to such an expectation. The year was 1956, a period of sanguine prosperity in the United States, when the population as a whole, and especially young families, were happily immersed in the rituals of everyday life. This phenomenon was no more apparent than in Franklin Park, Illinois USA, where the story of La Leche League began.

Prior to the late 1940s, Franklin Park had been a pleasant if decidedly sleepy little town along the Chicago and Milwaukee Railroad west of the city of Chicago. With the end of World War II, unprecedented numbers of young people married and started families, which in turn unleashed a pent-up demand for housing. Developers, seizing the moment, scurried to the outskirts of the nearby small towns and, harvesting the top layer of rich farmland, laid down rows of houses in its stead for first-time buyers. To young couples with high hopes and low budgets, the small, one-story brick homes were affordable and beautiful.

Among the new families were the Tompsons. Clement "Tommy" Tompson, a gracious man with an inventive turn of mind, and his wife, Marian, a petite young woman with warm brown hair, lived on Addison Street in the new part of town with their four young daughters.

A few blocks to the south on Calwagner across from the high school lived another young family, the Cahills—Chuck, Mary Ann, and their brood of five. Like many another homeowner at the time, Chuck was a do-it-yourselfer who enjoyed the challenge of bumping out roof dormers and finishing the enlarged space to accommodate a growing family.

Around the bend on Lonnquist Drive were the Wagners: Bob, friendly and outgoing, Betty, his wife, who was pregnant at the time, and their four children. Their oldest, Gail, was a mature eighth grader, older than most of the other youngsters in the neighborhood. On summer evenings when the dads were home and the older children were busy at play, Betty and Mary Ann would set out for a leisurely walk, each with the littlest one in a stroller. It was a welcome opportunity for the two young mothers to talk. Mary Ann, the one with the red tones in her hair, was drawn to new ideas and loved the mother-to-mother discussions they generated. Betty, slim with thick, dark hair, kept her feet firmly planted on the ground. Practical by nature, she was also decisive. Her quick, hearty laugh made her especially good company to be with. Before they knew it, the streetlights went on and it was time to call the children in for bedtime.

Over on Rose Street in the older section of town where large, mature trees shaded front lawns, Edwina and John Froehlich and their two boys occupied a gray-sided house with a good sized living room that opened onto an equally spacious dining room, perfect for large gatherings. John had a love for sports and poetry, the former as a spectator and the latter as a serious practitioner. Edwina, tall and slender with sparkling blue eyes, a bright smile, and dark curly hair, brought immense enthusiasm to whatever she set her mind to.

On the other side of the railroad tracks that bisect the town, and directly across from St. Gertrude's Catholic Grade School, sits a two-story frame house set off by an enclosed front porch. In 1956, it sported a red door and was the home of the new doctor in town, Dr. Gregory White, his wife, Mary, and their six children. Trained in family medicine and obstetrics, Dr. White began his practice in 1949 in a storefront on Franklin Avenue, the main street in town. He soon made a reputation for himself. Among childbearing women, opinions were seldom neutral. Some considered him totally outrageous and out of sync with the new techniques of anesthetized childbirth and bottle-feeding, while others were ecstatic to find a doctor who was devoted to supporting a mother in an unmedicated delivery and breastfeeding. Mary White, of quick mind and wit, took it all in stride. Without trying, Mary could even make parenting six children look easy.

Beyond the fact that all these families had young children and most were patients of Dr. White, all were involved in one way or other in St. Gertrude's Roman Catholic Church, either through the women's sodality or a program known as the Christian Family Movement (CFM). CFM served as a training ground for taking the initiative, for looking around one's immediate world and considering needs, and then, in the company of others, doing something positive to make things better. Five or six couples would meet monthly at each other's homes and, following a prepared format, discuss their findings and arrive at a plan of action. The introductory series began with the question, "Who is my neighbor?" It provided the nudge for the members to reach out and discover how small, seemingly inconsequential actions aimed at helping one's neighbor can make a difference, even against strong odds.

Whether or not CFM with its penchant for action spurred the start of La Leche League is probably a moot question. What is known is that it brought people together and built self-confidence. It also legitimized taking a small step, doing what is doable, rather than spending limited time and energy on theorizing about a grand plan. In the 1950s, in matters of infant feeding and child care, small steps were all that could be taken.

Marian Tompson

MAC: *Let's go back in time to 1956. Describe, if you will, the composition of the Tompson family in 1956.*

MT: In 1956 I was a mother at home. We had one car, so I had no way of getting away from home, even if I wanted to! But don't get me wrong—I loved being a mother at home. That was where I wanted to be.

Our first baby, Melanie, was born in February 1950. The next three came along pretty quickly after that. Deborah was born in 1951, Allison in 1952, and Laurel in 1955. So when La Leche League got started in 1956, I had four children, all daughters, and all under the age of seven.

MAC: *Marian, what kinds of childbirth and breastfeeding experiences did you have before La Leche League got started?*

MT: My first three babies were born in the hospital. But I didn't enjoy my experiences in the hospital at all. I was appalled at how indifferent and insensitive the hospital staff was to the mother in labor.

MAC: *Can you give us an example of what you mean by "indifferent and insensitive"?*

MT: Well, I remember with my first baby, the nurses threw a sheet over my head as I lay on the delivery table, and then they kept on talking about their boyfriends and their social activities, almost as if I wasn't there! No one was talking to me. Nobody said, "Isn't this exciting? You're going to have a baby! It won't be long now."

I think the hospital staff was able to get away with that because, in those days, most women in labor were sedated. But I wasn't drugged, so I could see that very little attention was paid to the needs of the woman in labor.

MAC: *Where was Tom when you were in labor with your first baby?*

MT: He was out in the Fathers Waiting Room. He certainly wasn't allowed in the delivery room. In fact, he wasn't allowed in the labor room if another woman's husband was there.

I actually remember saying to Tom, "I don't think that women should be left alone when they are in labor. When our children are grown, I'm going to sit at the bedside of laboring women just so that they will have someone with them when they are in labor."

I guess I didn't think that anything would change over the years. Of course, years later I did get to sit beside friends, and later my own daughters, when they were in labor, and that has been wonderful. So I was able to fulfill that dream, but in a different way than I had imagined back then.

MAC: *Marian, why do you think that you wanted to breastfeed your children when so many other women from our generation seemed content with bottle feeding their babies?*

MT: I remember wanting to breastfeed at least as far back as high school. I don't know why exactly. I guess it just made sense to me. I had seen my aunt breastfeed her children. I don't recall if I ever saw my mother breastfeed.

Of course, the baby books at that time said that it didn't matter if you breast-fed or bottle-fed, the baby could be healthy either way. But I remember saying to Tom, "You know, I want to breastfeed even if it doesn't make any difference nutritionally because I want to have that feeling of closeness with the baby."

MAC: *Did you have any problems getting started with breastfeeding?*

MT: No, I never had any problems getting started at all. All of my babies took to the breast right away. They were all strong nursers who gained weight steadily. So I had no serious problems in that area.

However, with Melanie, my first baby, there was a problem with her spitting up. It probably meant that she took in too much milk, too fast. Nowadays most Leaders would probably recommend that a baby with that problem be nursed more frequently, but for shorter periods of time at each feeding, so that the baby doesn't take in so much milk at one time.

But the doctor that we had at that time suggested that we give Melanie a bottle after she nursed each time. So Melanie had formula as well as mother's milk. Of course, that meant that we had to do that whole sterilization thing.

Sterilizing bottles was a big deal in those days. It turned your kitchen into something resembling a scientist's lab. You had to use tweezers to put the bottle nipples into the boiling water in a pan on the stove, because you couldn't touch anything with your hands. If you touched something, you had to start all over again, because the bottles or the nipples weren't sterile. And often you would be doing this in the middle of the night when you weren't thinking clearly because you were still half asleep. So it was quite a chore.

MAC: *Do you remember how long you nursed Melanie?*

MT: I am almost embarrassed to admit it, but with my first three babies the longest I nursed was six months.

I had three different doctors. All three of them said pretty much the same thing—that six months was a good time to wean the baby. I remember that the third doctor said it was very common for women who have toddlers or other children to lose their milk even sooner, supposedly because they are so tired. I don't know how many women he ever saw who breastfed but that's what he thought and that's what he told his patients. And in those days, you really paid attention to what your doctor said—he was the "expert."

MAC: From what I understand, Marian, you had your first home birth even before La Leche League was founded, at a time when having a home birth was almost unheard of. How did that come about?

MT: Yes, that's true. Laurel, my fourth baby, was born at home in 1955, more than a year before La Leche League got started.

From my fourth pregnancy onward, I was fortunate enough to have Dr. Greg White as my doctor—as our family doctor, actually. He not only delivered our babies, he took care of the whole family. we always knew that his help was just a phone call away, day or night.

MAC: How did you find Greg White, and what made you want to go to him as your family doctor?

MT: I asked one of the priests at our parish, St. Gertrude's in Franklin Park, if he knew of any good family physicians. He suggested that I might want to go to Greg White, who had recently set up his office in Franklin Park, and was also a parishioner. Also, Greg and Mary White lived in the neighborhood, where they were raising their already large family—I think they had six children by the time we got to know them.

The Whites belonged to the Christian Family Movement, a discussion group for young couples that was very popular in Catholic parishes in the 1950s. Tom and I were part of that, as were many of our friends and neighbors. So that was another way that we knew them.

MAC: Tell us about your husband, Tom. What was he doing in the 1950s?

MT: He was involved with the family. He didn't have any outside interests really. He was just a family man. Tom was an electro-mechanical engineer and an inventer. With our first babies, when I didn't know if my milk was good enough, or if I had enough milk, he used to get nervous at times. But as far as breastfeeding, and the time it took to take care of the children, he was totally supportive. I just felt that we were meant to be together, because when La Leche League came into our life, he was totally supportive of that too. I was lucky.

MAC: Did you receive other support for the choices you made?

MT: My mother gave me so much freedom as a human being, freedom to be who I really was. I would make decisions—like having a baby at home or breastfeeding past a year, or later on joining another church. And she would always say, "Well, I am sure that you and Tom talked about it and prayed about it, and if this is what you feel that you should do, then that is what you have to do."

She had lived a very sheltered life—for example, she and my father were never alone in a room together before they were married. But she always stood behind our decisions and never expected us to be what we weren't. And so that's how I tried to raise my children, too.

I feel that everybody's in the world for a purpose. I was always trying to discover who each child really was—I would never think of putting my expectations on a child as to what they should do or be when they grow up.

Mary White

MAC: Mary, going back to 1956, tell me something about a day in the life of the White family at that time. I remember that you lived in a house with a red door.

MW: Did we have a red door? I guess we did. I must like red doors, because we have one now. What I remember are the lilacs along the alley side of the house. Big bushes—oh, they were marvelous. The more we'd prune them, the more flowers we would get the following year.

MAC: But getting back to the family.

MW: Let's see. Michael was born in the spring of 1957, so Jeannie must have been the baby in 1956. Boy, did she keep me hopping. She was one of those real "live-wire" two-year-olds who just wanted all of my time and attention.

MT: How many children did you have at that time?

MW: We had Joe, Bill, Peggy, Katie, Ann, and Jeannie—six in all, at that time.

MAC: And Joe was how old?

MW: Joe was born in 1945, so that would have made him 11 years old in 1956. All of our school-age children went to St. Gertrude's, the parish school across the street from us. They could practically fall out of bed and into their classrooms! That was great.

It was one of those good old-fashioned Catholic schools run by really dedicated nuns who somehow were able to manage huge classes and still teach. For instance, when Joe and Bill were in seventh and eighth grades, there were 63 students in each room. There were two eighth grades, and each of them had more than 60 students. But somehow those children were well taught—they were right up there in terms of educational standards.

MAC: Mary, what was Greg doing at that time?

MW: Greg had a family practice in Franklin Park. We had moved there in 1949. His friend, Dr. John Kelly, was the one who had encouraged Greg to set up his practice in Franklin Park. John lived in the area, and he thought that Franklin Park could really use another doctor. Greg set up his office on Franklin Avenue, the main street in town at that time.

MAC: I remember Greg as having a large maternity practice. Was that true even when he was just starting out?

MW: He was a family doctor, actually. I guess word just got around about his being "different."

Greg had taken an obstetrics residency at Loretto Hospital under Dr. George Wickster. So when we had our first three children, Dr. Wickster delivered them. They were born in the hospital, of course. Dr. Wickster was a very fine obstetrician, but he didn't know beans about natural childbirth. And, at the time that we had Joe, we didn't know anything about natural childbirth, either.

But shortly before Bill, our second baby, was born, Greg came home one day and handed me a book to read. It was called, *Childbirth without Fear*, by Dr. Grantly Dick-Read. Greg said, "I was just reading this and I thought that you would like to read it." I was eight months pregnant at the time. It was August, and fiercely hot, but I read it. And after I had read it I said, "You know, what he is saying makes a lot of sense. It sounds great to me."

So that's how Bill became the first "natural" birth in our family. He was born in the hospital, but I didn't use any anesthesia, which was very disconcerting to the poor obstetrician. He wasn't used to having his patients wide awake. But it all worked out fine. And then our third, Peggy, was also born in the hospital without the use of any drugs or anesthesia.

Then, when we were expecting Katie, our fourth baby, Dr. Wickster was going on vacation at the time that she was due. And Greg said, why don't we just stay home with this one—save all the hassle at the hospital, and leaving the other children, and so on. Greg said that Dr. Ratner, who was a good friend, could come over and serve as the "official" doctor. Greg would actually "catch" the baby, but Dr. Ratner would be listed as the official physician on the birth certificate.

I said, "Sounds like a good idea." So when I went into labor, Herbert Ratner and Dorothy (his wife) came over and we were all sitting around in the living room. I was in the rocking chair. And then Peggy, who was 19 months or so, let me know that it was time for her nap. She started crawling upstairs, and I was going slowly behind her, pausing for a contraction every few steps. And then, shortly after that, I delivered the baby.

Dorothy had taken our two older boys out for a walk—it was October—and when they came back there I was, sitting in my rocking chair again, holding the new baby. When the boys came in I said, "Look here, you have a new little sister. Her name is Mary Catherine." But they barely took a glance at her! Instead, they headed for the kitchen, because we had promised to have a birthday cake when the new baby was born. So off they went to find the birthday cake.

And after that, all the rest of our children were born at home.

MAC: So tell me a little bit more about what family life was like for the Whites back in the late 1950s. Seems I've heard that a typical day for you would start with going to the early Mass at St. Gertrude's?

MK: Yes, I would often sneak over for the 6:30AM Mass on weekday mornings. Of course, as I mentioned before, the church was right across the street from us, so it took no time to get there at all. In fact, I remember going to Mass on the morning after Katie was born, I felt just fine—great, actually. So I bundled her up in a blanket, slipped out the front door, and went to Mass.

Well, it turns out my dear friend, Marge Boerner, was there that morning. And she wanted to know all about our home birth. I think that she was really quite taken with the idea. So I told her about the birth and said that it had been a very positive experience for the entire family. Marge seemed impressed, but kind of flabbergasted. Being sort of the "town crier" type, Marge went out and "spread the word" that I had had a home birth, and that I had been in church the very next morning with this brand new baby. For a while it seemed that our home birth was the talk of the town. But I didn't think that much about it one way or the other—it didn't seem strange or particularly difficult to me. Home birth just seemed like something that was natural, and right for our family, and a whole lot easier than all the rigamarole that's involved with going to the hospital to have a baby.

MAC: *So tell me more about a typical day at the White household in those days.*

MW: Greg always said that he didn't want his girls to get their hair cut until they were out of eighth grade. So they all had long hair, that they mostly wore in braids. So on weekday mornings, we had a regular routine. The girls would each take out their braids from the day before. And then they would line up, each one with a brush, from tallest down to smallest. I would do Peggy's braids—she was the oldest—while she was doing Katie's and Katie was doing Anne's and so on. Our system worked quite well—everyone had their hair newly braided every day, in a reasonable amount of time. Later on, when they were in high school, they got their hair cut to about shoulder length. For sentimental reasons I kept a set of braids from each girl. All that long hair in plastic bags is still upstairs in a dresser drawer.

MAC: *Mary, you mentioned that your own mother bottle-fed her babies, so it must have been quite a change for you to switch to breastfeeding and natural childbirth, when that was different from what everyone else in your family had done in terms of childrearing practices.*

MW: Greg was very receptive to more natural ways of caring for mothers and babies, in part because his own mother had struggled with the common childrearing practices of her day. The Holt method of baby care, which was popular in the 1920s and 1930s was named after a doctor who advocated putting babies on strict schedules, and sticking to those schedules, no matter how much the baby fussed or cried. The Holt method taught that a baby would suffer irreparable harm if the mother picked up the baby or fed the baby at any time other than the time dictated by the four-hour schedule.

Even though Greg's mother desperately wanted to pick him up when he cried, she felt that there was nothing for her to do except let him cry it out. Actually,

Grammy White was in complete sympathy with what we were doing. She was a very warm, loving person.

MAC: Tell us about what influence Dr. Herbert Ratner played in the development of Greg's thinking about baby care and family life?

MW: Yes, of course. Herb Ratner played a significant role in the development of Greg's thinking about breastfeeding, natural childbirth, the care of infants and babies, child care, and family life in general.

Herb taught preventive medicine when Greg was a medical student. He had a little office where medical students would go after class and sit around and talk. Herb was a remarkable person, and quite a philosopher. Greg picked up a lot of his ideas on the care of mothers and babies and families in general. And then he passed those ideas along to me, and basically we took it from there.

In regard to the way I was raised, I'm the oldest of eight children myself— I had six brothers and one sister. So I had a lot of experience with children even before I had my own. I picked up a lot of good ideas from my parents on how to raise children. My parents really loved their children—did everything they could for them. So we did have that feeling of being loved and cared for. Nevertheless, there was a stricter kind of discipline back in those days. As I said, there was always an emphasis on getting the baby on a schedule. The attitude was, "The child's been fed, he's had his bath, his diaper has been changed—now put him to bed." It was thought that if you did not put the baby on a schedule, you would be at his beck and call every minute, and you would end up raising a "spoiled" child.

Interesting enough, in later years my mother became one of La Leche League's most staunch supporters. She thought it was marvelous. So I'm really thankful that I married the guy I did, because I know for certain that if it had been left up to me, our children would have been raised quite differently. Greg was the one who picked up on the idea of doing things "nature's way," and he passed that philosophy along to me. And for that I will be forever grateful.

Edwina Froehlich

MAC: Edwina, let's talk about the Froehlich family and where you were in 1956.

EF: I had two children then—two sons, Paul, who was six, and David, who was four. But even having the two was kind of a big deal for me because I was older— 34 years old, actually, when I got married. So I didn't have quite as much time as the other Founders had to create a family.

MAC: And your husband, John, what was he doing back in 1956?

EF: John was working for his father's construction company then. Later on he got a job with the government.

As for me, when La Leche League got started in 1956, I was already 41 years old. I knew my biological clock was running out. As I said, I had two children at that time, but I was still terribly eager to have another baby.

After the first two planning sessions, I remember coming home and saying to my husband, "John, I really love this group and I enjoy talking with these women, but I really don't know how long I can continue to go to the meetings unless I get pregnant because everyone there either has a baby in her arms or in her womb."

You see, even though I had two wonderful, healthy children, I still had a strong desire to have another baby. So I thought, okay, I'll just go to a couple more meetings, and then I'll decide whether to keep attending. And then, wouldn't you know it—before the very next meeting I had missed a period!

However, I didn't know if that was a sure sign of pregnancy or not. In those days we didn't have those at-home test kits to give us the good news. So I didn't say a word about it when I first suspected. But then, by the time the next meeting rolled around, I was able to make my announcement. That was really wonderful. Because I very much wanted to be a part of this new breastfeeding club, but I didn't feel I should join if I didn't have a nursing baby.

I've always felt a great deal of compassion for women who are trying to get pregnant. I know what it means if you're the type of person who really, really wants to have a baby. My desire to have children was so intense that even my own sister said that she had never known anyone who wanted a baby more than I did. And I felt that way with every one of my pregnancies, including the two miscarriages that I had.

MAC: So that bring us up to the birth of your third son, Peter. Peter was born at home, wasn't he?

EF: Yes, he was. We were living in a third-floor walk-up in Chicago, right alongside the "el" tracks when the first two were born. But, by the time Peter was born in June 1957, we were living in our own home in Franklin Park.

Mary Ann Kerwin

MAC: Tell us about your life in 1956, Mary Ann.

MAK: When the Founders first got together, I was almost 25 years old. I had graduated from Barat College, Lake Forest, Illinois in 1953. After I graduated from college, I worked as a teacher and as a travel agent. Some friends had a birthday party for me in October 1953 and invited Tom Kerwin. They wanted us to meet each other. They told me he was from a very nice family. Tom was one of eight children, the oldest of whom was named Mary. As I discovered later, Mary Kerwin had married Dr. Greg White in 1944.

Tom and I dated for about one year, became engaged, and were married on December 27, 1954. We moved into an apartment in Oak Park, Illinois, a suburb of Chicago and lived there for a year and a half. Tom, a young lawyer, was an associate with a downtown Chicago law firm. We both came from strong Catholic backgrounds, so one of the first things we did was become members of the local Catholic parish, St. Edmund's. Also we joined the Christian Family Movement (CFM) in our parish. This was an activity for couples. Tom and I liked the idea of doing things as a couple. CFM encouraged participants to become involved in social action. The workbooks used by CFM were directed toward a goal that was summarized in the maxim: "Observe, Judge, Act." As a result, Tom and I became more conscious of our obligations to our community as well as to the oppressed and hungry throughout the world. This experience game me the right mindset when we started LLL and I made my commitment to volunteer my time to help other mothers breastfeed their babies.

I got off to a great start both with childbirth and breastfeeding primarily because of the strong support and guidance I received from the Whites. Also my parents gave me strong support. As soon as I thought I was pregnant, I read *Childbirth without Fear* by Dr. Grantly Dick-Read. Dr. Dick-Read made childbirth seem so wonderful—not at all scary as was the common perception at the time. I decided that the kind of childbirth that Dr. Dick-Read advocated, which he called natural childbirth, was just right for me. Tom and I asked Dr. White to be our doctor and help us have the kind of childbirth we wanted.

One of my expectations was that my husband would be with me throughout my labor and birth. To my consternation, Dr. White told me it was against the law in Illinois to allow fathers into the delivery room. (Fortunately this law was withdrawn many years ago.) I was not only shocked; I also felt devastated. I did not think I could give birth without having my husband with me to help me each step of the way. I felt very depressed and told my mother, knowing she was very supportive of Tom's and my "radical" ideas. My mother told me she had just read an article published in a women's magazine entitled "Babies Should Be Born at Home" by Dr. Ashley Montagu. She gave me the article and I read it eagerly.

I had been born at home in 1931 but did not think this was acceptable in the 1950s. My home birth came about because my father was very upset by the hospital procedures in Milwaukee, Wisconsin, when my older brother was born in 1929. My father felt that he was totally unwelcome at the hospital. He said he was treated as if he had no business being around my mother when she was giving birth. The next three babies, including me, were born at home. Dr. Montagu indicated having a baby at home was a normal, safe, and appropriate place to give birth even during the 1950s. He did not make the home appear to be a perilous environment in which to have a baby. And, best of all to me, the father could participate in the home birth!

I decided to ask Dr. White if he would assist me in giving birth at home. I showed him the article and he was not surprised by Dr. Montagu's advocacy of home births. Dr. White added that he had been doing some home births already. He told me that if everything looked normal toward the end of my pregnancy he would be willing to come to our home to deliver the baby. After he said that, I began looking forward with great anticipation to the birth of my first baby.

MAC: And did you plan to breastfeed your baby?

MAK: Yes. I wanted to breastfeed but Mary White was the only person I knew who was breastfeeding. None of my friends, acquaintances, or other relatives were doing so. All my friends who already were parents were certain they were experts on the subject of babies. When I mentioned I intended to breastfeed, they all told me I must buy some baby bottles "just in case." So I asked Dr. White if I should get some bottles "just in case." When he told me I would not need any bottles, I suddenly knew for sure that I was going to be able to succeed in breastfeeding my baby. I practically floated home from Dr. White's office.

MAC: And how did everything work out?

MAK: It led to the joyous home birth of our first son, Thomas More, on November 27, 1955. Getting started with breastfeeding, however, proved to be challenging. It took almost one week for our nine pound baby to really latch on to my breast. The vigilance and strong support of Dr. White were key in my finally succeeding with breastfeeding. He visited me every day to see how things were going and offered some practical advice. He suggested I try using a rocking chair. So Tom and I bought a second-hand rocking chair. I found using the rocking chair calmed me as well as my frustrated, hungry baby. As we rocked, the baby kept trying to latch on to my somewhat engorged breast and finally did. Without Dr. White's absolute confidence in me, I would have been another mother who tried to breastfeed but failed. Every day I felt grateful not only for my husband and baby but also for the lifestyle that had unfolded since the birth of our baby.

My mother stayed with me throughout the first week helping in any way she could. She affirmed my efforts to breastfeed even though she had not breastfed me or my siblings. Her doctor had discouraged her from doing so. Although my mother tried to breastfeed my older brother, she did not even try to breastfeed the next three babies. Of course, she received no support. After seeing my struggles to get my baby to latch on, and seeing my eventual success, my mother said that if her doctor had helped her as much as mine did, she also would have succeeded with breastfeeding. She was a wonderful mother. Even though I was not breastfed, I was lovingly mothered.

MAC: Mary Ann, a few years later you had a baby who died of SIDS. Tell us about that time in your life—how that affected your family.

MAK: Yes, certainly. Well Joseph was born on February 11, 1959. he was our third baby, and also third son. Joe died on March 17, 1959. So he was about five months old when he died.

On March 17, 1959, my husband, our three little boys, and I went to church to celebrate St. Patrick's Day. Joe fell asleep in my arms on the way home. When we got home, I put him in his little bassinet in a nearby room. I took care of the needs of our older boys and did a few other things around the house. Then I went to pick up Joe because I thought it was about time to feed him. To my horror, I found him in his bassinet looking black and blue, as if he had fallen. But I had been near him the entire time. I knew he never cried out for me. I scooped him into my arms. His body was warm so I thought he was okay even though he was black and blue.

Quickly I tried to get help. I called my husband but could not get him. It was about noon and he had left his office to get some lunch. Next I tried to get my doctor, Greg White. He also was unavailable. Then I tried my parents and could not reach them. After that, I called my sister-in-law, Mary White, but could not reach her. Desperately I called another sister-in-law, Kay Ryan, for help. Kay reminded me that a doctor who was a friend of ours had his office close to our home. She suggested I call him. She gave me his phone number.

As I dialed the phone number of Dr. Bill Cusick, I was still clutching my baby; I could not let go of him. I kept thinking and hoping he would be okay. I continued to desperately hold onto him as if just by holding him I could keep him alive. At the same time, I was thinking that I did not know what I would do if the doctor wanted me to drive to his office even though he was just a few blocks away. I was so distraught. I was sure I could not drive even a few blocks. Also I could not let go of Joe. When Dr. Cusick answered his phone, I told him briefly that my baby was black and blue. He quickly said he would come right over. His words were music to my ears. I was sure now that help was on the way.

Dr. Cusick arrived in just minutes with his little black case. I watched him open his case. He took out some instruments. My hopes soared. I felt sure he would be able to do something to help Joe. Because Joe's body was still warm, I kept hoping he would be okay, even though he was black and blue. Later I learned that the body of a baby often does not stiffen in death (no rigor mortis) and may remain warm for quite a while.

Gradually, I faced the horrible truth. Joe was dead. The unbelievable had happened. This was the worst suffering I had ever endured. I felt as though I had lost a part of my body. My empty arms ached with longing. It was heartbreaking to have milk for my baby but not have my baby to breastfeed.

There was some consolation in knowing that I had given Joe the best possible start in life. At that time, little was known about what caused "crib death" which is now called Sudden Infant Death Syndrome (SIDS). But it generally was believed that breastfeeding was the best safeguard against all babies' illnesses. Joe was totally breastfed throughout his short life. Additionally, I had a feeling right from the start that he was extra special. He had been a so-called easy baby to care for—he nursed for long periods of time and then slept peacefully for a few hours at a stretch. So I had eagerly welcomed him whenever he needed me.

MAC: *I would imagine there was some concern about engorgement because of the baby's sudden death.*

MAK: Yes, my breasts did become engorged. Dr. White suggested I hand express my milk to relieve the pressure. I did this but I was aware that any physical discomfort was insignificant in comparison to the emotional and psychological pain I was experiencing. Within days, the physical discomfort was gone but my grief seemed to almost paralyze me. Caring for my two older boys forced me to keep functioning, however.

Fortunately my family and friends did everything possible to help me through this difficult period. La Leche League was less than three years old at that time but already had become an important part of my life. I felt sustained in particular by the support and kindness the other Founders showered on me. Also LLL Meetings provided one of the few "safety zones" where I knew I could find friends who understood my seemingly unbearable grief.

Tragically during the intervening years since Joe's death, many other babies, including fully breastfed babies, have become victims of SIDS. It took decades for researchers to discover that simply putting babies to sleep on their backs, rather than face down, helps prevent SIDS. At last, there has been a dramatic decline in the number of SIDS deaths. Apparently the slogan "Back to Sleep" has already saved the lives of many babies and significantly reduced the number of parents who have had to grieve forever over the loss of a healthy baby.

MAC: And this happened in 1959. So you were still living in the Chicago area at that time, and you were involved in La Leche League then.

MAK: Oh yes. As you know, La Leche League was only about three years old then—not even three years old, actually. So we were still a rather close-knit group. The support that I got from La Leche League Leaders, and particularly from the other Founders, was wonderful and meant so very much.

In contrast, I went to my high school reunion not long after Joe died. But I quickly realized that I had made a mistake. There was no sensitivity, no understanding there. It wasn't their fault—they simply didn't understand what I was going through. It was too much, too soon. I couldn't handle it.

MAC: As a result of what you went through at that time, what would you suggest that friends do or say to help a woman who has suddenly lost a child or a baby? How would you comfort her?

MAK: Joe only lived for six weeks. During that time he was totally breastfed. He never had anything else, no water, no vitamins, nothing—just breast milk.

The point I want to make is that, while there are fewer instances of Sudden Infant Death Syndrome with breastfed babies, breastfed babies can still die of SIDS. Doctors still do not really understand what causes SIDS. So it isn't right to think that the parents didn't do what they could have, or should have, to prevent this from happening. Sometimes these things happen, and we don't really know why or how they occur.

In regard to how it affects a woman physically, I remember that Greg White told me to try to express milk, and take aspirin as needed.

But that's the least of it, I think. For me, as with most women in that situation I would imagine, it didn't bother me so much that my breasts were hurting. It was having the milk and no baby. The psychological and emotional pain was what mattered, not the physical pain.

That's why the understanding and support that I found through La Leche League meant so much to me. Now, occasionally we hear about women who say that they can't stand to go to La Leche League Meetings after their baby dies because of all the other babies there. So each woman has to decide for herself how she feels about going to meetings in these kinds of situations. All I can say is that I found understanding, sympathy, and support there. La Leche League was there for me when I needed it.

MAC: And soon after that, your family moved to Colorado and you found you were pregnant again, right?

MAK: Yes. Thirteen months after Joseph had died, I gave birth to Gregory Joseph. When I found out that I was pregnant, I considered going back to Chicago to have the baby. When we lived in Chicago, I had had home births (with all three of my children). But no one in Denver was doing home births at that time. My main reason for wanting home births, though, was so that I could have my husband with me.

In Denver, I had no problem finding a doctor and a hospital that would allow Tom to stay with me in both the labor and delivery rooms. As long as I could have Tom with me, I didn't really care if I was at home or in the hospital. So I was very satisfied with my birth experience with little Gregory.

MAC: So once again you had a newborn. Did that help you get over your grief somewhat?

MAK: Yes, it helped a lot. I know that there are differing opinions on whether a woman who has lost a baby should try to get pregnant again right away. But for me, having a baby as soon as possible after Joe's death was the best thing that could have happened to me.

Of course, you never forget the baby you lost—certainly no other baby can take the place of a baby who has died. But having a new baby to love and care for did help me to endure my grief. With the birth of Gregory Joseph, the feeling of emptiness began to subside.

Betty Wagner

MAC: Betty, let's go back to 1956, the year that La Leche League started. Describe a day in the life of the Wagners at that time.

BW: At that time I had four children and I was expecting a fifth. Gail was 13, Robert was 11, Wayne was in kindergarten, and Mary, our youngest, turned two years old in June of 1956. Our fifth baby, Margaret, whom we call Peggy, was born on November 30, 1956.

All of our school-age children were enrolled at St. Gertrude's parish school, where Mary White's children also went to school.

MAC: So you were living in Franklin Park—how long had you been living there?

BW: We bought our house in Franklin Park in 1946, when our second baby, Robert, was about six months old.

MAC: So you had been there a good ten years when La Leche League got started?

BW: Yes, and I ended up living in that house 40-some years—until 1993, when I sold it to marry my second husband, Paul Spandikow. So I lived in Franklin Park quite a while longer than I ever imagined when we bought the house.

MAC: What kind of work did Bob Wagner, your first husband, do? And what were you doing in 1956?

BW: Bob was working for the post office, and I was a "stay-at-home" mother.

MAC: Of course, weren't we all?

BW: I was 19 when I married Bob in 1942. I had worked at the Continental Bank before I was married. And later, when Bob was away at war, I worked at Montgomery Wards in the accounting department.

But by 1956 I was a full-time mother and I loved it. My mother had been a full-time mother when we were growing up—she didn't go to work until all of us had left home. So I always wanted and expected to be able to stay at home with my children, too.

MAC: You were active in the community, too, weren't you?

BW: Yes, I was active at church in the Altar and Rosary Society, which was fun. In fact, that's where I first met some of the other Founders. And I was a judge of elections—that's how I met Marian Tompson.

MAC: In 1956 you weren't nursing a baby, but you had nursed your older children, hadn't you?

BW: Yes, I nursed all of them until they were about nine or ten months old. I weaned them at about that age, mainly because that's the time everybody told me you should wean. I was told that they would wean very easily at that age. They're just becoming aware of things around them, and they're so very busy. They're crawling and they're pulling themselves up—they're very active.

I weaned Gail to a bottle, but the rest of them I weaned to a straw. It worked very well—it was very easy.

MAC: Did you nurse some of the later children for longer periods of time? I mean, after La Leche League got started, did you see advantages to longer nursing?

BW: Oh, yes, sure. After we got into our discussions, we woke up. We got to talking, and I learned so much from everybody.

MAC: Let's talk about the influences that made you want to breastfeed in the first place. At the time you started your family breastfeeding was not a popular choice, was it?

BW: No, it wasn't. Gail, my firstborn, was born in 1943. I didn't know anybody in my own age group who was nursing. Actually, I never knew many women who were breastfeeding until we started La Leche League.

On the other hand, my mother was a strong advocate of breastfeeding. She had breastfed all of her children. I remember seeing my younger brothers being breastfed. I was pretty big by the time they came along. They are eight and ten years younger than me. So I have a pretty clear memory of them as babies, and seeing my mother nursing them.

So then, when I started having my babies, my mother encouraged me to nurse them, just as she had done. It just seemed so easy and natural. It just seemed to be the right thing to do.

I remember my mother telling me not to worry about the four-hour schedule, that I should just nurse whenever the baby seemed hungry. She said that if you really insist on putting the baby on a schedule, make it every three hours. That was the longest she thought that any baby should go between feedings.

So my mother was there for me, and she helped me. I don't remember having any problems with nursing those babies, except for the orange juice that one doctor prescribed for the baby when I left the hospital. That caused problems—the baby broke out in hives. That was a mean thing to do to her! But, once we got rid of the orange juice, we sailed along fine.

Viola Lennon

MAC: What was happening in your life in 1956?

VL: In 1956 we lived on the northwest side of Chicago in a lovely neighborhood. Bill could take the train to downtown Chicago, where he worked as an attorney. Our oldest, Elizabeth, was in kindergarten. Mark, the next in line, was three years old, and the baby, Melissa, was born in June of that year. I didn't know it at the time La Leche League began in October that our fourth child, Rebecca, would be born the following June. Our three-bedroom house was getting crowded, though I loved our big backyard and the way neighbors supported each other. It was like a small community of young families with lots of children.

MAC: *Let's go back to when you were growing up, Vi. What were the influences in your life that ultimately made you want to breastfeed your children? What were your ideas about having a family, about the best way to care for babies, and the best way to raise children—all those things that a young girl begins to think about and then carries on into womanhood.*

VL: Probably the most important influence in forming my philosophy of baby and child care was my own family. I was the oldest of three children—two girls and a boy. My mother breastfed me, and she always spoke very lovingly about breastfeeding.

MAC: *Do you remember seeing your mother breastfeeding your baby sister or brother?*

VL: No, my mother nursed me, but she didn't nurse either of my siblings. She didn't breastfeed my sister, Patricia, who was three years younger than me, because my sister was a sickly baby. In those days (the mid 1920s), if you had a sick baby, or a baby who was not gaining weight, a mother was told to switch to formula. Formula was considered more modern, more "scientific," whereas breastfeeding was considered old-fashioned and not as reliable as formula in terms of monitoring how much the baby took in and so on.

So that was the advice that my mother got from one of the leading pediatricians in Chicago at that time—to switch to formula for my sister. And then with my brother, I guess my mother thought that if formula was better for my sister, then maybe it would be better for him, too. Of course, now we know that's not right at all, but that was the thinking in those days.

But, as I say, in later years, my mother always spoke positively and fondly of having breastfed me when I was a baby. So the suggestion that breastfeeding was an enjoyable experience that would bring you closer to your baby was an idea that stayed with me into my own adult years, and influenced what I wanted to do for my own children.

Aside from my own family, I think the strongest influence on me and my outlook on life came from a rather radical group of Catholics of the 1950s called the Young Christian Workers (YCW). Although I had always wanted to marry and have children, I think that the idea of wanting to cooperate with nature was strengthened by being involved with YCW, because cooperating with nature was one of the major tenets of this organization. Marrying and having children just seemed to fit in with that philosophy of "doing things naturally."

MAC: *You and Bill Lennon married in 1951, and about a year later, along came your daughter Beth. How did the breastfeeding go with your first baby?*

VL: Perfect. Edwina Froehlich was a good friend—I knew her mainly from YCW. Edwina had nursed her first baby, Paul, who was born a couple of years before my Elizabeth. So I turned to Edwina quite a bit for breastfeeding advice. In fact, I think that I must have talked to her every other day for the first four months or so of Elizabeth's life.

And, of course, I also had probably the best doctor in the Chicago area when it came to giving breastfeeding advice and encouragement, namely, our own Greg

White. I was referred to Greg through my good friend, Dr. Herbert Ratner. I knew Herb from Catholic University in Washington DC. By the time that I was expecting my first baby, Herb was Health Commissioner in Oak Park, Illinois. Herb didn't have a private practice at the time, so he referred me to Gregory White, who had been a student of Herb's in medical school.

So I was a lucky young mother, because I was able to turn to both Edwina and Greg White for encouragement, information, and advice. Consequently, I had no real difficulties at all in nursing my first baby, or any of the children that I had after that.

MAC: So Vi, how did you manage with so many children? That is a question that we often get from young mothers today who feel so busy with far fewer children.

VL: Certainly, we were busy. But there weren't as many organized activities as I see the children doing today. The neighborhood we lived in was pretty interesting for children even without a lot of organized activities. Almost everyone had big families in those days, so there were lots of children up and down the block for them to play with.

And all of the mothers were at home, so there were lots of adults around to keep an eye on things. of course, we took it for granted that we would be home with our children.

MAC: Of course. We couldn't imagine not being home, especially with the size of our families.

VL: It was nice because there was always someone around to talk to, or someone who could watch your little ones for a few minutes if you had to run to the store or something. And then, too, my own mother didn't live too far away. She would come over to help out when I had a new baby, or if I wasn't feeling well. So, unlike what you hear from some of the young mothers today, I don't remember feeling isolated or alone. It seemed that there was always someone around to talk to.

MAC: You had how many—ten children in all?

VL: Yes, ten children—Beth, Mark, Mimi, Rebecca, Matt, and then the twins, Charlotte and Cathy were born on Matt's birthday two years later. Charlotte died in 1982 though, in an automobile accident.

Winding up the gang were Martin, Maureen, and finally Gina in 1967. I was 44 years old when I had my last baby.

Mary Ann Cahill

MAC: We numbered seven in October 1956, the year La Leche League began. Besides Chuck and myself, there were the school-age children—Bobby, age seven, our adopted son who had joined the family as a two-and-a-half-year-old, and Elizabeth, also seven, whom I had "tried and failed" to breastfeed as a baby.

On school mornings, lunch in hand, they walked to St. Gertrude's school on the other side of town in the company of older neighborhood children.

The Cahills who were not yet of school age were four-year-old Timmy, his sister, Teresa, sixteen months younger, and the baby, Mary. Timmy and "Tee Tee" were great buddies. They enjoyed each other's company and were a constant source of entertainment for the baby.

Chuck was putting in long hours with a public accountant firm, especially during the tax season, and needed the only vehicle we had to get to and from work. Most church and other meetings involving women normally met in the evening, when dad and the car were home.

The days developed a rhythm of their own, filled with the work of feeding, clothing, and caring for our brood. Looking back now, I wonder how we managed it all, though at the time it seemed perfectly natural and, besides, the other young couples around us were equally busy with their families. I enjoyed being at home. It was my world, and this was my time to be close to my children. Actually, I saw myself as having quite a few things going for me that made life easier.

Following Teresa's birth, we had purchased a clothes dryer, still something of a luxury at the time. Chuck promoted the idea, having ventured into hanging the laundry to dry on the lines stretched across the basement. All those little socks! With baby Mary's arrival, we invested in a dishwasher, even more of an innovation. Also, I had arranged with the independent grocer in town to order the family's groceries by phone. I'd make a list, phone it in, and Sam the grocer would have it filled and delivered to my door at no extra charge. Most other shopping was done "up town" in Franklin Park, within walking distance. For major excursions, I could call my parents, who lived a short distance away in Chicago.

They were a wonderful help in many ways, often popping in unexpectedly. My father was skilled at home repairs. Young Bobby never missed an opportunity to be at Grandpa's side when a project was under way. The two had come to an agreement of sorts, with Bobby not crowding Grandpa and not walking off with Grandpa's tools. (Now grown-up, Bob is himself a master repairman.) Grandma would occasionally surprise us with homemade cookies and, on catching sight of a pile of laundry in the basement, seemingly had it washed, dried, and put away in short order, with Chuck's shirts crisply ironed and hanging in the closet.

We missed them terribly when my mother died in March 1959 of cancer. The last three months of her life were spent at our house, a time that the older Cahills still remember well. As her care grew more intense, neighbors rallied to help. Six months later, my father died suddenly.

Chuck and I were well aware of the power of having the love of family and friends to support us. When the idea came up of helping mothers learn to breast-feed their babies, there could be no hesitation. It was all part of the wonderful adventure we saw ourselves being part of.

Chapter 2 — ONCE UPON A PICNIC

In July of 1956, the Whites and Tompsons found themselves at a CFM picnic in Wilder Park in Elmhurst, Illinois. Mary and Marian sat together talking and nursing their babies on that warm, sunny Sunday under the shade of a tree. Picnic tables were piled high with food and cool drinks, dads were talking and laughing, and youngsters were chasing each other across the broad lawn. Mary and Marian had no worries about milk for their little ones. Their healthy, happy babies were ample proof of the wonder of natural supply and demand.

Mary, whose children were older, was the more experienced mother in terms of years on the job. She and her husband, Greg, had espoused breastfeeding even before their first child was born. As a medical student, Greg had been impressed by the teachings of Dr. Herbert Ratner, a professor at Loyola Medical School and later the Public Health Officer of Oak Park, Illinois. Herb was as much a philosopher as he was a physician; he had a keen appreciation of the purpose and power of nature and the natural order of things. For Dr. Ratner, the rightness of this process could be found in the way a mother's body so beautifully meets her needs and those of her baby in childbirth and breastfeeding.

Under a shade tree in Wilder Park, the convenience of having a milk supply that is always pure and never runs out became the topic of conversation as Mary and Marian talked with other mothers. How simple it all was! No worries that the milk would go sour as the day warmed. No nipple contaminated by a tumble into the dirt. No jars of baby food to pack. What was the secret, the mothers wanted to know, of Mary's and Marian's success?

There were no secrets, Mary and Marian both knew. After struggling to breastfeed her firstborn, Mary learned to follow baby's lead, and thereafter, there was never a bottle in the house. The Whites' confidence in breastfeeding carried over to Greg's practice in Franklin Park, where the waiting room was often crowded with pregnant women and mothers with a nursing baby in arms or on a lap. In the course of an office visit, Dr. White might casually refer one mother to another mother in his practice on questions of breastfeeding. As is typical of a small town, many of his patients knew each other, and talking to another nursing mother about the everyday care of a child could be extremely helpful.

Marian and her family were patients of Dr. White, and it was through his guidance that she had turned the corner on breastfeeding. With her first three, the longest she had breastfed was six months. But the satisfaction and joy it brought to her was something Marian never forgot. Talking to the mothers at the picnic made her wonder once again how she could help others know the same fulfillment.

Mary, too, was acutely aware of the lack of good, practical information for mothers. What would it take to share what they had learned with other interested mothers? They were thinking in terms of Franklin Park and thereabouts, nothing more. Yet Mary and Marian were both already busy with their growing families. Could they take on yet one more thing? What kind of response would they get? Were there others who would help—friends who were also breastfeeding babies? They decided to find out.

Once back home, Marian placed a call to her friend Edwina Froehlich, whom she knew from St. Gertrude's Church and CFM. Breastfeeding was something they had discussed at various times previously, but now she was eager to tell Edwina of the latest development. A meeting was planned for the following week at Mary White's house to further discuss the idea. Would Edwina be able to make it? Did she know of anyone else who might be interested? Edwina's response to both questions was an enthusiastic "Yes!"

The Froehlichs' five-year-old son, Paul, had been Dr. White's first home birth outside his own family, and three-year-old David Froehlich had also been born at home and had nursed well. Edwina quickly called her long-time friend from the days of their mutual involvement in the Young Christian Workers Movement, Viola Lennon of Chicago. Vi was also a Dr. White patient and breastfeeding mother, and she and her husband, Bill, were the parents of three at the time, all of whom had been breastfed. Vi was intrigued with the proposed idea. Other than Edwina and Mary White, whom she had talked to only by phone, she was unacquainted with the other players in the drama.

Mary White, for her part, was also busy making calls. She phoned her sister-in-law, Mary Ann Kerwin, a proud first-time mother who was happily breastfeeding nine-month-old Thomas More Kerwin. The youngest of the group, Mary Ann greeted the news with enthusiasm. She, too, would be meeting five of those attending for the first time.

Mary's next call was to another Mary Ann—Mary Ann Cahill, across town on Calwagner Street. Mary Ann had experienced both bottle-feeding and breastfeeding, having tried and failed to breastfeed her firstborn, Elizabeth, seven years earlier. She remembered the sense of loss she experienced at the time and the ambivalent feelings of hope and inadequacy that she felt when putting her second baby to the breast for the first time. Moving to Franklin Park and finding Dr. White had made a dramatic difference in the life of the Cahills.

Mary Ann, too, was excited at the prospect of helping mothers avoid what she had gone through. It also seemed only natural to check with her dear neighbor and breastfeeding advisor, Betty Wagner. Betty herself had had no problems breastfeeding her babies, and wondered aloud why something so natural should need so much attention. She quickly added, however, that she'd be happy to come to the meeting.

And so it was, seven women and an idea, the beginning of a dream to bring gentleness to giving birth and joy in the womanly art of breastfeeding. None of the seven women imagined that the dream would travel around the world, stem the tide toward artificial infant feeding, change how people thought about child care and, in so doing, reverse a societal trend. At the time, they saw their lives as already busy and fulfilling and not too unlike those of other young wives and mothers. Again, in ways they could not imagine, this was about to change.

Marian Tompson

MAC: So tell us about that famous picnic at which, as legend has it, you and Mary White hatched the idea of starting a "breastfeeding club."

MT: Yes, right. It was a CFM picnic at Wilder Park in Elmhurst on a Sunday in July 1956. Mary and Greg White were there, and Tom and I were there, and all of our children. In fact, there were quite a few couples there, and children all over the place.

Women we knew from CFM kept coming up and talking with us as we were breastfeeding our babies. Several of them said they had tried to breastfeed their babies, but that they had had "problems." So they had given up on breastfeeding and switched to formula.

This came as a revelation, an illumination, to me. Up until then, I thought that the women who were bottle-feeding simply preferred to feed their babies that way. I didn't realize how many women were out there who wanted to breastfeed, but gave up on it when they ran into difficulties.

As I started thinking abut this, it bothered me that women who wanted to do right by their babies, who wanted to breastfeed their babies, weren't succeeding because they couldn't get any help. So I said to Mary, "What if we would arrange a get-together with friends, women who have breastfed, and share our experiences with women who are pregnant?" We debated. Mary had six children at the time, and I had four. When were we going to find the time for something like this?

MAC: So did you plan the first meeting right then and there?

MT: Oh no. As I said, we had to mull it over for a while. I remember that I was pregnant at the time, so I was visiting the doctor regularly. Whenever I would go to the doctor, I would stop over at Mary's and we would talk about a lot of things. After the picnic we started talking about the possibility of starting a breastfeeding discussion group.

And, then one day as I was leaving Mary's—and even now I can see it as clear as day in my mind's eye—I was standing on the steps of her house and we were debating for the umpteenth time whether or not to do this. And I finally said, "You know, Mary, if we can help mothers nurse their babies, then we will be helping families, and if we are helping families, we will be helping society. So I think we ought to try it." So that's when we made the decision to go ahead with it.

Mary White

MAC: Let's talk about the picnic, that famous picnic. You and Marian were at a picnic, nursing your babies, when the idea came up to do something to help other mothers who wanted to nurse their babies. Describe that day as you remember it.

MW: Well, as you mentioned, we were at a church picnic. It was actually a CFM picnic—Christian Family Movement. This was a movement within the Catholic Church in the United States that was very popular at that time. CFM was composed of young couples who got together periodically and discussed things. The motto of CFM was, "Think, judge, act." So I think that we brought some of that attitude, that way of doing things, into La Leche League once it got going.

But, I'm getting ahead of myself. The picnic that Marian and I both attended was held at Wilder Park in Elmhurst one Sunday in July. So we packed picnic lunches and our children and went to the picnic. I remember that the Tompsons were sitting with us. And I guess it came time to nurse whoever was the baby at that time—let's see, it was 1956 so Jeannie must have been the baby.

Anyway, I was nursing a baby and Marian was nursing, too. And we were saying, "Isn't this great? We can just sit here and enjoy our picnic lunch, and hand out food to the family without having to worry about heating a bottle or mixing formula, or worrying about formula spoiling on a warm summer afternoon." And one thought led to another and we found ourselves saying, "You know, it's too bad that more mothers can't do this." And I mentioned that Greg had said he wished we could help some of his patients with breastfeeding because he didn't have any personal experience with it. He thought it would be great if some of the experienced mothers could get together with some of the new mothers and give them a few pointers.

MAC: I was always under the impression that Greg had already started an exchange of information, woman-to-woman, in an informal way through his medical practice. I recall when I went to him, before we had La Leche League, that it seemed that he would often refer his patients to other women who were breastfeeding.

MW: Yes, I think that's true. Greg did think that having what is now called a "support group"—we didn't have a name for it then—was a good idea because, obviously, it is the women who have nursed their babies who know the most about it, who have the most practical experience with the whole process.

So, to make a long story short, Marian and I decided to call a few of our friends and get together at somebody's house—mine as it turned out—and see what we could come up with in regard to getting some kind of breastfeeding support group started in Franklin Park.

MAC: At that time, Mary, if I have correct notes, you already had six children and Marian had four. Did you ever wonder if you had time to get involved in starting a new organization?

MW: Yes. I guess it does seem odd, when you have all these little ones and you are so busy already, that you would even think you had the time or energy to get a big project like LLL up and running. Of course, we didn't know that it was going to turn into anything like what happened later. But we were young and full of energy, and we thought, "Sure, we can do that. No problem."

MAC: That brings me to my next point. What motivated you to take on the extra work involved in starting this group? Because you certainly had a sizable family by that time, and more than enough work to keep you busy, I would imagine.

MW: Well, yes, but this was a different kind of challenge. It was something outside of the day-to-day household. It was a good excuse to skip washing the kitchen floor! Seriously, though, starting a group that would be talking about breastfeeding and mothering and the best ways to raise children was an intellectual challenge. It was stimulating and enjoyable to get together with like-minded women friends and discuss the various challenges and concerns that presented themselves to us as we were raising our families.

Edwina Froehlich

MAC: Edwina, do you recall Marian phoning you and telling you that she and Mary had been talking about starting a breastfeeding discussion group?

EF: Oh, yes. I think it was soon after the picnic, that famous picnic. I was enthusiastic about the idea as soon as Marian suggested it. You see, I have always been a "joiner." I've been a member of many organizations in my lifetime, and I've helped start more than one organization. So when Marian called, I almost immediately said, "Count me in—I want to be part of this."

MAC: So then you called Vi Lennon?

EF: Yes, that was it. I called Viola Lennon. We had been great friends from way back, back to the days before we were married when we were both "working girls." Vi sounded interested, especially when I said that we would be discussing "mothering" as well as breastfeeding. Anyway, Vi pretty quickly agreed to come with me to the meeting at Mary's house.

Mary Ann Kerwin

MAC: Let's talk now about when La Leche League first got started. Who approached you about joining this fledgling discussion group?

MAK: Mary White. Of course, you know that Mary is my sister-in-law—she is my husband's sister. Yes, Mary called me soon after she and Marian went to that picnic, that famous picnic. I remember being amazed at how quickly the meeting was scheduled after our initial conversation. My recollection is that it was, like, two weeks from the time that Mary asked me about helping to start a breastfeeding support group until the time we had our first meeting.

MAC: When you say "first meeting" do you mean the core group of just the seven Founders, or are you referring to the first general meeting?

MAK: I mean the core group.

MAC: Okay then, yes, I agree with you. It was not a long period at all from the time that we hatched the idea until we had our first couple of planning meetings.

MAK: In any case, that's my recollection—that it all came together very quickly. You know, sometimes people propose ideas and then they simmer for quite a while. But this idea took shape and was acted upon very soon after that.

MAC: Do you have any further recollections about our original planning meetings? Any "first impressions" about the other Founders?

MAK: Yes, I remember being almost dumbfounded when I came to that first meeting and met the rest of you. You see, up until that meeting I didn't know anyone there but Mary White. Pretty much everything I knew about breastfeeding and natural childbirth I had picked up almost entirely from discussions with Greg and Mary White.

So when I came to that first meeting, and saw these other women breastfeeding, that was quite a thrill. And you were all such nice people. You didn't seem like oddballs!

MAC: Do you remember anything else from those early days?

MAK: Well, I just remember that we had the first series of four meetings together. But already, by the end of that first series, there were getting to be too many people at Mary's house. So Mary and Marian Tompson and I stayed together, and the rest of you formed a second group. You didn't exactly "break off" but you did start another meeting because there were simply too many people to fit everyone comfortably into Mary White's living room.

MAC: Yes, we held our meetings at Edwina's, because she had the largest living room.

MAK: It seemed like a natural decision.

MAC: Mary Ann, do you remember the "flavor" of the early meetings? Are there any situations or stories that particularly stand out in your mind from those days?

MAK: Yes. In particular I remember being very surprised when a mother who already had seven children came to us for help in breastfeeding her eighth. She had not succeeded in breastfeeding any of her other children.

That made a big impression on me—that this mother, who was expecting her eighth child, was still very much interested in mastering the art of breastfeeding, and that she would come to us for help in learning how to do that.

And she did successfully breastfeed her eighth baby—of course she did. And that made me realize how important it was to have a support system, to have other mothers to talk to when little problems or obstacles came up. I decided that, if we could help a woman who had tried and failed seven times, and then succeeded in breastfeeding her eighth baby, we could probably help just about any mother, as long as she wanted to learn.

MAC: Do you remember the atmosphere among the seven of us, the Founders, in those early days?

MAK: Yes. In retrospect it seems incredible. Now maybe I'm exaggerating, or maybe my memory has gotten foggy, but I just don't seem to remember a lot of difficulties or problems between us. I think it was partly because we were just so happy to have found each other, and to have other women to share these experiences with. All I remember is that the seven of us seemed to get along beautifully in those days—we really worked well together.

Betty Wagner

MAC: What were your impressions of the other Founders?

BW: Well, I had met several of them before. I met Marian Tompson for the first time when she came to the polling place where I was an election judge. She had three darling little girls with her—one was blond, one was a brunette, and one was a redhead. I thought that was unusual. According to the records, Marian was not registered. So we said, "No, you can't vote." And she said, "But, I know I'm registered. I went to city hall, and got registered, so I should be able to vote." Somebody went to call downtown. It took a while to check it out, to find out if she was actually registered. And while she was waiting, we got to talking. We found that we were in the same parish. I thought, "I like her. She seems nice." And I liked her little girls. And, finally the other election judge came back and said,

"Yup, she's registered. She can go ahead and vote." So that was the first time that I had met Marian Tompson.

MAC: I didn't know that's how you and Marian met. I thought that you had met at church. Do you remember how you met any of the other Founders?

BW: I met Edwina when my friend Dorothy and I picked Edwina up for a meeting at church. She was so bubbly and full of information and stories. And then, on the way home, she was just as bubbly and talkative as she had been on the way over. When she got out of the car, Dorothy said, "Wasn't she awful—she talks way too much!" and I thought, "How could she say that? I liked her so much!"

MAC: Anyone else you remember meeting before that first La Leche League meeting?

BW: Well, let's see. I remember when I met Mary White—it was at an Altar and Rosary meeting. There was a woman there giving a book review. She used some big word that hardly anyone recognized. And she said, "Does anyone here know what this word means?" And Mary White was on her feet in an instant, and boy, she knew that word, and I am sure every other word that woman used. Mary is very smart.

And, of course, I remember meeting you, Mary Ann. You and I met when you came to the door doing the census. You had just moved into the area, and in order to get acquainted with people you were going door-to-door for the census. So we met, and yes, we did go walking on many evenings. You had little Elizabeth in a stroller when I first met you, and later Tim was your baby. And I always had a baby with me, as well. So that's how we got to be friends.

And then there was Vi Lennon. I didn't meet Vi until the second or third planning meeting because I think she was sick at that first meeting. Vi makes a very striking appearance, as though she just stepped out of a fashion magazine. Vi makes you feel very good about yourself. So naturally I liked her.

And then, last but not least, there was Mary Ann Kerwin. I met Mary Ann for the first time at that first planning meeting at Mary White's house. She seemed very nice, very sweet. It took me a while to decide if she was really as sweet as she seemed. But later I decided that, yes, she really is like that—she really is very sweet.

So that's how I met all of you. I liked all of you, and I felt that all of you were very smart and very nice and very interesting people. I felt fortunate to be in your company, and to call this group of women my friends. I still do.

Chapter 3—GETTING STARTED

Following the picnic and the phone calls that followed, the idea was quickly converted into action. A date was set for a planning meeting to be held at the White's house, and when the evening arrived, six of the seven assembled, Viola being unable to attend. Mary and Greg's home had the pleasant and comfortable look of a house that is thoroughly lived in by its occupants, hand-me-down sofa and upholstered chairs nicely dented, a collection of mix and match, high-backed chairs around the large dining room table. The group easily settled down to the business at hand.

The tone of the meeting was relaxed but with a tinge of anticipation. The agenda was filled with actions to be taken and decisions to be made. Whom would they invite to their meetings? What would they tell the mothers who came? What information was available to use as resources? A search had already been made of printed materials and had yielded only a few possibilities—some popular magazine articles and, most promising, a little-known periodical, *The Child-Family Digest,* published by John and Charlotte Aiken. It was like a voice crying in the wilderness in support of a natural and loving approach to birth and child care. It was encouraging and inspiring to the group.

Apart from the fact that a beginning had been made, one of the most noteworthy things to come of the evening was the sharing that went on among the women about their own personal birth and breastfeeding experiences. A similar exchange was to become a regular part of LLL Meetings in the future. The talk that evening was unstructured and lively, with one or another member of the group picking up on and verifying points that another had made. Breastfeeding, the joy of it and the challenge of making it work, was unquestionably the focus, yet a wide range of subjects was covered, from childbirth to the fact that hospitals routinely limited a mother's opportunities to breastfeed her baby. Through it all there surfaced a seemingly endless array of worrisome stories that were often passed along to any woman contemplating breastfeeding.

This photo of all the Founders, except Vi Lennon, was taken in 1957.

With reluctance, the hour growing late, the group departed, having first agreed to meet again and continue the planning. The decision had also been made to announce a meeting open to other mothers in the community, their neighbors and friends to begin with. All women would be welcome, without exception. As for the approach to their new endeavor, it was understood from the beginning that it would be positive, with the emphasis on the benefits of breastfeeding. No attacks were ever contemplated against infant formula or bottle-feeding. Whether a mother had previously bottle-fed her baby was of no import; what counted was that she was now interested in breastfeeding. The group would be there to help her.

For the seven, it was an exhilarating time. Their phone lines buzzed with calls back and forth to iron out details. What steps needed to be taken to give structure to their efforts? Even for those least interested in organizational matters, the question that demanded an answer was—who would be doing what?

At a subsequent meeting, the matter of selecting officers for the new organization was quickly dispensed with. The choices just fell in place. Marian was named President, when, as she seems to recall, she momentarily left the room. Edwina was a natural for Corresponding Secretary, and the same could be said for Betty in the role of Treasurer. Who else, it was decided, but Mary White for Research, with her access through Greg to the medical literature. Mary Ann Cahill was named Recording Secretary, a duty she kept up for only a short time. Mary Ann Kerwin, with her deep love of books, readily volunteered for the position of Librarian.

Naming the new organization was more problematic. Choices were limited, since the word "breastfeeding" was not used in "polite society" at the time. References to the breast were reserved to medical reports or were totally avoided. Women had "bosoms," and mothers "nursed" their babies. Suggested names had been ranging from the mundane to the ridiculous—the Milk Maids, for instance. Then one evening Mary White ventured a suggestion that her husband Greg had mentioned to her earlier. What did the group think of La Leche League, taken from a title for Mary, the mother of Jesus, "Our Lady of Happy Delivery and Plentiful Milk"?

There was an intriguing element to a name which, when translated, meant "the milk," yet didn't offend sensibilities. Clearly, the early Spanish settlers who had erected the shrine by that name in the 1500s in what is now St. Augustine, Florida, had had a keen appreciation of the value of mother's milk. Those hardy explorers also understood the importance of mother-to-mother help, albeit in the form of heavenly aid. So it was agreed, again unanimously, that La Leche League would be the name of the new support group for breastfeeding mothers. Interestingly, some of the Founders' first attempts at pronouncing the name gave it a French, rather than the correct Spanish, accent.

In no time, it seemed, summer had waned, days were getting shorter, and the leaves on the trees lining the streets of Franklin Park were turning red and gold. Newspaper headlines chronicled an uprising in Hungary against the Russians and the rise of a civil rights movement in southern parts of the United States. A young musician out of nowhere named Elvis Presley was taking the country by storm. Fashion dictated that a fashionably dressed woman wore a one-piece dress, zipped up the back, with a fitted bodice and full skirt. It was October, and the first-ever La Leche League meeting was scheduled for the Whites' home, 2932 Gustave Street in Franklin Park. Meeting time was 8:30 in the evening, which gave mothers time to get their older children ready for bed. The nursing baby, of course, would accompany mother.

The exact date of that first meeting is lost in obscurity, though years later in response to repeated requests for a date for the first-ever La Leche League meeting, Betty Wagner, then Executive Director, chose October 17, 1956. It is as good a date as any. What is important is that there was a meeting and that five young pregnant women, friends of the Founders, showed up. The seven Founders were all present, cheering Marian on as she led the meeting, a presentation of an article from *Reader's Digest*, "Breast Fed Is Best Fed." The newcomers listened politely but said little. Refreshments followed, coffee and a dessert, most likely something sweet and unquestionably homemade. There is no record as to whether the visitors attended subsequent meetings or, if they breastfed their babies, for how long.

As for the Founders, they were pleased that they were able to put their plan into action, and they searched for ways to make it even better. Marian expressed interest in a new format, one that would allow greater participation. Everyone agreed that women who had been home all day with young children looked forward to talking to other adults on an evening out. They wanted to test their own ideas and share new ones. This was never truer than with mothers discussing their babies.

It was soon realized that when there are other experienced breastfeeding mothers in the group, they, too, are a rich source of information that should be tapped. It became apparent that breastfeeding did not stand alone, that events as diverse as the kind of delivery a mother experienced and what she ate or didn't eat could affect the outcome of her breastfeeding. The consensus was that new mothers needed to know about these other topics as well, and so attention turned to organizing the information. The outcome was a division of the material to be delivered over the course of several meetings.

For the first meeting, the material just naturally presented itself—The Advantages of Breastfeeding. It was a story waiting to be told. The second topic was equally compelling—Overcoming Difficulties. "Why can't I breastfeed?" mothers wanted to know. This was the time to address old wives' tales and not-so-old tales of attempts to breastfeed that had not been successful. It was felt, too, that childbirth, which in so many ways sets the stage for breastfeeding, had to be included, and so the third meeting consisted of a discussion of birth and moved on to tips for getting breastfeeding off to a good start—The Arrival of the Baby. And then there was the matter of what a breastfeeding mother could or couldn't eat and when to start the baby on solid foods. A discussion of nutrition developed into the fourth meeting along with weaning—Nutrition and Weaning. The Series, as this lineup of four meetings came to be known, was augmented by a "fathers only" meeting at which dads could share their concerns in a frank discussion with Dr. White or Dr. Ratner. Again, sharing experiences was at the core of the give and take.

Fathers were not the only ones who had the privilege of fielding questions to a supportive doctor. Quite often, when a meeting at the Whites was winding down, Dr. White would arrive home from a long evening of seeing patients, pull up a chair and answer questions, or just talk about babies and families. A new understanding of what natural birth and childrearing meant was taking shape for many of those present.

Group Meetings were held monthly and, month by month, the number of mothers attending increased steadily, somewhat to the surprise of the Founders. As winter took hold, mothers with babies carefully wrapped against the cold, and pregnant mothers equally bundled up and not quite sure what to expect, all crowded into the Whites' living room. Blankets were spread on the floor in protected areas on which to lay sleeping babies, and those who could would sit on the floor. Meetings inevitably began with each mother introducing herself and telling as much as she cared to about her current or previous experience with breastfeeding or her hopes for doing so in the future.

The response heartened the Founders and confirmed what they had sensed in their hearts—mothers bloomed in a positive environment and were eager for every snippet of information. Also, they loved the chance to meet and talk to other nursing mothers. As a way to strengthen this sense of belonging, and to cover the costs of handouts, the Founders decided to offer memberships. Dues were one dollar a year. Asking for money was not a priority at the time, and the announcement of dues at a meeting was often handled rather apologetically. To a woman, the seven worried that a mother might feel she could not come to the meetings because of budget constraints.

Yet in true entrepreneurial fashion, the Founders produced a brochure announcing their meetings and giving a phone number that mothers could call at any time for personal breastfeeding help. This offer of mother-to-mother help with no expectation of payment continues to this day and has been a hallmark of La Leche League's volunteer Leaders over the years. As was true with most of La Leche League materials then and for years to come, the brochure was truly a "home-made" piece, in the sense that it was produced at home with the help of loving family. One of Mary White's daughters, Peggy, drew the sketch for the cover.

By the beginning of the new year, it was evident that meetings were outgrowing the Whites' combined living and dining rooms and so, in February 1957, Edwina opened her home to the second Franklin Park La Leche League Group. Marian, Mary White, and Mary Ann Kerwin continued to share leadership of the group south of the railroad tracks, while Edwina, Betty, and Mary Ann Cahill were the core members of the north group. With Edwina's enthusiasm and skill as a discussion leader, and Betty and Mary Ann's support and readiness to chime in, the new group was soon firmly launched.

Between group meetings, the seven, or as many of them as could make it, continued to meet on their own, usually during the day. Children who were not yet in school came along. The pace was brisk and decisions were made quickly. If someone had a good idea, they moved on it. Even so, there was a lot to discuss. Invariably, once business-like matters were disposed of, the talk reverted to their main interest—breastfeeding. What it was all about, what made it work, the importance of all the many other things a mother did for her baby besides feeding. The sum of it all—giving birth, breastfeeding, mothering—became known as La Leche League's Philosophy. How they perceived this and how it was to be passed on to others would dominate their thinking for years to come.

Marian Tompson

MAC: Marian, do you recall the first time that we got together as a group and started figuring out just what we were going to do?

MT: I don't remember in detail. I remember the whole idea of wanting to get organized. I remember that, because Betty Wagner had worked in a bank, we decided that she should be the treasurer. And, I remember that I thought Edwina should be president because she had worked longer than any of us before she got married, and because she seemed to be the most organized. So I nominated Edwina for the job. Then I went into the kitchen to do something—I think I made some more coffee. And when I came out, the rest of you told me that you wanted me to be the president. That surprised me because I was very quiet and shy in those days. But, I wasn't one to oppose what others thought should happen. So I accepted the presidency of our little group, never dreaming of what that job was going to entail, or the places that it would take me, someday, down the road.

MAC: Marian, what do you remember about the first meeting when we invited women from the community? In other words, the first "general" meeting?

MT: I remember that we held our first regular meeting for all women interested in breastfeeding at Mary White's house in October of 1956. Greg White stayed in the kitchen because he wasn't supposed to be part of the meeting. Later on I remember him saying that he had learned so much that night, just by eavesdropping. Because, you know, women talk to each other about these kinds of things differently than they would talk to their doctors.

Three of the mothers at that first meeting were my friends from church, and I picked them up and drove them to Mary's house. Two of them, Margaret O'Brien and Betty Reiling, went on to nurse their expected babies although they had thought they didn't have enough milk with earlier children.

MAC: Anything else that you remember, Marian, from that first meeting?

MT: I remember that I read "Breast Is Best" from the *Reader's Digest*—which is something that we would never suggest that any Group Leader do now. We were really just feeling our way. I remember that one of the women had already weaned her eight-month-old baby. She wasn't pregnant, but she kept coming to meetings anyway. I was really curious as to why she was still coming. So one day I asked her and she said, "Marian, you women seem to love being mothers so much. I am hoping that if I keep on hanging around you, it will rub off on me." So that's one of the times I realized that what we were giving people was more than information. It was also an attitude, a feeling about being a mother.

MAC: Marian, are there any telling moments that stand out for you from those very early days?

MT: I just remember that I liked having a new baby and going over to Mary White's house to lead the meetings. I remember being surprised at all the mail we were getting. I had some problems dealing with that. I used to feel guilty because I didn't have time to write to my relatives, but here I was, answering all of these letters from people I didn't even know. It was an interesting time.

MAC: Marian, weren't you the one who came up with the name that we chose for our organization—La Leche League?

MT: The name really came from Dr. White. As you probably remember, we couldn't call ourselves anything that actually used the word "breast" or "breast-feeding" because that was considered pretty vulgar language in those days. But then, through the Whites, we heard about the shrine in Florida to Nuestra Senora de la Leche y Buen Parto, Our Nursing Mother of Happy Delivery.

That was Spanish, of course, although at first some of us were confused and thought it was French. So at first we were pronouncing the name of the organization as "la lesh" as if it was a French name, instead of "la lay-chay" as it is pronounced in Spanish.

In any case, we decided that the La Leche name would make a "good cover" for what we were trying to do. We never realized that it would be a name that would travel all over the world.

MAC: *So Mary, tell me, what are your recollections of that first get-together of what I would call the "core group"—the seven of us. Because we certainly weren't thinking of calling ourselves "the Founders" at that time.*

MW: No, we certainly weren't. Well, one of my recollections is that the group sort of fluctuated. We would invite different people to this meeting or that meeting. My recollection is that it was very loose, not set in stone.

MAC: *Right, I would agree with that. But the seven of us did some official organizing like picking a name for the new group and deciding who the officers were going to be. And in doing that, we seven became a sort of core group, wouldn't you agree?*

MW: Yes, I would agree with that. That's pretty much the way I remember it too. We seven were the core group and the others came along at various points.

MAC: *I remember the discussion of who would be president. You said, "Let's make it Marian."*

MW: Yes, Marian, of course, always says that the reason we picked her was that she was out of the room at that time. She went to make coffee or something. But we all thought that she would make a good president.

MAC: *Speaking for myself, I think the rest of us thought it should either be you or Marian because you were the ones who came up with the idea, so it seemed fitting that one of you should be president of this new group.*

MW: Well, I thought having Marian as president was a great idea, and I still do. She was an excellent president, very articulate. Marian was comfortable speaking in front of groups and to health professionals. I thought she did a great job as LLL's president for all of the years that she held that post.

MAC: *Mary, if you were to describe La Leche League to someone who didn't know us, what would you say are our identifying points—how we operated and how we reached out to others.*

MW: I think I would say that we originally got together to see if we could help mothers who wanted to nurse their babies, plain and simple. We realized that they needed a lot of support and encouragement. And, of course, they also wanted basic "how-to" information. But from the very beginning we realized that new mothers needed more than just "how-to" information. They needed the company of other like-minded women.

The group idea really seemed to fulfill this need. So that was the basic premise of La Leche League Meetings—support and encouragement for the new mother, coupled with solid research and reliable information about breastfeeding.

MAC: And didn't we decide on a discussion-type format for our Group Meetings right from the beginning?

MW: Yes, that's right. The whole idea was to share ideas and experiences. We also decided early on to have somebody leading the discussion who could keep it going in the right direction.

Edwina Froehlich

MAC: Okay, so moving ahead to that first meeting for mothers held at Mary White's house, do you have any vivid recollections of that meeting?

EF: Yes, I do. I remember that Marian was kind of running the meeting. And that Dorothy Ratner was sitting next to her. We were thrilled to have Dorothy there because she was a doctor. I don't think that she had ever really practiced medicine, but she was a bona fide doctor. And she was also a mother who had nursed her own babies. So it was wonderful to have her there, to have that kind of back-up. Because in those days nobody took you seriously when it came to giving child care advice unless you had medical authorities backing you up. So we felt that having her there gave our group a certain credibility, a certain legitimacy that we wouldn't have had otherwise.

MAC: Do you remember if Dr. Greg White was at that first meeting?

EF: I don't know if he came to that meeting or not. I do remember some meetings where Greg White would come in near the end of the meeting, and we would throw questions at him. But he wouldn't sit in for the whole meeting. We know what would have happened if he had done that. Anytime we had a doctor sitting in on a meeting, all questions were directed to that doctor. That doctor, for all intents and purposes, took over the meeting. That's one of the things I think we always appreciated about Herb Ratner and Greg White—they could have easily taken over and dominated our meetings, but they never did. Dorothy Ratner wasn't like that. She attended some of the early meetings but she was a mother too, so she contributed to the discussion as a mother not as a doctor. But she helped build our confidence by being there. We knew she would let us know if we were giving mothers the wrong information.

MAC: Okay, you've been describing the first meeting where we invited mothers from the community. But, let's go back a bit before that. Do you have any recollections about the planning sessions that were attended by the seven of us Founders before we had that first general meeting?

EF: Well, as I recall, we had to get our planning going pretty fast. And so, when the seven of us got together, we very quickly chose Marian as our president and Betty as

In 1990, Edwina visited the shrine of
Our Lady of La Leche in St. Augustine, Florida.

our treasurer. I offered to be secretary because that's how I had made my living for so many years before I was married and had children, so that seemed logical.

We also decided to charge dues for this club we were starting. A very small amount, but we did have a membership fee. We thought it would help mothers feel they "belonged" to the group and we also needed money to cover our expenses. But we never restriceted our meetings to only include members. We were always willing to help anyone who called.

MAC: And then, of course, we had to choose a name for the group. Edwina, do you remember what a hard time we had finding a good name for the group? Our husbands were making up all sorts of names for us, like the "Busty Broads" and the "Milk Maids." We laughed at their teasing, but we really were kind of stuck for a while about what to call ourselves.

EF: Right, right. We knew those names wouldn't work. We had a hard time choosing a name because the newspapers and various places where we advertised the group didn't want us to use the word "breastfeeding."

MAC: As I recall, it was actually Greg White who came up with the name that we ultimately chose, wasn't it?

EF: Yes, it seems that a patient of Dr. White's sent him a postcard from St. Augustine, Florida with a picture of an old Spanish shrine. The statue was supposed to have been brought to the New World by Spanish explorers in the 1500s. The name of the statue was Nuestra Senora de la Leche y Buen Parto.

We were excited when we learned about this shrine. We thought, "Hey, that's it! That's the name for us." The name La Leche League solved our problem in regard to not having to use the word "breastfeeding" in the title of our organization. In addition to that, we kind of felt that, if we named ourselves after Our Lady of La Leche then she could, in effect, be a sort of sponsor for our fledgling organization. We felt that because Our Lady of Leche was a breastfeeding mother, she would understand what we were trying to do, and guide us in the best way to go about accomplishing our goal of helping new mothers to breastfeed. So we just kind of put the whole thing in her hands.

MAC: How would you describe the information that we passed on to the mothers who attended those early meetings? I mean, nowadays we have such a vast background, but back then we didn't know much beyond our own personal experience.

EF: Right, right. Well, actually we didn't have a whole lot to go on. There was very little published material on breastfeeding at that time that was available to the general public. But we had various sources.

For one thing, Mary White combed through everything she could find of Greg's to see what she could come up with. And I remember that we also found a magazine, *Child-Family Digest,* that was put out by Charlotte Aiken and her husband, John, down in New Orleans. So we had that. And I also remember Marian Tompson reading an article from the *Reader's Digest* at some of the early meetings. It was called "Breast Is Best."

We were also in touch with Mildred Hatch, I remember, in California. Mildred was a nutritionist, and very much into natural foods. She may have been the one who put us in touch with Charlotte Aiken. Mildred told us, "There's this woman in New Orleans who is right up your alley. You are one in your belief about doing things the natural way, especially when it comes to children."

We found one or two articles in various issues of *Child-Family Digest* that were relevant to what we were discussing at the meetings. So that's the way we started our meetings. Marian would read whatever printed information she had. That was very valuable to us because it gave us a source, it gave us references. We had to have that in order to combat the medical advice that was being handed out all the time that was strictly about bottle-feeding.

So at each meeting, Marian would find something somewhere that she could read to us, and we would discuss what the article said. Then we would devote the rest of the meeting to talking about our own experiences or those of the other mothers who were there.

MAC: Edwina, at the time we started La Leche League we certainly had no idea that a neighborhood discussion group would eventually turn into an organization providing information and support for breastfeeding mothers worldwide.

EF: No, we certainly didn't.

MAC: Knowing what we know now about how groups grow and evolve, do you think that it would be easier to get an organization up and running today than it was 40 years ago? Or do you think that the conditions were "just right" in 1956, and that it would actually be more difficult to get a group like La Leche League up and running now?

EF: Well, I do think that timing had something to do with the success of La Leche League. In the 1950s people knew that they wanted to have families—that was the dominant theme of the post World War II family. Having children was thought of as a good thing, not something that "dragged you down."

So there was that—young married couples wanted to have children. But beyond that, they also wanted to raise those children somewhat differently than they had been raised—more naturally, with perhaps fewer "rules and regulations." So people, young married couples, were open to new ideas, were open to the idea of doing things "nature's way." It was La Leche League's good fortune to come along and tap into that feeling at a time when people were open to what we had to say.

MAC: *Edwina, does anything in particular stand out for you from those early La Leche League meetings? Was there anything that surprised you, or any particular nursing questions or situations that you remember being discussed at those first few meetings?*

EF: Yes. I remember one mother at the first meeting who came with a new baby. She was breastfeeding this baby, but she didn't feel that it was going very well. Turns out that her doctor had told her to put the baby on a four-hour schedule, and stick to it. We told her that she probably wasn't nursing often enough, and that if she started nursing the baby every couple of hours, her milk supply would gradually increase. We reassured her that that was a perfectly normal nursing schedule, especially for a young baby. She seemed relieved to hear that.

And then I remember that there were a couple of other mothers who were friends. They were not nursing babies at the time of that first meeting. As I recall, they both told stories about how they had tried to nurse, but for one reason or another, had not been successful. They had come to the meeting hoping to pick up a few tips, so that the next time they had a baby, they would have a better chance of having a positive nursing experience.

One of the mothers said that she was always saving her milk from one nursing period to the next because her doctor had told her, "Be careful, or you will drain all of the milk out of your breasts in one nursing period, and you won't have enough milk the next time the baby wants to nurse." And the other mother had been told, "Don't nurse too long or you will get sore nipples and then you may have to stop nursing altogether." So that was the kind of misinformation that was coming from the medical establishment in those days.

Betty Wagner

MAC: Betty, what do you remember about the first "real" La Leche League meeting— the one that was held at Mary White's house in October 1956?

BW: Well, let's see. I remember Marian Tompson read that "Breast Is Best" article from the *Reader's Digest*. And then we discussed the ideas in that article. And I remember that Mary White had gathered together some books on breastfeeding and childbirth. She had Frank Richardson's book, *The Nursing Mother*. So we had the beginnings of a little "lending library" for mothers who wanted to do some additional reading on breastfeeding and child care and other related topics.

I remember that six of the Founders were there—I don't remember Vi being there. And there were two or three other women there who were patients of Dr. White's, and another one or two who were friends of someone else in the group. So I would say that there were about a dozen women present at La Leche League's first real meeting.

I also remember that the seven of us didn't continue going to the same group for very long after that first meeting. After just two or three meetings, we split into two groups. You (Mary Ann Cahill), Edwina Froehlich, and I were in one group, and Mary White, Marian Tompson, and Mary Ann Kerwin were in the other group. And Vi—hmmm—I think that I remember Vi coming to our group once. I don't know if she went to the other group as well.

MAC: Betty, what are your recollections of setting up our organization—choosing a name, deciding on the format of the meetings, things like that?

BW: Well, we had a lot of meetings that didn't include outside people when we set things up. It was all done pretty quickly. The idea of the four-meeting series was decided on pretty early on.

MAC: Yes, setting up a structure wasn't particularly important to us. Basically, we just wanted to get this information about breastfeeding out to mothers. But then, at some point, we had to have a name, since we wanted to publicize the group.

BW: Yes, and that's when we found out that we couldn't use the word, "breast." We considered using the phrase, "natural feeding," which was sort of clumsy, and I don't think most people knew what we were talking about with that phrase. So eventually we settled on the name, "La Leche League," which a lot of other people also didn't understand. But there was a story behind that name, of Our Lady of La Leche, and the shrine down in Florida.

So that's the name that we decided on, and that's what we've been ever since.

Viola Lennon

MAC: *So, Vi, tell me what your memories are of our first few La Leche League Meetings—how we got the organization up and running, choosing officers, and a name for the group—all of that.*

VL: Well, Edwina, of course, was the one who called me to tell me about a group that was getting started to talk about breastfeeding and mothering. Now if Edwina had simply said, "We're going to start a group to talk about how to breastfeed," I probably would not have gone to the meeting. I already had three children by that time—Beth, Mark, and Mimi—and I figured that I had the breastfeeding thing pretty well figured out. But, Edwina used the word "mothering" to describe what we were going to talk about. That caught my attention. I wasn't quite sure what she meant by that. We didn't really use words like "mothering" in those days. Another word we never used was "nurturing"—that wasn't even in our vocabularies back then. The idea of mothering sounded interesting to me, so I decided I would go to the meeting after all, and find out what this "mothering" business was all about.

MAC: *Do you remember that first meeting at Mary White's house?*

VL: I sure do. I have a funny reason for remembering it. I went to the White's house and, not long into the meeting, I started feeling terribly ill. And I realized that one of the things that was bothering me was that they were painting somewhere in the house, and the smell of paint was beginning to sicken me. But I decided to stick around anyhow. What I didn't realize was that the reason the paint smell was having such an effect on me was because I was pregnant with Rebecca. My third baby, Melissa—we called her Mimi—was only about four months old at that time, so being pregnant again so soon was the furthest thing from my mind. But, that's what the situation was—I was pregnant with my fourth baby, Rebecca. Melissa had been born on June 13, 1956 and Rebecca was born just a little more than 12 months later, on June 30, 1957. They were my "Irish twins" (a term usually used to designate two babies in the same family who are not actually twins but are born less than a year apart). So, I definitely remember that first La Leche League meeting.

MAC: *What do you recall about the planning meeting that we held prior to our first general meeting? I mean, the meeting where we picked officers for our fledgling organization.*

VL: In truth, I don't remember much about that. In fact, I may not have even been at that meeting. You have to remember, I'm the one who was the Chicagoan, and the rest of you were pretty much living in Franklin Park. So sometimes I didn't make it to some of the meetings.

Mary Ann Kerwin

MAC: *Mary Ann, talk a little bit, if you will, about how we organized La Leche League in the early days, and how we chose the name of our fledgling organization.*

MAK: Okay, Well, my recollection of choosing the first officers of LLL is that the whole process was very informal and based on logic and common sense.

For instance, Edwina was a natural for secretary of the group because she had worked as a secretary for many years—more than a decade—prior to her marriage. And I was the one who suggested that Betty should be our treasurer—she had worked in a bank, so she seemed to be the logical choice. Betty volunteered to take on that job, and we were glad to have her do it. As for myself, I volunteered to be the group's librarian, mainly because I liked to read! Seriously, though, I liked to stay current on topics that interested me. Even before La Leche League was started, Mary and Greg had passed along articles and references to information on breastfeeding and childbirth because those were topics that I was interested in. So I guess I seemed like a logical person to be the group's librarian.

So, no, I don't remember any formal "elections" as such. It was just sort of a voluntary process based on who wanted to do what.

MAC: *Yes, that's pretty much the way that I remember the whole process of "choosing officers," too—we just volunteered for different jobs, and everyone said, "Fine, now we have that settled." But we did have a trickier time choosing a name for our little "breastfeeding club" though, didn't we? Tell us what you remember about that process.*

MAK: Oh, yes—our name. We really had to struggle to come up with our name. We explored many options, but we seemed to be striking out on all of them.

We quickly decided that using the word "breastfeeding" was out. Somehow actually using the word "breast" or "breastfeeding" seemed to embarrass people or make them uncomfortable. And we had reason to believe that, if we chose a name with the word "breastfeeding" in it, we would have a hard time getting publicity—that newspaper writers and others would hesitate to write about us because they would be uncomfortable writing abut a "breastfeeding club."

After we ruled out having the word "breast" or "breastfeeding" in our name, we tried to come up with names that used the word "nursing." For instance, I remember that someone suggested the name, "Nursing Mothers Anonymous." But we ruled that out because it sounded rather ambiguous, and we were afraid that people would think that we were a group of nurses.

Basically, I remember that we batted around dozens of different ideas, some of which were quite amusing and even ridiculous, but we still couldn't seem to come up with something that everyone liked. I remember we were at the White's house for one of these planning sessions, and we were talking once again about what we should call ourselves. And apparently Greg heard us, because he wandered into the room and said, "Why don't you name your group after this shrine in Florida?"

We seemed to be out of other options. So we rather quickly, and without a lot

Marian Tompson, on the left, with Mary Ann Kerwin.

of discussion, agreed that "La Leche League" would be the name of our organization. I don't know if we were all thrilled with that particular name, but it seemed like our best option at the time.

MAC: How did you feel about the name "La Leche League"? You don't sound particularly enthusiastic about it.

MAK: In all honesty, I didn't especially like the name, but I knew we had not been able to come up with anything better. I guess that I felt a little sorry that the name of our organization had to be, in effect, a disguise. Also, in that time and place—Franklin Park, Illinois in the 1950s—Spanish was not spoken by the vast majority of the women who came to our meetings. I felt that newcomers would trip over the words, that they wouldn't understand what it meant, and that we would have to be explaining ourselves all the time. And that's pretty much what did happen.

MAC: So you didn't envision us becoming a worldwide organization where having a Spanish name might actually be an asset?

MAK: No, oh no. My vision was initially just helping mothers in the neighborhood. Then, with a little bit of publicity we began to spread to other suburbs in Chicago. And then, after a year or two, we began to get inquiries from other states.

No, in the beginning I don't think that any of us ever envisioned that La Leche League would spread throughout the United States and eventually to countries around the world. So trying to choose an "international" name was the last thing on my mind as a consideration in choosing a name. But, don't get me wrong. We were unanimous in our decision (to use the name "La Leche League"). I don't think there was any one of us, including myself, who felt that any of the other names that had been suggested would be better than the name we chose. So that was it—we became "La Leche League" and eventually, "La Leche League International." So maybe it was a good choice after all.

Chapter 4 — Defining the Philosophy

For a mother, indeed for her whole family, breastfeeding marks a beginning, a starting point on a journey of discovery. The Founders knew in their hearts that helping a mother become proficient in feeding her baby at the breast was not their only goal. Tapping into a new and more rewarding way of mothering the baby was also part of the process, the flip side of the breastfeeding coin. Defining this process or philosophy involved peeling back layers of truth that had come close to being lost in the modern world.

It was a world of two working parents, the father "earning a living" in a job outside the home, and the mother working full-time caring for the children and house. In an incongruous reversal of values, the house had almost come to be more important than the little people in it. Women were judged on their ability to keep a spotless house, one where children's things were kept in perfect order. There was to be no evidence, such as fingerprints or muddy shoe tracks, of the children themselves. It was not uncommon for a mother to confine her toddler in a playpen or crib so that she could clean her house undisturbed. The baby's bottle was propped, and if the baby fussed, it just had to be tolerated. When parents had an evening out, it was understood that the baby remained at home.

Again, Drs. White and Ratner were invited to be part of the discussions as we worked on defining our philosophy. On more than one occasion, Dr. White could be heard saying, "A baby's wants are a baby's needs." It was one of those short, pithy axioms that sticks with a person, but it was also a radical idea. Everybody knew that "giving in to the baby" was akin to "spoiling" the child and was sure to create untold problems in the future. But for those who bucked the trend and put this more responsive parenting into practice, the outcome was a happier baby and a more relaxed family.

As Public Health Officer of Oak Park, Illinois, a vibrant, mid-sized town adjacent to Chicago, Dr. Ratner had been conducting a forum for parents for a number of years. All of the Founders had participated in these thought-provoking forums and had subsequently adopted the ideas into their own parenting. Later, their personal experiences proved invaluable in defending the wisdom of "loving guidance" as a basis for discipline.

Many of the beliefs encompassed in La Leche League's philosophy were accepted without question. The superiority of a mother's milk for her baby was one. Also, the Founders were of one mind on keeping the baby with the mother immediately after birth. A welcoming first nursing, followed by unlimited, leisurely, loving time at the breast, was a high priority. But achieving this ideal could be a frustrating experience for many parents, since even the most determined could be thwarted by the restrictive practices of doctors and hospitals. The generally accepted and extensive use of pain medication in childbirth posed one such roadblock. A mother and baby groggy from drugs already have a number of strikes against them, making breastfeeding an uphill battle.

Most of the Founders had sidestepped such difficulties by choosing to give birth at home with Dr. White in attendance. It was a wonderful arrangement, with the doctor coming to mother, rather than the other way around.

Word of these unorthodox home births soon spread throughout La Leche League, though no attempt was made to promote home births at LLL meetings. The contrast spoke for itself, helped along no doubt by the sight of a glowing mother at an LLL meeting telling of her joyful, never-to-be-forgotten experience giving birth in the familiar surroundings of her own home, surrounded by family, not strangers.

Yet not everyone in La Leche League bought into this idyllic picture. As LLL Groups proliferated and spread farther from the center, a movement developed that questioned why childbirth should even be a part of Series Meetings. How a mother chose to give birth was a matter for her and her doctor to decide, and the business of La Leche League was to come in at the point when she wants to breastfeed the baby. Those who questioned this had the best of intentions—the dissatisfied Leaders felt they would reach more mothers if childbirth was left out. They asked "Is La Leche League a breastfeeding organization or what?"

It may have been the first time that question was asked, but it would not be the last. Over the years, discussions have repeatedly surfaced as to whether La Leche League's mission is about breastfeeding or, for instance, mothering. It is not an unhealthy exercise, since each generation of mothers must wrestle with the question and make the answer its own.

By the time the childbirth question came up, the two Mary Anns had moved; the Cahills to Libertyville, Illinois, about 30 miles north of Franklin Park, and the Kerwins, a much more distant thousand miles away to Denver, Colorado. The miles did not exclude them from the circle. When the hotly contested childbirth issue came to the fore, calls went out and each Founder was polled on the matter. Polling the Founders became a standard practice that has persisted through the years.

The response of all those years ago on the childbirth issue was unanimous: Mary, Marian, Edwina, Betty, Viola, and the two Mary Anns all agreed that a good birth experience is an important step to successful breastfeeding. And so the connection remained, yet distinctions have been made, with added attention placed on helping mothers understand the types of birth options available to them.

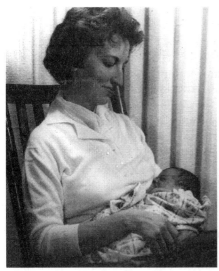

Mary Ann Cahill, on the left, and Betty Wagner posed for breastfeeding photos with their babies to show how mothers could breastfeed discreetly; these photos were used to illustrate brochures and pamphlets.

Eventually, other voices were also raised in support of a good birth, as a number of excellent books came out on the subject.

Yet immediate agreement among the Founders was not always the order of the day. An understanding of just what LLL Philosophy encompassed evolved over time. The "relief bottle" was a case in point, often suggested as a way to make life easier for the breastfeeding mother and family. But, it was what the proponents didn't know that posed the problem.

In the past, both Betty and Mary Ann Cahill had given their babies an occasional "relief bottle" consisting of cow's milk, water, and a little sugar. Betty had passed the "recipe" to Mary Ann, and neither could recall having any problems with it, though Mary Ann remembered her Timmy preferring to wait until she came home rather than ingest the strange concoction. For the most part, it was the dad or grandmother caring for the baby who was relieved to have something to fall back on, "just in case." Why these two mothers had not expressed their own milk isn't clear, though it must be said that giving both breast and bottle, i.e., other milk, was pretty much an accepted practice at the time. By most, perhaps, but not Mary White.

Mary knew the pitfalls, especially the risk of allergies down the road for the baby. The discussion went on for some time, with one or another mother stopping momentarily to "latch on" the baby for a breastfeeding session or perhaps dig out an apple from a diaper bag, cut and scrape it with a spoon, and feed the sweet "sauce" to an older baby who had started solids. In the end, Betty and Mary Ann were won over, and the overall good sense of taking the baby along, even when it goes against social norms, was ever more firmly planted in the Founders' minds.

La Leche League functions had always been geared to mothers with babies in tow, and soon countless stories were circulating on how to accommodate one's little "travelin' buddy." Baby carriers went mainstream and could be seen in multiple circumstances worn by mothers and dads alike, a bright-eyed youngster riding front or back, happily surveying the world.

Along the way, Mary White became known as the "guardian angel" of the mother-baby relationship. Mary never hesitated to speak out. Circumstances might change, she'd remind the group, but a baby's needs do not.

For all the emphasis in La Leche League as an organization for and by mothers, there was never any question as to the importance of fathers. Each of the Founders could recall numerous instances of how crucial her husband's support had been to her as a mother. Breastfeeding the baby is a commitment, one that often takes precedence over others' needs or wants. Without a husband's understanding, this could cause problems. For La Leche League as a whole, the advent of the Women's Movement brought parental roles into question. Why couldn't—shouldn't—a father be the caregiver for the baby? Who's to say that fathers can't be as nurturing as mothers?

La Leche League says so, not because fathers can't be nurturing, since they can, but rather because they nurture differently, and besides, everything in the young child's makeup cries out for mother. Father and mother are each a specialist in his or her own right. When the Founders defined LLL philosophy, care was taken to include the Father's Role.

Perhaps the most contentious issue for the greatest number of LLL mothers in the early days had to do with solids. La Leche League's strong stand on not starting solids for the healthy, full-term baby until six months of age put it in direct opposition to the prevailing medical opinion of the time. Many doctors were telling mothers to start solids as early as six weeks, and mothers were getting the impression that withholding the prescribed cereal and vegetables would have all kinds of dire consequences, from depriving the baby's brain of vital nutrients to causing a child to reject the spoon.

Mothers were in a quandary, on the one hand feeling an obligation to follow the doctor's orders, while at the same time being impressed over and over by the healthy, happy, totally breastfed six-month-old babies to be seen everywhere at LLL meetings. Grappling with this dilemma occupied many a discussion at the Series Meeting on "Nutrition and Weaning." Probably the majority of the mothers at the time chose not to confront their doctor but to continue exclusive breastfeeding. As long as their babies were doing well, they felt safe and even vindicated. A few brave souls questioned their doctors and, to their credit, some doctors took a second look and went along with the mother's wishes to delay solids, broadening their own knowledge of the breastfed baby.

Even more trying was the situation of the mother whose baby did not gain according to the standard weight-gain charts then in use. The baby might be either below or above the standard, but in either case, the breastfeeding always seemed to be blamed for the perceived problem. It was not until many years later that the scientific community took on the task of revising the tables, which had been based on data from formula-fed babies. New evidence supported what breastfeeding mothers already knew in their hearts; their healthy, active breastfed babies might follow a different curve on the chart, but slim or chunky, they are just right.

In the meantime, mothers found support in their LLL Groups to continue breastfeeding against the odds. They also found a whole new approach to feeding the family. Good nutrition was a key component of La Leche League's basic message.

When looking at the seven, it could be said that all were nutrition-minded, but Edwina truly lived and breathed the subject. Her enthusiasm, devotion to learning, the joy she took in preparing good food, and her faithfulness to the high standards she set for herself, all inspired countless families over the years. Again, La Leche League was ahead of its time in promoting a healthy diet. Fresh was in, as were also whole grains, low sugar, and non-processed foods. Armed with information gained at LLL meetings, mothers began reading food labels when shopping and started co-ops among themselves to get the best buys on the best products. It is not uncommon among LLL families for the children, now grown, to reminisce on how they had been the only ones in their class to bring sandwiches on whole-wheat bread in their school lunch box.

Weaning was an issue where the Founders themselves had a lot to learn. Back when La Leche League started, weaning seemed rather simple. Based on their own experience at the time, the Founders concluded that babies lose interest in the breast at around a year old, and the chapter titled "Weaning, Gradually and with Love," in the early editions of THE WOMANLY ART OF BREASTFEEDING blithely says as much. Later editions of the manual set the record straight and addressed the many joys and challenges of breastfeeding the older child.

The topic of discipline, now, challenged both parents and La Leche League. While mothers readily espoused the idea of a baby's wants and needs being the same, they were often unsure of how to distinguish between the two as their child grew older. It became a matter of learning how to set limits for parents and child. Discipline without physical punishment, which La Leche League advocates, was something of an anomaly at the time, and parents searched for alternatives to the slap on the hand or spanking that were the accepted, even expected, practice for making children "mind." Again, the Founders drew on experience. Those who had older children when La Leche League began had already gone through a number of stages and had decided that there are better ways than hitting to guide a child in being a good, kind, and caring person. Loving guidance, they concluded, is work, but it works.

So does setting priorities, and for the women involved in this new and increasingly time-consuming venture, "Family First" became a guiding principle. It was never voted on, just acted upon. When a mother had a new baby, it was taken for granted that she would devote herself to her baby and family and that others in the group would pick up her LLL work for a time. A lofty philosophy has meaning, they realized, only when people believe in it and live it. The fact that more and more people were making it their own was tremendously exciting. The people who joined in the effort to make it known were pioneers, the early heroes. They were exceptionally generous and gifted, and each has a story worth telling.

Marian Tompson

MAC: *Some people have described LLL philosophy as "an attitude, a special feeling, about the importance of mothering." How would you define or describe LLL philosophy, Marian?*

MT: Speaking personally, the philosophy that Tom and I had as we embarked on raising a family was simply to do the best we could for our children. That idea, that "philosophy" if you will, took different forms over the years.

For instance, it was the idea of wanting to do what was right and best for our children that caused me to want to have unmedicated births. And that's also why, even before my first pregnancy, I planned on breastfeeding my babies.

I don't know exactly how my own philosophy and whatever we define as "LLL philosophy" intersect or diverge. I guess the one thing that both my personal philosophy and LLL philosophy have in common can be summed up in one sentence: "Be sensitive to the needs of your children."

MAC: *Looking specifically at the baby and toddler period, how did La Leche League philosophy influence your parenting during that phase of your children's lives?*

MT: Well, I believe that the foundation of LLL philosophy is the idea that the baby has legitimate needs. And secondly, the baby is capable of making those needs known to his or her mother. You should also realize that every baby is different. Some are cranky and high strung. Others are placid and laid back; they don't cry very much.

Nevertheless, they all have the same basic needs. Your job as a mother is to pay attention to what your baby is trying to tell you. Then you will have a happy, healthy baby who thrives on having his or her needs met.

MAC: *Marian, would you say that your own parenting was affected by being involved in La Leche League? League?*

MT: Well, it had already been affected by being exposed to Dr. Ratner's talks on parenting. I remember the first time Tom and I went to one of those talks, and we came out of it and I just said with relief, "Tom, we've been doing the right thing all along."

Because what we had been doing was so different than what anybody in our neighborhood was doing. I had thought that I was behaving the way I did because I had a weakness. I couldn't bear to spank my children, I couldn't bear to have them cry it out. I would carry them around all the time. And I thought it was because of a weakness in me. Then, when I heard Dr. Ratner talk I realized I had been responding to the needs of my children. So that was an enormous relief.

I am sure that being around women who felt the way I did about parenting strengthened my resolve to act in a way that felt right to me as a mother. Mary White was a big influence in that regard, with her casual attitude toward a lot of things that I had previously gotten very uptight about. I think she and Greg made a real strong impression on us, and were really helpful in helping me understand a different style of parenting.

MAC: Vi, do you remember our discussions with Dr. Ratner?

VL: Yes. I remember being very interested in Dr. Ratner's ideas on mothering, his theories on the importance of motherhood, both to your own baby, to the woman herself, and to society as a whole.

That appealed to me very much. I had some vague ideas of my own on the importance of motherhood as a calling, as a vocation, if you will. But I had not thought them out very clearly. I don't know that anyone else in the group had either, quite frankly.

But I did have some experience with creating and helping to articulate a group's philosophy. When I was in Young Christian Workers (YCW—a Catholic group for working people that was especially active in Europe right after WWII) we spent a lot of time discussing the relationship of work and life—the proper role of work in your life, how to integrate work into your life, what is meaningful work—that kind of thing.

So it didn't seem too terribly strange or far-fetched to me to apply the same questions, the same kind of analytical thinking to the concept of mothering. After all motherhood is at least as big a topic as work.

MAC: Yes, it certainly is. So, do you remember what kind of questions that we discussed with Herb Ratner in those dialogue sessions on the nature of mothering?

VL: Well, some of the questions and concepts that we discussed were: What is a good mother? How does a woman, particularly a new mother, learn how to mother effectively? What role does breastfeeding play in the development of a woman as a mother? In what ways does a woman change when she becomes a mother? Those were the basic questions and concepts that we discussed.

Of course, it was one thing to raise the questions. But it took some of us quite a while to work out the answers to those questions—in some cases it took years.

MAC: Did your ideas about mothering change with your involvement with La Leche League?

VL: Yes, definitely. In particular, I think that the biggest change in my thinking was in regard to discipline. Like most everybody else in those days, I equated discipline with punishment. But after LLL came along, we began discussing questions like, "What is the purpose of discipline in raising children? What are your goals in administering discipline? What are the most effective ways of disciplining children?" and so on.

And then, after I had been in La Leche League for a while, and had a chance to talk these questions over with the other Founders, it all came together for me. That was when I realized that the proper role of discipline in raising children was not to punish them. The proper role of discipline is to provide loving guidance for your children. The job of a parent is to teach your children how to make good choices. If you have done that, then you can say that, as a parent, you have been an effective disciplinarian.

The other thing that I would like to mention is that I think breastfeeding, in and of itself, gives you some vision of what a human person is. To me, breastfeeding your baby leads to self-discovery. I think that's an important aspect of nursing that is seldom discussed.

MAC: Were there any other areas or topics where your ideas were changed in a significant way by your involvement with La Leche League? For instance, did you change your mind about what it meant to "spoil" a child after you got involved with La Leche League?"

VL: Oh, yes, I changed my mind quite a bit in regard to "spoiling" a baby. I think that I had a lot of the same cultural attitudes that almost everyone else had about "spoiling" a child. You know, that if you pick up a baby every time he or she cries, you will "spoil" the baby. And, of course, that you cannot "give in" every time a toddler wants you to do something, or wants his own way in a particular situation, or you will "spoil" him.

MAC: I understand what you are saying. My ideas on "spoiling" changed after I was in LLL for a while too. But sometimes LLL mothers are accused of being too easygoing. So do you think that it is possible to spoil your children by being too permissive with them? In other words, is it possible to have too much of a good thing?

VL: Oh yes, absolutely. I'll give you an example. I am generally looked upon as being a pretty easygoing grandmother. But I remember one time I was taking care of three of my daughter's children—they were six, four, and one at the time. The second oldest and most spirited of the boys hit his brother. So I corrected him. He let a few minutes pass and he hit him again, so I corrected him again. He let a little more time pass, and then he hit his brother a third time. So I picked him up and put him on a chair and said, "Okay. You didn't listen to Grandma so you are going to have to sit here until you turn back into your nice self." His response was, "Grandma, I can't believe you are doing this to me!"

So you see, to me it is quite clear that there is a difference between loving guidance and excessive permissiveness. It has to do with age, with intent, and with knowing your child—or your grandchild. I think there's a lot of misunderstanding nowadays in recognizing the difference between loving guidance and being overly permissive. The two are not the same.

MAC: In the early days, I think you will agree, we were under a lot of pressure to endorse the idea of a "relief bottle." New mothers were told by their doctors and friends that they ought to give their baby at least one bottle a day so that if a mother had to be away from home for any length of time, the baby would know how to take a bottle. And of course, they were talking about a bottle of formula—hardly anyone expressed milk as a "back-up" in those days. So what were your feelings about getting your baby accustomed to the bottle, just in case?

VL: Except for Mimi, I never gave a bottle.

MAC: You had an unusual experience breastfeeding Melissa, didn't you?

VBL: That's right. At about three-and-a-half months of age she stopped nursing. She just flat out wouldn't nurse anymore. I took her to the doctor. He watched as I tried to nurse her, but she just turned her head. I don't think he believed me until he saw for himself that she was refusing to nurse. We tried everything. We tried to starve her. We gave her a little water. No matter what we tried, Melissa simply would not nurse. It was really strange.

But then, nine months later, Rebecca was born. So I wonder, did the constitution of the milk change? Did it somehow taste different to her, even just a couple of weeks into my pregnancy. That's the only thing I can think of. All I know is that we tried everything and nothing worked. So I had to put her on formula. I had never even made a formula. I had no bottles in the house. Mimi was the only Lennon who was ever given formula. I didn't want to do that, but that's what we had to do.

MAC: And our approach to childbirth? Of course, you started out with Greg White as your doctor, which put you one step ahead of most of us in being accustomed to the idea of home birth.

VL: Yes, but it still took me three babies to move into home birth. Nevertheless, I don't feel that the concept of home birth is or should be considered essential to LLL philosophy.

I think that home births are wonderful, and I am very glad that I had as many home births as I did. I never went back to the hospital after I started having my babies at home. At the same time, however, I don't ever think that we should try to give the impression that having a home birth is required in order to be a "real" La Leche League mother.

MAC: And what about the concept of "nurse early and often." Do you remember having any thoughts on that part of LLL philosophy?

VL: As far as "early and often" is concerned—of course I believe in that! That's the only way breastfeeding is going to get off to a good start. And it's also the only way that a woman is going to build up an adequate supply of milk. So you'll get no argument from me on that.

MAC: What about delayed solids?

VL: With my first baby, Elizabeth, I didn't delay. I fed her solids beginning at three months of age. As you know, Greg White was my doctor. He didn't exactly agree, but he didn't particularly try to talk me out of it, either. As I look back on it, the main reason I gave Elizabeth solids was because all my neighbors were feeding their babies solids at three months, or even sooner. Not a very good reason!

So I guess you could say that I was a victim of my era and my neighborhood. But when I was expecting my second baby I did some reading, and decided that maybe it would be a good idea to hold off on the solids until the baby was maybe five or six months old. It's too hard to feed a three-month-old baby solids.

MAC: Weaning—what are your thoughts on that topic?

VL: My weaning experience with Elizabeth was not very pleasant, to say the least. It was a terribly hot summer that year. Elizabeth was cross and crabby and sort of disinterested in nursing. So I decided that it was time to wean. It was very hard, because it was just miserable all around Chicago that year. And remember, we didn't have air conditioning back in those days.

So I weaned her, and we just got on with our lives. But with Mark I nursed much longer. And with all of the subsequent Lennon children I just seemed to nurse longer and longer. I had adjusted to the fact that baby-led weaning is the way to go.

MAC: Were there any incidents that stand out in your mind in regard to our discussion of LLL's basic philosophy? I am thinking, for instance, of the controversy about childbirth. Many of the mothers who came to our meetings asked why we were talking about childbirth if we were supposed to be a breastfeeding organization.

VL: In regard to childbirth, while La Leche League doesn't necessarily recommend any kind of childbirth specifically, an educated natural childbirth is a marvelous entrance into breastfeeding.

I must say that I came to that conclusion on my own, rather than because of LLL meetings. I think that each woman has to "walk through" her own experience, and realize that you are growing and learning. Some may decide to have home births with their first babies, some with later babies, some not at all.

But by no means is La Leche League saying that, unless you have a home birth, you are not a "good mother." or that you won't have a good experience in breastfeeding your baby for as long as you wish. The vast majority of LLL Leaders around the country have never had home births, and never intend to have a home birth.

So the bottom line is that a woman has to trust her own instincts, her own feelings, and her own sense of what will work for her with each baby. If you do that, you and your baby will be fine, and you will get off to a good start with breastfeeding.

Mary Ann Kerwin

MAC: Let's talk about our motto. In browsing through a lot of our old newsletters I saw that, for a long time, our motto was "Good Mothering through Breastfeeding." Not with the very first issue, but starting with maybe the third or fourth issue of the newsletter. Do you remember how that came to be our motto?

MAK: I think that motto came about as a result of a meeting that the seven of us had with Dr. Herb Ratner in March of 1958 to discuss our philosophy of mothering—what it meant to be an effective, caring, and involved mother.

MAC: So the "Dialogue with Dr. Ratner" was the impetus for formalizing our thoughts on mothering and breastfeeding into what we now call La Leche League Philosophy?

MAK: Yes. Basically that meeting precipitated the broadening of our purpose to include a particular philosophy in regard to mothering. Breastfeeding was seen as just one component of good mothering—a very important component of course, but just one component.

As a matter of fact, I recently found an article in one our old LLL newsletters that described the "Dialogue with Dr. Ratner" as the occasion that precipitated the broadening of our purpose from teaching the how-to's of breastfeeding to new mothers, to a more comprehensive philosophy of what constitutes good mothering.

That article concluded by saying: The Founders unanimously agreed that the purpose of La Leche League shall be: "To help mothers successfully breastfeed their babies, so as to help them to successfully mother their babies."

So that's how we came up with La Leche League's stated purpose, and with La Leche League's official motto.

MAC: Yes. I vividly remember our meeting with Dr. Ratner. He really helped us clarify our thoughts and our ideas about what constituted good mothering. And I remember that we discussed the wording of our goal for quite a while. We wanted the statement of our goal to really reflect what La Leche League is all about.

MAK: Yes. So that's how "Good Mothering through Breastfeeding" became the motto of our organization.

MAC: But, as time went on, there were some variations on that theme. For instance, I seem to remember that, at one point, we changed the motto to "Better Mothering through Breastfeeding."

MAK: Yes, we but we only used the "Better Mothering" motto for a short time.

MAC: Yes, that's right. That motto didn't last long, did it?

MAK: No. Eventually, though, we changed the motto again. Now our motto is simply, "Mothering through Breastfeeding" with no reference to "good" or "better." Because in the end, that is our goal—to help women mother their babies by helping them to breastfeed their babies.

MAC: Are there any issues that stand out for you, Mary Ann, from the early days that exemplify LLL philosophy? Do you recall any specific situations or controversies that showed how LLL philosophy applied to everyday life?

MAK: Well, solid foods were a big issue. When I had our first baby in 1955, I managed to hold off on introducing solids until he was five or six months old. As the baby got beyond infancy, I felt as though a lot of people disapproved of the fact that he was getting all of his nourishment through milk. You know, the idea that "You're starving that baby!" It was a very volatile issue.

And the same could be said of breastfeeding "on demand." In the 1950s most doctors, and most mothers, too, thought that babies should be put on a four-hour feeding schedule. If you deviated from that at all, you were said to be "spoiling" the baby by giving in to his every whim. All in all, it was a very negative environment for those who tried to follow their instincts when it came to mothering.

MAC: If you got negative feedback on delaying solids and feeding on demand, I can only imagine the criticism you must have taken for having home births.

MAK: That's right—I had my first home birth even before LLL got started. Yes, most friends and acquaintances thought I was crazy, just absolutely nuts, when we had our first baby at home. But I had talked to Mary and Greg White. They had already had at least a couple of their children born at home by the time I was having my first.

After I talked it over with them—what to expect, whether it was dangerous or not, the difficulties, but also the benefits—well, then I became pretty clear in my own mind that this was something that I wanted to do. And Tom was in agreement with me, he was happy to do whatever I felt comfortable doing.

We had home births with our first three children, and everything worked out fine. But yes, before we had our first, I got to the point where I didn't even tell people what we were planning to do, because we were getting so much negative feedback from people about having a home birth.

MAC: You must have been pretty excited when you came to our first meeting, to meet other women who felt the same way about breastfeeding and natural childbirth as you did.

MAK: Oh, yes. You see, I didn't know anyone except Mary White who was breastfeeding, let alone who had had a home birth.

I was the youngest of the seven Founders and the least experienced mother. So to meet the other Founders, all of whom had more babies and broader experience than I had, was really quite a thrill.

MAC: Mary Ann, do you remember any discussion of using formula supplements in those early meetings? Because in the 1950s, it seemed that if a woman did breastfeed her baby, it was almost always with supplements. Do you remember where we stood on the question of supplements in those days?

MAK: Yes, that is my recollection as well. Almost every woman who came to us who said that she was breastfeeding was also using formula supplements. It was considered almost impossible, almost unheard of, for a woman to be totally breast-feeding her baby. That was thought to be simply too difficult, that it would place unrealistic demands on the mother.

The idea was that every mother needs a break. And then too, there seemed to be some thought—and this idea was spread mainly by the doctors at the time—that the formula would work as a sort of "insurance policy" so that if a mother had "poor quality" milk, or not enough milk, the baby wouldn't suffer because of those deficiencies on the part of the mother. So we had to combat those misconceptions.

MAC: Yes, we did. And the same can be said about when to introduce solid foods—we had to challenge a lot of misconceptions there as well, wouldn't you agree?

MAK: Yes, we had to counteract a lot of misinformation in that area, too. In those days, many mothers introduced solids much sooner than is recommended today. It was not uncommon for mothers to begin giving their babies cereals and baby food from jars as early as three or four weeks of age.

MAC: Yes, that's right—that's what I remember too.

MAK: The main idea seemed to be that, if you fed the baby something besides mother's milk or formula, your baby would be more likely to sleep through the night. This was what both doctors and other mothers would tell you.

But right from the beginning of La Leche League we were pretty consistent in telling mothers that human milk was by far the best food for their babies up through about the first six months of life. They didn't always want to hear that, but that's what we told them—and we were right.

MAC: What is your recollection of the development of our mothering philosophy? Do you remember whether our thoughts on LLL philosophy evolved over time? Or did it seem to you that all the major components of our philosophy were there pretty much from the beginning?"

MAK: I think that most of the components of LLL philosophy were pretty much there right from the start.

MAC: *What would you say were the main ideas that both Greg White and Herb Ratner tried to pass along to us?*

MAK: I would have to say that the central idea was simply respecting the baby's needs. For instance, experience told us that letting a baby "cry it out" was not the best way to mother a child—not good for the baby and, really, not good for us, as mothers, either. Because, as you know, Mary Ann, there's nothing more difficult to do than to listen to a crying baby and not pick up that baby.

MAC: *That's for sure—and that's the way that nature intended it to be, don't you agree?*

MAK: Absolutely. We know now that crying is nature's way of getting the baby's needs met. When the baby cries, he or she is trying to tell you something. Maybe he's hungry, maybe he needs a diaper changed, maybe he just needs some comforting. Whatever it is, the best thing for the mother to do is to pick up the baby and try to meet that need. But that's not what most of society was telling mothers then—or now, for that matter. If we picked up the baby every time he or she cried, we were accused of "spoiling" the baby.

And another thing that new mothers were often told was that they should "get out more often." This was repeated over and over, even if the mother insisted that she didn't want to leave her baby, especially a brand new baby.

So these were the kinds of ideas that we were up against in the early days. Without the support of doctors like Greg White, as well as the support that we found at La Leche League meetings, I am sure that many of us would have ended up caving into some of these pressures—to our own detriment and, of course, to the detriment of our babies.

MAC: *What are your thoughts on weaning?*

MAK: In 1956, about a month before we started LLL, I weaned my first baby. He was about nine months old. Almost everybody as well as every child care book told me the appropriate weaning time was about three months and the latest point at which weaning should occur was by nine months of age. As a rule, I turned a deaf ear to all the negative influences and inaccurate information about babies and mothering prevalent in the 1950s. But aside from wondering if my baby would ever wean, I was eager to become pregnant and have another baby. At that time, I thought I could not become pregnant while breastfeeding even if my baby was eating solid foods well. With my baby breastfeeding just once a day in the morning as soon as he woke up, I decided to ask my husband to feed him breakfast in place of my nursing him. So my husband willingly gave our baby breakfast without questioning the wisdom of my plan. Meanwhile I kept out of sight. Looking back 45 years later, I know this was ridiculous! Also this was a painful and upsetting experience for both my baby and me. Had I been patient, I suspect he would have weaned on his own in a few more months.

After that I decided never to force another baby to wean. All of our other babies weaned at their own pace without any trauma whatsoever. Our second baby weaned himself when he was 13 or 14 months old. It was summertime in Chicago and the days and nights usually were hot and humid. Our baby started pointing to the water faucet at night when I would offer the breast before putting him to bed. So I gave him some water to drink from a glass. In his case, it was the night feeding that he had held onto the longest. I found each baby nursed a little longer.

Although I had nine babies, I never had to tandem nurse. When our ninth baby was almost due, our eighth baby was almost two years old. He still was nursing a bit but not regularly. I thought I might actually have to tandem nurse this time because the next baby was due any day. Then about a week before his baby brother was born, I realized the older baby had not nursed for about a week. Thus he had weaned himself after all. The youngest baby nursed the longest which seems to be typical in large families. As I recall, he nursed until he was between two-and-one-half and three years old. His weaning was gradual. I did not really know he had weaned himself until I realized one day he had not nursed for about two weeks.

Mary White

MAC: What about the struggle we went through to get the baby soon after birth, instead of waiting 12, 24, or however many hours. Nobody was talking about that at the time, were they? I mean, the importance of mother and baby being together—what later came to be called mother-infant bonding. Do you have any thoughts on that, Mary?

MW: Right. No one in mainstream health care was really taking a close look at that issue in the 1950s. Mothers and babies were routinely separated after birth, with the baby being taken to the nursery, and the mother to the recovery room. During the mother's stay in the hospital, babies were usually brought to the mothers on a strict four-hour schedule. There was no such thing as "rooming-in" or having the baby brought to you on "on demand."

MAC: Family-centered maternity care, with all that that entailed, was something that we worked very hard on over the years, wasn't it?

MW: Yes, very much so. And a lot of people contributed to that effort. For instance, Charlotte Aiken with her *Child-Family Digest*, which was such a treasure. She had been putting out her magazine for years before La Leche League even got started. Charlotte had all these wonderful stories about the importance of the mother and baby being together after birth—rooming in, nursing right after birth, and so on. It was thanks to Charlotte, and others who followed in her footsteps, that all of that finally began to change.

MAC: On another topic, what are your thoughts on the subject of the "relief" bottle? That was a hot topic in the early days, wasn't it?"

MW: Yes, oh definitely, that was a major issue in the early days of La Leche League. One of the big problems that people seemed to have with breastfeeding was the concept of "being tied down." That was a big thing in those days. The thinking was that, if I've got to be there all the time to nurse this baby, I'll never be able to get out to the movies with my husband. Or, how can we go away for the weekend, and so on and so forth, if I am so "tied down" with breastfeeding.

MAC: Yes, that's right. And some women even raised the question of, "What if something should happen to me?" The thought seemed to be that you would really be doing a disservice to the baby if you didn't give him or her an occasional "relief bottle."
Of course, we have to remember that, even among the Founders, some of us had occasionally given a bottle as a supplement or a "back-up" to our breastfeeding. Betty Wagner, for instance, would leave a bottle with the babysitter so that there would be something there in case the baby woke up and mother wasn't there. Betty was pretty much my sole source of information on breastfeeding before La Leche League got started. I remember she even told me exactly how to mix the formula for this bottle.

MW: Yes. And I can understand why you would listen to her advice, because Betty had successfully nursed several children by the time that LLL got started.

MAC: Yes. In fact, Betty says that she remembers that, in the early days of La Leche League, she tried to promote this idea of the "relief bottle" or the "back-up bottle," but that you wouldn't hear of it. Of course, there are good reasons why you shouldn't leave a bottle of formula—allergies and such.

MW: Exactly. But even more important than concerns about allergies, is what using a relief bottle can do to the mother-baby relationship. It's one of those habits that's so easy to slip into. If you have the bottle in the house, it's so handy to use it as a back-up. You tell yourself that you will use it "just this once." And then, a few days later, you need to use it again. And before you know it you are not really totally breastfeeding anymore. So I think that it's just better to avoid that "slippery slope."

MAC: Can you describe how we came up with topics for the "four-meeting" Series?

MW: We were trying to decide on the topics that needed to be covered. So we said, okay, it would be logical to start at the beginning and talk about mothers with newborns. Then somebody said, "Yes, but what about childbirth? Doesn't that affect whether the nursing relationship gets off to a good start?" And the rest of us agreed that the childbirth experience can have a tremendous impact on mother-infant bonding and the subsequent breastfeeding relationship. So we decided that one of the four meetings should focus on childbirth and the immediate postpartum breastfeeding experience. Then later on we added nutrition and weaning since, after all, the baby does transition from breastfeeding to solid foods, and eventually stops nursing altogether. So those topics—childbirth, nursing infants, introducing solids, baby-led weaning became the basis of the four-meeting Series.

MAC: Wasn't discussion about childbirth kind of controversial in the beginning?

MW: Oh, definitely, yes. There was the belief that mothers who came to us for help with breastfeeding didn't want to hear about childbirth.

MAC: The thinking was, "Why is a breastfeeding organization talking about child-birth?"

MW: Yes, exactly. And you see, it was so clear to us that there is a very close rela-tionship between having a positive childbirth experience and getting breastfeeding off to a good start. It just seemed logical to us to include childbirth among our discussion topics.

But, of course, everybody wants to defend her own experience. And you have to remember, this was the 1950s, the high-water mark of medicated childbirth. We never tried to force anybody into anything. But we thought, we've got to at least tell them about the link between natural childbirth and a good start in breastfeeding.

MAC: And on the topics of nutrition and weaning, do you remember any reaction to those topics? Especially "baby-led" weaning—people really questioned us on that point, didn't they?

MW: Yes, that was very controversial at first. I remember when our first was born I asked Greg how long I'd be nursing him. He, in his infinite wisdom, suggested "about six months." I was horrified. That was such a long time.

That's why we developed meetings on nursing toddlers, when to wean, and so on. How do you know when "wants" and "needs" are not the same? Does this lit-tle child need to nurse, or does he just want to nurse because he's bored?

We had to keep emphasizing to the mothers that the deciding factor should always be, "What is best for this child at this time?" Now with a baby, of course, picking the baby up and offering the breast when he is upset or crying is usually what the baby both wants and needs.

But later on the child may be asking to nurse because he can't think of any-thing else to do. Instead of breastfeeding, perhaps what the child really needs is for you to read a book to him, or play a game with him. Or maybe he just needs a nap. That is what meeting the needs of the child really means—meeting their real needs at that particular stage of their development.

MAC: Of course, we all started out thinking that babies should wean themselves at about a year.

MW: Yes, that was pretty much the standard advice on weaning in those days, even among the seven of us.

MAC: Then we realized that isn't always the case, that isn't always the best choice for your particular child. Most of us started to wean our babies later and later— we nursed on average until they were at least two years old, or older.

And then we moved into an era where mothers were tandem nursing two and even three children at a time. You have some definite ideas on this topic, don't you, Mary?

MW: Well, yes. You see, sometimes you have these older babies who are seemingly showing no signings of readiness for weaning and I have always thought that sometimes what they need is "other mothering." Sometimes they don't need to nurse; they just want their mother's attention.

For instance, it's so easy to just keep right on talking on the phone and pick that toddler up and "plug him in" and let him nurse because it keeps him quiet and out of trouble and you can go on about your business. Or mothers who are running around all the time, and then when mother finally comes home and sits down, the little one is trying to make up for lost time.

On the subject of tandem nursing, I have never had to do any "tandem nursing." Most of our children were two to three years apart, and somehow it just worked out that one child would be weaned before the next one came along. We came close, though.

MAC: What would you say to a mother who has an older child who is still nursing a lot in the middle of the night?

MW: Well, if the toddler is waking in the middle of the night and asking to nurse then, yes, sure, you lie down next to him and nurse him. But in the daytime it's different. You have to know if your child really needs to nurse, or if it's just become a habit. Dr. James Hymes used to talk about "habits vs. needs." He said a habit is easy to change but if a certain behavior represents a "need," it's not so easy to change it. Maybe a child who is asking to nurse doesn't really want to nurse, he just wants your undivided attention. So then you can read to him, or sit in a rocking chair and sing a lullaby until the toddler falls asleep. Different things work for different people. You have to experiment to find out what works for you and your child. If he really still needs to nurse, he'll let you know!

MAC: Another topic that stirred up some heated arguments in the early days of La Leche League was discipline. La Leche League was generally perceived as being "soft on discipline," wouldn't you agree Mary?

MW: Oh my, yes. I remember that, in the early days, my own mother would shake her head and say, "Your children are going to grow up to be spoiled brats." Well, maybe she didn't use the word "brats," but I do remember her saying that our children were going to be spoiled by a lack of "proper discipline" in our home. Of course, in later years my mother was among LLL's strongest supporters. I guess she realized that our children had turned out pretty well, despite the supposed lack of discipline.

MAC: But don't you agree, Mary, that some LLL parents take the idea of "gentle discipline" to an extreme? I mean, I think we have all seen parents, both mothers and fathers, who don't seem to know when to put some restraint on their child's behavior.

MW: Yes, that's true. That's why we developed a whole session on weaning and toddlers and all the rest of that—the toddler meetings. In those meetings we address questions such as, "How do you know when the 'wants' and the 'needs' of a toddler or a young child are not the same? If the toddler or young child wants something, does he have to have it right this minute, or can he wait a while?" That kind of thing.

The bottom line is, "Is this for the child's own good?" That's where your judgment as a parent comes in. Using La Leche League philosophy of loving guidance does not mean that you just let your children run wild, and do anything they want at any time of the day or night. Again, it's mostly a matter of using common sense, tempered with the loving kindness of a parent who really wants what is best for her child.

MAC: Mary, we have been talking about the ways that we really stuck our necks out in the early days of La Leche League, when everything we did and said seemed to run counter to what was popular in the general culture, as well as with most health care professionals. Can you think of any other areas where you feel that we set ourselves apart?

MW: Well, I think that the just whole idea of having a "club" for nursing mothers was, in itself, quite controversial. You see, in the beginning, there were three main obstacles to breastfeeding: doctors, hospitals, and social pressures, which at that time were terrible. There were even nurses in hospitals who liked to say that your baby was "their baby" until it left the hospital, if you can imagine that!

But then, when La Leche League came along, there was a forum, a gathering place, for discussing ideas like family-centered maternity care, delaying solids, baby-led weaning, and so on—all of the ideas that have come to be associated with the name La Leche League.

I think that it's probably true that we were quite naïve about what we were undertaking. And in our naivete and our enthusiasm, we didn't really listen to the people who raised objections. In a sense, they didn't even exist for us.

So we just cheerfully went on our way, doing what we had set out to do from one meeting to the next. We didn't have to use the "hard sell" on anybody. We weren't promoting a product that people had to be convinced about. And the fact that we got such a tremendous response from everybody who heard about this sort of seemed to vindicate us.

MAC: What other recollections do you have about how we defined our philosophy?

MW: In the beginning our philosophy was great influenced by Herb Ratner. He was the one who kept after us, who would say to us at various points along the way: "What is it that this new group of yours is all about? Is it about breastfeeding? Or mothering? Which is it?"

So I guess you could say that Herb was the one who really drew us out on that topic. He made us realize that the purpose of our little discussion group was not just to teach the "how to's" of breastfeeding. That it was really about the kind of mothering that you give your baby, and about what constitutes successful breastfeeding and mothering.

MAC: *Those words, "successful mothering," almost constitute fighting words with some people. People outside of La Leche League, and inside, too, on some occasions, have questioned over the years what we mean by "successful mothering." We have also been asked on many occasions why La Leche League built its philosophy around the idea that there is a "right way" to care for your baby, your toddlers, your family as a whole.*

Let's face it, the whole idea of "successful mothering" annoys some people. It upsets some people. Because when you have a "right way" to care for your baby, that implies that almost every other way is the "wrong way." Or at the very least, that every other way of caring for babies is less desirable, less satisfactory, than the way LLL recommends caring for babies.

So what do you think, Mary? Do you think that we "overstepped" the boundaries of what we, as an organization, should have been about? Do you think that we should have simply stuck to the how-to's of nursing, and let mothers decide for themselves what constitutes "successful" mothering?

MW: Well, you're absolutely right, Mary Ann. The word "successful" is a "hot button" word, especially when it is used in conjunction with the topic of mothering. People get very touchy when the word "successful" is paired with the word "mothering." Because you are making a value judgment on various mothering styles. If you say that, this woman is "successful" because she is using this particular breastfeeding or mothering technique, then it almost by definition implies that someone else, who is doing things differently is "not successful." Or at the very least, that the second mother is not as successful, not as effective in her mothering skills as she might be if she did things the "LLL way."

MAC: *So how do you respond to that? What do you say to people who say that an organization that was originally set up to help women breastfeed their babies has no business making those kinds of value judgments?*

MW: Well, I say, yeah, that's right. Maybe "Mother B" is not as successful as "Mother A." And maybe there are, in fact, effective ways of breastfeeding and mothering, and other ways that are not as effective. That's just the way it is. We are there to help mothers become the best mothers that they can be. We don't force them to do things our way, not at all. But we won't dilute our message just because some people don't want to hear what we have to say.

And you know, Mary Ann, it is possible for women to "grow" in both their mothering philosophy and their mothering skills. I mean, I myself was not successful in nursing our first baby. I think that most of the Founders would probably say that they were not successful in breastfeeding their first babies.

MAC: That was certainly true in my case. I was not able to successfully breastfeed my little Elizabeth, who was my firstborn.

MW: Right. And then, even with our subsequent babies, many of us did not nurse as long as we did later on, after we got involved with La Leche League. Or we introduced solids too early, or we used "relief bottles" on a regular basis—these are things that you begin to do differently as you learn more, and as you grow in your mothering skills.

So yes, I would say that there are varying degrees of success in mothering skills. And if that bothers some people, well, so be it.

MAC: Continuing along that line of thought, another word that we hear mentioned in a negative way in connection with La Leche League is "guilt," as in, "I don't like to go to La Leche League meetings because they make me feel guilty about how I am caring for my baby." Do you have any comments on that?

MW: Ah yes, guilt. Well, yes. We have all had experiences where someone reacted very negatively, very indignantly because La Leche League had presented something as "fact" that someone else preferred to think of as "opinion."

Apparently the idea is that, if you tell someone that something is true, and then, for whatever reason, they decide to do something else instead, that La Leche League should be held responsible for making them feel "guilty."

For instance, we tell the mothers who come to our meetings, in a positive sort of way I hope, that breastfeeding is better for their babies than bottle-feeding—better nutritionally and better in terms of mother infant-bonding. This is true; this is a fact. And yet we meet resistance to that piece of information, even from those women who voluntarily came to our meetings to learn about the benefits of breastfeeding. It seems as though some folks would have us believe that, simply by presenting the facts, we have made these mothers feel "guilty."

Well, I am sorry, I just don't buy that. You cannot force a woman to breastfeed her baby. We in La Leche League do not attempt to force or coerce anyone into breastfeeding. New mothers come to our meetings of their own free will. We share information and the collective wisdom of what we have learned from our mothering experiences. But after listening to what we have to say, it is up to each woman. Each mother makes her own decisions about breastfeeding—how long to breastfeed, whether to supplement, when to wean, and so on.

The decisions are all theirs. We just want to make sure that they are making informed decisions.

Edwina Froehlich

MAC: *Do you remember whether we talked about any topics that would come under the category of "mothering" rather than just the "how-to" techniques of breastfeeding in our early meetings?*

EF: Oh, yes, definitely. Right off the bat we were talking about the importance of holding the baby, picking up the baby rather than letting him "cry it out," breast-feeding "on demand," and so on.

You see, in those days most family doctors and pediatricians gave first-time mothers the impression that the crib was a better place for the baby than mother's arms. You were told that they would enjoy being in their crib—that they would have plenty of room there to kick their legs and flail their arms about, and that babies liked doing that. Mothers were also told that they should put a mobile over the crib, because it would teach the baby to focus their eyes on an object in their line of sight, but not too close.

So there was no shortage of advice for new mothers on how to distract or comfort or quiet babies. But the real message seemed to be that, the less time that mother had her baby in her arms, the better off the baby would be, and the better off the mother would be, too. That was really the message that was being given: "everything but mother."

I think that is why the mothers who attended those early meetings clung to us the way they did. Their maternal instincts were telling them one thing, but their doctors and the prevailing societal norms were telling them just the opposite. When they came to LLL meetings, they found support for what they instinctively wanted to do anyway. We were saying to them, "Listen to your heart! Do what feels right for you and your baby!" That made the new mothers feel good about their mothering instincts and abilities. Not surprisingly, they kept coming back for more.

MAC: *Edwina, I think you would agree that, right from the beginning, we seemed to feel that the breastfeeding mother had a right to know that we saw breastfeeding within a larger context of a certain kind of mothering. What are your recollections of how our philosophy developed and came together over time?*

EF: I think that in the beginning we didn't think so much in terms of having a specific "philosophy" for our fledgling little organization. But I remember that we had only had a few meetings when the seven of us had a series of discussions with Dr. Herb Ratner—what we now call, the "Dialogue with Dr. Ratner."

He helped us to see that we were not just giving mothers breastfeeding information and techniques. What we were really talking about was a philosophy of mothering. The idea was that breastfeeding was just one component of this larger philosophical issue that we called "good mothering."

I think that we realized early on that it was pretty hard to succeed at breast-feeding unless you had an overall acceptance of the idea of being there, in person, for your baby—what we called "mothering" the baby.

This was not a problem for any of us Founders. In fact, to a great extent, that is what excited several of the Founders about this new little discussion group that we were forming—that we would not just be talking about breastfeeding, but that we would also be talking about this larger, less clearly defined topic of "mothering." I remember Vi Lennon, in particular, commenting on how the topic of "mothering" was what actually motivated her to come to our early meetings, and to keep coming back.

Because you see, by the time La Leche League got started, all of the Founders except Mary Ann Kerwin had more than one child already. And even Mary Ann Kerwin had successfully breastfed her first baby already, and even had a home birth. So if the topic of La Leche League meetings had been limited to the techniques of breastfeeding, the seven of us would have probably lost interest in this little group fairly quickly.

But our meetings weren't just limited to breastfeeding techniques. They included this larger topic of mothering. And that topic became a sort of umbrella topic that came to include all kinds of related topics, like natural childbirth and baby-led weaning and nutrition and our thoughts on discipline—what is punitive and what constitutes what we called "loving guidance."

All of these ideas were just bubbling up and evolving and coming together as we met and talked, first among ourselves, then with Dr. Ratner, and finally at regular meetings with the mothers who came to us for guidance and support.

So yes, I would say that LLL philosophy was something that evolved over time, but it was also part of the very foundation of what La Leche League was all about, right from the start.

MAC: Edwina, can you tell us about your own philosophy of motherhood—how it grew and developed? And how was your own mothering career affected by your involvement with La Leche League?

EF: Yes. Strangely enough, it all came together for me in a single moment, kind of like the story of St. Paul in the Bible, being hit by the bolt of lightning and falling off his horse. It happened like this: I was crossing a wide street in Franklin Park one afternoon with my two young sons—Paul and David. This was before Peter was born, so it must have been around 1955.

I was pushing the buggy with David in it, and at the same time I was holding Paul by the hand. But before we could get all the way across the street, the light changed, and cars started coming at us. So immediately, instinctively, I put up my hand as if to tell all of those cars, "STOP! Let me cross. Don't harm these young children."

And they did stop. And I found myself thinking, "Wow! They realize that I am a mother, that I am responsible for these young lives."

I was just totally taken with my role as a mother, both the power and the responsibility of being a mother. I suddenly found myself thinking of the contribution that mothers make all over the world in caring for the next generation, not just in my time, but since the beginning of time. It was really what today we would probably call an "epiphany"—a moment of enlightenment or special understanding.

MAC: *Edwina, next to Mary White herself, as I understand it, you were the first one of Dr. Greg White's patients to give birth at home. And you had a home birth with your very first baby. Will you tell us about that experience?*

EF: Yes, certainly. Well, even before I was married or pregnant, I gave some thought to how and where I would like my babies to be born. You see, I was born at home, as were my two sisters. And my mother always spoke very positively about those birth experiences—she had very fond memories of her home births.

So when I found that I was expecting my first baby, I began to wonder if it would be possible for me to have a home birth. This was in 1950, and nobody, absolutely nobody that I knew would even consider doing such a thing.

But Greg White was our doctor. He was known for doing things very naturally. And I knew that his own wife, Mary, had had one of their babies at home. Plus, I had gotten hold of *Childbirth without Fear* by Grantly Dick-Read. He advocated doing things as naturally as possible, up to and including giving birth at home.

So I made up my mind that on my next prenatal visit I was going to bring up the subject with Dr. White. After he had finished examining me, I remember saying to him, "This may sound like a crazy question, but what do you think are my chances of delivering this baby at home—of having a home birth?"

Imagine my surprise when he said, "Your chances are very good, actually. I don't see any reason why we couldn't do that." I almost fell off my chair when I heard him say that!

So as it turned out, our first baby, Paul, was born at home in November 1950. I was already 36 years old at that time. Despite all of my neighbors' and in-laws' dire predictions, everything went smoothly—we had no problems whatsoever. My husband, John, was there. He participated in the birth, and he thought it was wonderful, too. And then, in 1952 and 1956, our other two sons, David and Peter, were also born at home.

So I did get a chance to live my fantasy of giving birth the way the vast majority of women had given birth down through the centuries. I felt good about that because I felt that, in delivering my babies at home, I gave a boost to the home birth movement. Later on, most of the Founders followed suit and also had many of their later babies at home.

But I was the first, and I guess that I will always be proud of that.

MAC: *Edwina, when I asked "How did LLL change your life?" what struck me was how very much you felt you changed and grew as a woman as a consequence of becoming a mother. Did you also feel that you were changed specifically by your involvement with La Leche League? If so, how and in what ways?*

EF: Oh yes. I feel that I changed and grew as a person, a woman, and a mother specifically as a result of my involvement with La Leche League. The most important part of what I gleaned from La Leche League was that I had a chance to explore what we later came to call LLL philosophy—how to become an effective and nurturing mother to your children. Of course, we always believed that kind of mothering, of necessity, began with breastfeeding.

Betty Wagner

MAC: *As I recall, Betty, you breastfed all your children but at first you weaned them at about nine months. After La Leche League got started, you discovered some of the other Founders had nursed longer. What happened then?*

BW: Well, Peggy, our fifth baby, was nursed until she was about two. She was a little bit of a thing. All she seemed to want to do was nurse, but for some reason she never gained much weight. When she got to be about two years of age I said, "this is enough." I felt that it was time for her to learn to eat regular food, rather than just continuing to get most of her nutrition from nursing. So, I weaned her, but she didn't eat much better!

MAC: *She was just a petite person.*

BW: Yes, that's right. And she's still petite today. Then I had Dorothy in May of 1959. She was two and a half when she weaned. I was pregnant with Helen by that time, and I really didn't want to nurse two at once, so I decided to wean Dorothy. I must admit, neither Dorothy nor Peggy was happy being weaned, but I weaned them anyway.

MAC: *What approach did you use to weaning?*

BW: With Peggy, Bob would take her upstairs and lie down with her until she fell asleep. But that didn't work out so well. Because then, during the daytime, she would cling, cling, cling to me. She didn't want me to do anything except pay attention to her.

So when it was time to wean Dorothy, I decided to do things differently. She was nursing very little in the daytime hours. At night I just said, "No, no. You can have some juice or some water, but I am not going to nurse you (to sleep)." So, it took a little longer with Dorothy, but she didn't cling as much as Peggy had.

With Helen, she was almost three years old when she weaned. She just stopped. She was sleeping with her sisters upstairs, and it was too much trouble to come down looking for me, I guess. It was easy. I guess you could say that she weaned herself.

So you see, you can learn as you go along. You just have to have enough children.

MAC: *And did you resist the common practice of starting solids early?*

BW: Yes, I did. Again, because of my mother. She had come from Texas to this area, so she had no one to talk to about how to take care of babies. She had weaned my oldest brother at nine months because she had read Dr. Herman Bundeson who said that you should wean your baby at nine months.

She sat my brother in the high chair and gave him scrambled eggs and toast for breakfast, and Campbell's vegetable soup for lunch. He got very sick (not surprisingly!). She knew that wasn't the way to do it!

When I had my first baby in 1943, the suggested time of starting solids was three to four months. Start with vegetables and work from there. We made our own vegetables for the baby. I remember pushing those carrots through a sieve. There really wasn't anything on the market then. You couldn't just go buy a jar of baby food. Of course, once there was commercial baby food available, the push was on to start solids as early as possible.

Chapter 5 —
<u>FINDING LIKE-MINDED PEOPLE</u>

A year into its existence, the fledgling LLL gained an unexpected boost from a visitor from overseas, Dr. Grantly Dick-Read of England. Dr. Dick-Read had gained prominence for his unorthodox approach to childbirth, which he described in his book *Childbirth without Fear*. Based on his experience as a country doctor, he had come to realize that a woman's fear of childbirth often results in anxiety, which causes her to become tense and that in turn causes pain and prolongs labor. Dr. Dick-Read advocated that mothers learn a routine of how to relax and work with, rather than against, their bodies during the birth process. To those in attendance at the birth—doctors, nurses, and midwives—he pointed out that an important part of their job is to support and encourage the mother as she, not the doctor, brings her child into the world. And without delay, it should be the mother who welcomes and reassures the newborn by gently placing her baby at her breast, to the great benefit of mother and child.

In 1957, Edwina spotted a notice of an upcoming trip to the USA by Dr. Grantly Dick-Read. She quickly brought it to the attention of the other Founders. Would they want to invite Dr. Dick-Read to speak in Franklin Park? The response was mixed, with some wanting more information. As Corresponding Secretary, Edwina offered to write for details. No doubt Dr. Dick-Read charged a fee. How much was it? She had no idea. As Treasurer, Betty had the most reservations, but she, too, was willing to take a wait-and-see attitude. Realistically, it was a gamble. Could they hope to support such an undertaking?

Life on the homefront was busy for the seven. The year 1957 could have been called the "Year of the Baby," with the Tompsons welcoming their fifth daughter, Sheila, in March. Also in March, the Whites rejoiced in the birth of their third son, seventh child, Michael. The Froehlichs' third son, Peter, arrived in June, as did also the Lennons' fourth child, Rebecca. The month of June saw the arrival, too, of the

Kerwins' second son, Edward Michael. Mary Ann Cahill gave birth to Joseph, their sixth child, in October of 1957, while the previous November, the Wagners had welcomed their fifth, Margaret Ann "Peggy." Not only did the Wagners celebrate the birth of a new baby, they literally raised the roof of their house and added a complete second story. The Tompsons had moved to a larger house in Leyden Township, just west of Franklin Park.

La Leche League work was carried out in snatches of time, often by phone. A prized innovation was an extra long phone cord. The added reach would allow a mother to keep track of her toddler, prepare a meal, fold diapers, and of course, nurse the baby, all the while helping another mother on the phone. Finding room to do paperwork was more of a problem, especially when space was limited, which was the case for many of the Founders. For some a corner in a bedroom was set aside, for others the solution was to take over the dining room table, but only until dinnertime, when it would have to be cleared. The evening meal was unquestionably a family meal.

When Dr. Dick-Read's reply arrived, it stunned the seven, at least momentarily. His fee was $750, a veritable fortune to a group with less than $50 in the bank. The response to La Leche League from mothers and others had been steady, but not spectacular—not $750 spectacular! The local newspaper, *The Franklin Park Journal,* had published an article on the meetings being held in Franklin Park for breastfeeding mothers, and papers in other surrounding suburbs had picked it up. In June of 1957, a large Chicago newspaper, the *Chicago American* featured a story on La Leche League, complete with a lovely picture of Mary Ann Kerwin and her nursing baby. As a result of that publicity, an influx of mothers from Chicago and outlying areas had been coming to the Franklin Park meetings. As encouraging as this was, the question remained: Did the seven dare take on something as ambitious as a lecture with a price tag? What if they could not meet the cost? As several of their husbands had pointed out, they would be liable—they and their families.

Yet in Dr. Dick-Read there was someone with convictions as strong as their own, someone with an international reputation. The opportunity was too good to miss. Betty quieted her qualms, and the decision was unanimous; invite the good Dr. Dick-Read.

And so a date was agreed upon, October 21, 1957, and arrangements were made to hold the event in the auditorium of the local high school which, for the cost of the janitor's fee, was available for use by community groups. A large brick building on Rose Street, the high school was just a short distance up the street from Edwina's house. Time was short, and getting the word out about Dr. Dick-Read's lecture was seen as critical to its success. The Founders threw themselves into the task, creating a flyer and sending it to natural childbirth groups, hospitals, and doctors' offices in the surrounding area. The price of admission was set at $1. The question of how to keep track of ticket sales set off a minor difference of opinion, a matter of details, but when the big day arrived, spirits were high.

The weather that year was typical of fall in the Midwest with warm, sunny days and cool nights. Mary Ann Cahill had given birth to son, Joseph, five days earlier, and the family was enjoying the bounty of dinners and other goodies from friends

The Founders appreciated the support they got from their husbands; Mary Ann Cahill, on the left with her husband, Chuck, and Marian Tompson with Tom.

and neighbors that typically came with the birth of a new baby. Mary Ann decided to forgo the lecture and attend the reception afterwards for Dr. Dick-Read and his wife at the Whites' house, but her husband, Chuck, joined the six other Founders and their spouses in getting to the auditorium early. They were confident that all was under control, but never in their wildest dreams had they anticipated the streams of people coming through the doors. Busloads of people arrived, from as far away as Wisconsin and Indiana. All 1250 seats quickly filled, and eager ticket holders were sitting on the steps to the balcony when the fire commissioner arrived, citing chapter and verse of the fire code. The aisles had to be cleared and people turned away, for only then could Marian introduce the renowned Dr. Grantly Dick-Read so he could begin his lecture and film presentation on the birth of a baby.

The success of that evening was beyond anyone's expectations except, perhaps, for that of Dr. Grantly Dick-Read himself, who had predicted a good turnout. The Founders viewed the event as their first big triumph, the first indication of broader support for what they were doing. There was also the added bonus of a $350 profit after paying expenses. Former worries were quickly forgotten, and the mood was one of jubilation. Now they had the capital they needed for getting their message out. Without this unexpected windfall, it is highly doubtful whether work on their manual, THE WOMANLY ART OF BREASTFEEDING, would have started as soon as it did.

Nor were the benefits solely monetary. New contacts were made and friendships formed. One such was that of a plucky obstetrician in Indiana, Dr. Carolyn Rawlins who, on learning of the Dr. Dick-Read lecture, gathered a car full of other interested supporters and made the three-hour drive north to see what was happening. Dr. Rawlins herself had regularly encouraged the mothers in her practice to breastfeed their babies and so wholeheartedly endorsed La Leche League's approach. On returning home, she quickly established a breastfeeding support system in her own practice using the LLL model and went on to become a favorite speaker at LLLI Seminars for Physicians, renowned for her earthy and practical advice.

Word of another author, this one closer to home, had been passed on to La Leche League by the Aikins of *Child-Family Digest* fame. She was Niles Newton, PhD, a tall, gracious woman who spoke in measured tones and had written a wonderfully sensible and practical book, *The Family Book of Child Care*. A breastfeeding mother herself, Niles matter-of-factly combined her interest in science with her role of mother. A notable example was the experiment that she and her husband, Michael, an obstetrician, conducted on the let-down reflex as Niles nursed their baby.

On the day that the Whites had invited Niles to dinner to meet the other Founders, Niles arrived early in the afternoon. She and Mary were soon deep in conversation, so much so that Mary missed adding the sugar when making the rice pudding for dessert. It was barely noticed, since the raisins added more than enough sweetness to the pudding, and the exchange of ideas marked the beginning of a lifelong friendship between Niles and La Leche League.

Plans were also made for Niles to attend an LLL Series Meeting. At the time, Niles' fourth child, Warren, was still nursing and so accompanied his mother. Those driving Niles and her young child across town to Edwina's home, where the meeting was being held, recall an incident that typified a common concern of breastfeeding mothers, then and now. Rather than go into the house and risk offending others by nursing in front of them, Niles asked if she could nurse Warren in the car. As she was to learn later to her great delight, a La Leche League meeting is a safe haven for breastfeeding. A mother need not remove herself and her baby from the group; rather she can comfortably nurse and continue to join in the discussion. Often, too, no one would be the wiser that the baby is at the breast, since mothers quickly learn the delicate art of discreet nursing.

Niles recognized the immense value of mothers helping other mothers. She also placed great importance on the soundness of LLL information. Both she and Michael became lifelong supporters of La Leche League, and both served on the LLLI Health Advisory Council. Michael was head of the obstetrical department at Northwestern University at the time of his death in 1989. For years Niles subscribed to a search of the scientific literature for information on breastfeeding for the LLLI Center for Breastfeeding Information. She was also a frequent speaker at LLLI Conferences and served on the LLLI Board of Directors from 1980 to 1983. Her sudden death in 1993 was a tremendous loss to families and the cause of breastfeeding.

With word of the new organization percolating through the medical community, a number of other "true believers" were attracted to La Leche League. One was a pediatrician in the neighboring suburb of Glenview, who had more than the usual regard for breastfeeding. Not only did Dr. E. Robbins Kimball encourage mothers in his practice to breastfeed their babies, he worked with Evanston Hospital in Evanston, Illinois to establish a human milk bank for babies at risk. Tall, with an engaging smile, Dr. Kimball had witnessed the power of breastfeeding firsthand when, as a young doctor with the Armed Forces in the Pacific, he participated in the rescue of American civilians from prisoner of war camps. Food had been scarce and the adults were all malnourished. With no artificial infant food available, the babies who were born in the camp were of necessity breastfed. To the amazement of the medical personnel and the tremendous pride of their mothers, these babies were round and robust. Dr. Kimball quickly became part of the La Leche League scene, in particular sharing his research on the role of breastfeeding in preventing allergies.

Memorable, too, from La Leche League's early days was a colorful shaker of the status quo, Dr. Robert Mendelsohn, a young pediatrician who was later to become a newspaper columnist, lecturer, and the author of a number of books. Bob came on board because of his uncompromising belief in the value of breast-feeding to mothers, babies, and families. He stayed because, as he never hesitated to explain, he learned more from La Leche League mothers and fathers whom he came in contact with than he taught them. Those who heard him speak delighted in his irreverent way of looking at many of the accepted but questionable practices then in vogue in medicine. They also appreciated his insistence on the importance of parents in a child's life. Dr. Mendelsohn never missed an opportunity to put in a good word for La Leche League. His death in 1988 was a great loss.

Other interested doctors began to participate in the Medical Advisory Board, often because their wives became involved in the organization and they saw what a difference it made in their own families. These included Drs. James Good and Paul Busam from Ohio, Dr. LeRoy Goedecke from Arizona, Dr. Paul Fleiss from California, and Dr. Frank Countryman from Indiana. Often these dedicated physi-cians continued with La Leche League for many years.

Along with professional people, La Leche League was attracting an increasing number of mothers who wanted to be a part of the effort to help others. Initially they had come looking for answers to their own breastfeeding questions, then stayed to learn more and be part of what they perceived as "changing the world for the better." Intelligent, independent thinkers, they were self-confident and eager to carry the LLL message back to their own communities. The Founders were excited about the possibilities, but unsure where it would all lead them. What had started as a simple neighborhood group was taking on a new, much broader dimension. The challenge now was to keep all of the balls in the air.

Edwina Froehlich

MAC: *Edwina, you were the one who heard that Grantly Dick-Read would be touring the USA. Tell us what you remember about that.*

EF: I think we read about it in the paper, or one of the publications that we had access to at the time. And of course, we had a very small treasury—probably less than $50 in it. And so we thought, "Oh, wouldn't it be wonderful if we could sponsor him, and have him come out to talk to us." And we said, "Sure, that would be great but we don't have the money."

So when I got home that night after we had talked about it, I thought about the time that I went to Europe. I belonged to the Young Christian Workers (YCW) and we had this invitation. It was the first meeting after World War II and it was to convene in Europe. We all said, "Yes, my goodness, wouldn't it be wonderful to go but we don't have the money."

I remember that one of the young women called me on the phone the next day. She was a working girl, we were all working girls. And she said, "Edwina, I think we made a mistake. We dismissed the possibility too readily. We should be represented at that meeting."

And I said, "Well, we dismissed it because we don't have the money. Do you have any ideas on how we can get some money?" And she said, "If there's a way to get some money we've got to find it because we should be there."

Well, we did find the money—we found a way and we went to Europe.

So that night I thought, "We, of all people deserve to have Dr, Dick-Read come and talk to us. We're the ones who are talking about it and doing it (natural childbirth) here."

And with that feeling of confidence, I wrote to him and told him that we would love to have him come and talk to us. I told him that there was a high school nearby that could seat about a thousand people. I told him that we had no money, but we figured if we charged everybody a dollar apiece we could get together enough money to pay his fee, assuming we got a crowd. We didn't know whether we'd get 50 people or a thousand—I explained that to him too.

Well, the answer came back from his secretary, and it didn't say much other than, "This is the arrangement." She sent me a flyer and the information was that it would cost $750.

Of course, that really scared us because we didn't know how many people we were going to get and then I said, "Oh, surely he will understand if we don't meet it."

So we went ahead and planned to do it. We made up a little flyer, an inexpensive, mimeographed thing, and sent it around to a number of hospitals and to different doctors that we knew, and to childbirth organizations. There weren't many childbirth organizations at that time but there were one or two, and one was in Milwaukee, I think. The natural childbirth movement was just beginning at that time.

Naturally, they were all interested. We had a doctor from Indiana, Carolyn Rawlins, who spread the word in Indiana.

Anyway, it was a big commitment for us. We were in charge of this thing. I went and got the auditorium at Leyden High School which was just down the street from where I lived, and they said that we could have it for nothing because we were a community group. I think we had to pay $15 or something like that for lights. I talked directly to them, and wrote confirming letters so that I had it on file.

We kind of got wind that there were an awful lot of people who were interested in this, so we began to get the idea that we might have a pretty good crowd. We were trying to think how we could handle the ticket arrangement. I don't remember too much about it, but I do remember that we had quite a difference of opinion as to the most efficient way to handle tickets at the door and we did not come up with a very good system.

That night people came in droves. Never had that auditorium had so many people. The Fire Department came out because they wanted to make sure we were not overcrowding. We had people driving up in cars, people walking, busloads coming from way out on the south side of Chicago, from Milwaukee, Wisconsin, from Indiana, from Michigan. They had to turn people away because the Fire Department wouldn't let anybody else in.

There was a terrible bottleneck at the door as our ticket takers were checking people off as they came in. We had doctors who were begging to be allowed in— "Somehow, get me in." I can remember one doctor saying, "Edwina, get me in here." I remember turning him over to Mary White saying, "Well, maybe she can get you in. Ask her."

Anyway, it was a hugely successful night from the point of view of those who attended. It was the first time that many parents had seen a birth. It was depicted on screen. It was a large screen so all could see in detail this mother in labor.

And one of the maintenance men, or a fireman or somebody in uniform, said to me, "Oh my gosh. Look what they're showing on the screen. Oh, no." He walked away in disgust. But most of us were thrilled, thrilled to be seeing a birth for the first time in our lives.

Of course, the younger generation that we are dealing with now see marvelous pictures far superior to that photography, but for us that was a first, and it was a tremendous experience.

Dr. Dick-Read's message was that, if you stand by and give a woman support and keep your hands off, and keep the drugs away, she'll do the job. And, of course, that appealed to us.

You know, women don't like to think that their bodies have failed them when they can't bring the baby into the world by themselves. There's a tremendous feeling of accomplishment, almost a triumph, to bring that baby into the world under your own power. We can't do it alone; we need to have the support of the physician.

Of course, women in the past, millions of them, have given birth to babies without physicians' assistance, but this was our culture and that was what we were used to. Most of us couldn't have done it (given birth naturally) if we hadn't known that there was a physician standing by if we needed him.

So that was the message. A woman's body is made to do it. Let her do it. Help her, but don't try to take it away from her.

MAC: *The success of Dr. Dick-Read's talk was a real triumph for La Leche League, and we ended up with a little pot of money. But, belatedly, the high school wanted to charge us, didn't they?*

EF: Yes, it was the talk of the town, of course, what had happened. It really was a big thing to have all those buses come in, and to have the Fire Department come out. The most successful program Leyden High School had ever held had never drawn that kind of crowd.

The next day one of the school board members called me and said, "I understand you had quite a crowd." I said, "Oh yes, it was marvelous," and I went on and on. And he said, "Uh huh, well you know, your huge turnout made it a commercial venture, so you'll have to pay $1,000 for the rental of the school."

I almost dropped the phone! I said, "I didn't hide anything. I explained to you when we booked the auditorium that we didn't have a large treasury. Besides, we are benefiting the community." And he said, "Well, the way I see it . . ." and he kept repeating his point and just went on and on.

So then I said, "I have a copy of my letter." You see, it wasn't just a phone call. I said, "You talk to Mr. So and So. I have a copy of my letter to him and a copy of the letter in which he responded." And he said, "Oh, you do? I didn't know that." So you see, my years of being a secretary paid off. Having that carbon got us off the hook.

MAC: What else do you remember about Dr. Dick-Read's philosophy?

EF: I recall one thing he said that La Leche League used as a quote for many years. He said, " The newborn has but three demands: Warmth in the arms of its mother. Food from her breast. Security in the knowledge of her presence. Breastfeeding satisfies all three."

Hearing this renewed our commitment to do our best to help mothers fill those three demands of their babies.

The publicity surrounding Dr. Dick-Read's talk made everybody in town more aware of La Leche League and natural childbirth. And of course, there were some who thought that what we had done was in the realm of pornography. We were in a culture where bottle-feeding and medicated births were absolutely everywhere.

But the negative comments never bothered us. We didn't dwell on things like that. We were all so convinced that we were doing the very best thing possible. And when anyone, let alone a mother, is convinced that she's doing the best for her children and family, well, you know, it's hard to put a dent in that. Doing the best thing for your children is about the strongest motivation you can possibly have, and all of us had that to the fullest.

Viola Lennon

MAC: Let's talk about Dr. Grantly Dick-Read's visit in October 1957. I know we had all read his book. I had picked up a copy on a sale table at Marshall Field's in Chicago and he made a convert of me. I carried it to the hospital when I was ready to deliver my first baby and I was doing well until the doctors came in and said, "Oh gee, she's in transition. The routine says we give her a spinal." So that was the end of my natural delivery.

VL: Oh, I remember his visit well. I thought natural childbirth was a great idea. I had also read his book. It had helped me but I thought sponsoring a lecture was risky. I recall a conversation with my husband when I told him that we were going to have Grantly Dick-Read come. I forget the fee—some outlandish price. And I said if we don't succeed in getting a large enough turnout we'll just have to pay the difference, and he looked kind of surprised.

Anyway, when Dr. Dick-Read came, it was a marvelous evening. It was so crowded that half the people couldn't get in and it began to occur to me that there are women out there who are hungry for good advice on childbirth, breastfeeding, and doing things the natural way.

It was the beginning of what I found out later was answering a real need. Because women wanted to do things right, naturally, and there were not many people out there helping them. This was just one more proof that we were on the right track.

Marian Tompson

MAC: *Let's talk about the Aikens—they made such a tremendous contribution through their periodical,* Child-Family Digest, *way back before we even got started.*

MT: Right. A lot of people heard about La Leche League through their periodical, *Child-Family Digest.* They started the periodical to honor the memory of their son who was killed in World War II. They wanted to make the world a better place for children.

The Aikens were just remarkable people. They would drive up here with a box of sprouts in the back seat of their car. They ate very healthful foods. They were part of the pioneers who helped make people aware that there was a different way of doing things and a better way, too.

And Ashley Montagu, who helped us a lot right at the beginning. He visited us at Mary White's house, maybe that first year. Ashley Montagu died in November 1999. We stayed in touch. We talked at least once or twice a year and wrote notes back and forth. His handwriting was so legible and smooth. It's much better than mine. He was very impressive.

Oh, and Dr. Kimball—E. Robbins Kimball. He's now living in Florida. We first heard of him as being very supportive of breastfeeding. We later found out that what had convinced him that breastfeeding was really special was when he was part of the Army liberating the prisoner-of-war camps in World War II. He said that while the adults might be skin and bones, the toddlers that were being breast-fed were running around and were healthy. He realized that even if a mother was malnourished, she still could feed her baby very adequately.

MAC: *Tell me about Niles Newton. I know that you two were close.*

MT: Oh yes, Niles. She was such a special, special person. After her husband, Michael, died we would get together once a month and have dinner together and just talk about all of these things that both of us felt passionately about. I have had

Betty Wagner and Mary Ann Cahill with
Ashley Montagu in 1968.

some enormously wonderful people in my life. It seems that there are so many of them that if I start naming them, I am going to leave some people out who shouldn't be left out.

MAC: *Marian, when did you first meet Dr. Mendolsohn?*

MT: Dr. Ratner and I were attending the Illinois Maternal and Child Health Association meeting in Peoria, Illinois, when I saw that a talk on children in the hospital was going to be given by a Dr. Mendolsohn. I was surprised when Dr. Mendolsohn ended up encouraging parents to stay in the hospital with their sick child.

After the talk, I introduced myself and La Leche League and asked if we could have a copy of his talk to reprint for our members. He said (or pretended) he knew about La Leche League and yes, we could have a copy of his talk.

Then I sought out Dr. Ratner and it turned out he knew about Dr. Mendelsohn and suggested we ask him to be on our LLL Medical Advisory Board.

It was at Dr. Mendelsohn's first meeting with the other doctors, at Mary White's house, that he asked when he would get a copy of the minutes of the meeting. Minutes, I objected, we don't take minutes. "Well, you've got to get organized," was his rejoinder. With all we already had to do as wives and mothers, and our commitment to helping breastfeeding mothers, I wondered just when we would have time to get organized!

MAC: *Let's go back and talk about the Dr. Grantly Dick-Read visit.*

MT: That was so exciting. When we first talked about it, we wanted to just meet with him, and Edwina wrote to him and he said he would rather give a talk to a larger group of people. He was going to charge what seemed like a lot of money to us. But we said we would do it. That was the wonderful thing about those early days. We were a small group and we could just move on what we really felt was right to us and it usually was the right thing to do.

We sent out meeting notices all over the place. We weren't seeing them appear in any newspapers. I think there was one little paragraph in one Chicago newspaper. We found out later that the big Chicago papers had checked with the American Medical Association (AMA), and the AMA said that this man must be a quack for charging money to talk. So we really didn't know if anybody was going to show up.

I remember Dr. White and I drove downtown to pick him up, and I had Sheila, my nursing baby, on my lap. I went into the hotel and picked up Dr. Dick-Read and his wife, and we got in the car and Dr. White starts racing down the highway as if there's an emergency waiting. I remember talking very casually with the Dick-Reads and thinking in my mind of the headlines—"Famous Doctor Dies in Crash." I wasn't even worried about myself and my child. I was just thinking of this famous doctor getting in an accident because of us.

Then we pull up to the high school and there were buses in front of the auditorium and crowds of people, and people being turned away. My husband was there taking pictures of the crowds and we were totally flabbergasted. We had no idea we would get that kind of response.

People came from, I think, Wisconsin, Indiana, Iowa, and Illinois. I think somebody said four states. The Fire Department came because people were sitting in the aisles and they had to ask some people to leave. I introduced Dr. Dick-Read and he gave his talk and showed his film.

One local doctor commented that he thought the film was a fake. He didn't believe that a woman could give birth without anesthesia. The views in Dr. Dick-Read's film were all from what would be the foot of the table, views looking right into the vagina with the baby coming out, so how that could be faked, I have no idea. That doctor really didn't want to accept what was in front of his eyes.

It caused a lot of comment in town, but we had realized early on that most of the women who came to La Leche League had never seen their babies born. Since we knew an undrugged mother meant an undrugged baby, it meant a better start when they were both awake and alert. We used to talk about the advantages of having a baby without being drugged. Most women were drugged because they didn't even know any better, and they didn't have anyone to help them through the situation.

Mary Ann Kerwin

MAC: Do you recall any reaction to the film that showed the birth of a baby?

MAK: It was totally unheard of. I had never seen the birth of a baby before. But everything was so different then. All in all, it was just lovely. His film was wonderful. His talk was wonderful. He wasn't an entertainer, but it was the content and the reassurance of what we believed about childbirth and breastfeeding. He just underlined everything we were doing. And, of course, we had all read his book. It was just wonderful to hear him say all those things in person. It was a reaffirmation of what we were saying, which we badly needed. I mean, we were looking so much for acceptance. And respect. We wanted to be respected. We knew we were right but we weren't getting widespread support. But that night we got plenty of support! He gave a really good talk and we were so thrilled. And then there was the reception afterwards at Mary's, which was so lovely.

Chapter 6 — ORGANIZE WE MUST

Clearly, the first order of business to be taken up was truly a business matter—the need to incorporate in the state of Illinois. La Leche League was already an entity unto itself, with a name and bank account, and was incurring expenses and paying bills. Incorporating would define it as a legal, nonprofit organization and provide the Founders with some protection under the law. Bill Lennon, a lawyer, and Chuck Cahill, the accountant in the group, handled the paperwork. On September 3, 1958, incorporation was officially granted, with all the Founders signing the document except Viola, who was not able to make it.

In keeping with their new status, a simple constitution was written, and note was taken of the requirement to hold an Annual Meeting and record the minutes in an official minutes book In practice, meetings were called regularly in response to needs, though minutes of those early meetings are scarce.

Down the road, application was also made for a federal tax-exempt status, the kind that would allow donors to list charitable contributions to La Leche League as deductions on their federal US income tax returns. It is an invaluable asset for an organization in raising funds, though procuring it was more involved. La Leche League did not fit neatly in the usual categories for nonprofits. It isn't engaged in charity, such as feeding the hungry (though every breastfeeding mother could claim otherwise) nor is it a teaching institution in the sense of a school or other educational bodies. In the final analysis, LLLI received its tax-exempt status as an educational organization, and while such a designation is true, those who know and love La Leche League feel that no legal document begins to describe the scope of its work.

Much more exciting to the Founders than legal incorporation was incorporating the new LLL Leaders as partners in the work that needed to be done. To begin with, they were "family." When Lucya Prince, Gloria Watson, and Dolores Hoder, the first to start a group outside Franklin Park, struck out on their own, they were at ease with discussion-style LLL meetings. They knew the basics of breastfeeding and were familiar with the multitude of practical tips that make a breastfeeding mother's life easier. Printed literature on breastfeeding was scarce, but the Franklin Park LLL Groups had procured reprints of supportive material. An article in the magazine, *The Ladies Home Journal*, by the well-known "baby doctor," Dr. Benjamin Spock, was regularly passed out to the mothers at meetings. The new Chicago LLL Group followed the same practice and, like its predecessors, set up a library of books that could be counted on to be helpful. And when the new Leaders faced an unusual breastfeeding situation, they had only to call their friends in Franklin Park for advice.

All of the Founders were willing to help answer questions when they could, but for unusual situations, especially medical questions, the calls were invariably directed to the Whites. Mary and Dr. White were extremely generous with their time and knowledge, taking calls on a daily basis. Often it seemed that when a mother or baby had a problem, breastfeeding was the first line of attack, no matter what the condition, from gout to goiter. Almost invariably, before anything else was tried, the mother was told to wean her baby. Dr. White brought years of experience to these considerations and was ever mindful of the strong relationship between a nursing mother and her child. The young La Leche League could not have functioned without his expertise.

Chicago was the first of the new LLL groups to spring up outside of Franklin Park, but others soon followed and always, the pattern was the same; mothers from an outlying area who had been making the long drive to Franklin Park went out on their own and started La Leche League in their hometown. But like homing birds, they were drawn back. The resulting "homecomings" became know as "Board Meetings," and drew upward of 50 women to the old municipal building in Franklin Park where these meetings were held, since no home could hold everybody. They were happy occasions, where LLL Leaders could greet old friends, make new ones, catch up on family news and the latest breastfeeding information, carry on LLL business, share successes, vent frustrations, find inspiration, and renew their commitment. After LLLI published its loose-leaf manual, THE WOMANLY ART OF BREASTFEEDING, Betty Wagner, as treasurer, found herself extremely busy passing out books, collecting money for those sold, reimbursing those who paid for postage, and adroitly keeping it all straight.

Of course, it was only a matter of time until a request came to start an LLL group outside of Illinois. The pioneering mother who was anxious to break new ground was Martha Pugacz. She had been corresponding with Edwina for some time, and in June 1958, she introduced Cleveland, Ohio to La Leche League. And then, like seeds thrown to the wind, requests to start new LLL groups proliferated.

Here was a new challenge and further responsibility for the Founders. Instead of one or two mothers eager to become LLL Leaders, there were numerous caring, enthusiastic mothers volunteering to help. The prospect was exciting, but the reality daunting. How was La Leche League going to prepare the applicants for their new role? Who would take on the added work?

The Founders took up the topic of new Groups and Leaders at one of their regular "planning" meetings. As their toddlers played and the mothers contemplated the long-range effects of preparing many new Leaders, their minds turned, too,

*New Board Members, Mary Jane Brizzolara and Florence Carlson,
with five of the Founders in 1963.*

to their older children who would soon be coming home from school, to husbands arriving home from work, meals to prepare, and days crowded with activities.

The answer was evident; they needed help. Dealing with new Leaders was a job in itself, especially since the job holder would also be wife and mother of a family. The other side of the equation, supporting the Leaders once they were established in a group, amounted to another demanding position.

The decision to delegate was made easier by the presence of wonderful, bright women who cared deeply about helping other mothers and babies. One such was Mary Jane Brizzolara, whose husband had written an article about Dr. White, "Maverick Physician," that appeared in a national magazine. Articulate and a fine writer in her own right, Mary Jane took on the task of preparing new LLL Leaders. To help qualify the would-be Leaders, Mary Jane worked with the Founders to assemble a list of questions and situations that they dubbed "The Questionnaire." It had to be complete enough to cover what a new Leader needed to know, yet not so difficult as to frighten her away. The process itself has expanded and contracted over the years. Since LLL Leaders are central to La Leche League's identity, refining and defining the Leader application process has, as might be expected, occupied the attention of every member of the Board of Directors, Director of Leader Accreditation, Director of Leaders, and everybody in between, possibly every LLL Leader, going back to the days of "The Questionnaire."

But some of that was far down the road. In the late 1950s, La Leche League was still in the throes of getting started. Tapping at the door was another need, the need for more and better written materials. In the beginning, information was exchanged verbally for the most part, an LLL Leader to mothers at a meeting or over the phone. As the number of people who heard about La Leche League increased, so too did the number of written requests for information, all kinds of information, more often than not, urgent and most urgent. Again, the need was critical.

Mary Ann Kerwin

MAC: *In 1957 there was a feature article about LLL in the* Chicago's American.

MAK: Yes—that was important because the publicity helped us quite a bit. The article said that, at that point—June 1957—we had 50 members, and that included the seven of us. Then I saw something the following year that indicated that we had 150 members. So even though we were growing, the growth was still relatively slow. Fifty in a little less than a year, and 150 in the first two years.

MAC: *Well, some of that first year was spent in getting ourselves organized, figuring it all out—how we were going to present the material.*

MAK: Oh, yes. Yet we know that at the end of the first Series we already thought there were too many coming to fit in one house and we split into two Franklin Park Groups. Mary White, Marian Tompson, and I stayed together. Marian and I would lead the meetings. Mary White would stay in the background. She was the hostess. And I never knew if it was because she was the hostess or because she was Greg White's wife that she took a minor role back then. Because Mary knew more than any of us, she had more experience with breastfeeding and natural childbirth. But somehow or other, she took a less prominent role.

MAC: *She encouraged you and Marian to run the meetings?*

MAK: Yes. And I remember that the three of you were at another house. I think it was Edwina's.

MAC: *Yes, it was Edwina's. She had the largest living room—so it seemed like a natural division.*

MAK: We began to get inquiries from out-of-state within a year, didn't we?

MAC: *Yes.*

MAK: I believe Martha Pugacz may have asked how to start a Group in Ohio—Cleveland, I believe. Was that the first one outside of Illinois? She was certainly among the first.

If anybody wanted to start a Group, we were just glad to have them do it. There were no qualifications. In the case of Martha, we felt she was of one mind with us since she had been corresponding with Edwina for a while. I think she even came to Franklin Park for a visit. We didn't wonder at all about whether to give her the go-ahead.

MAC: And after that, when you moved to Colorado, LLL went with you, right? For many years, Mary Ann, you were the only Founder who was not living in the Chicago area. Tell us how it came about that the Kerwins moved to Colorado, and talk about the early days of LLL out that way.

MAK: Tom and I had talked about moving to Colorado, and after our baby died I thought it was probably as good a time as any for us to make the move. Our other two boys, Tommy and Eddie, were four and two years old at the time—good ages to move because they weren't in school yet, and they weren't yet old enough to be missing friends. Tom really wanted to move, and I was beginning to think that a change of place would be good for me, too.

So that's how it came about that the Kerwin family moved to Colorado in January of 1960. And we've been happy here ever since.

MAC: So how long after your move to Colorado was it before you were able to get a La Leche League Meeting going there?

MAK: Oh, not long at all. I mean, we got there in January, and I think I hosted the first Colorado La Leche League Meeting in February, 1960. We didn't even have all of our boxes unpacked when I hosted the first meeting.

MAC: And did there seem to be much interest on the part of women in Denver to learn about breastfeeding, and to get involved with a group like La Leche League?

MAK: Oh, yes—very much so. You see, we had been planning to move, and talking about moving, for some time before it actually happened. So during the period when we were still in the planning stages, Edwina started passing along all the letters that La Leche League was receiving from anyone who lived in the Western states.

MAC: What La Leche League now calls the "Mountain States area," right?

MAK: Right, the Mountain States—Colorado, Wyoming, Idaho, California—all of that. So by the time that we actually moved to Colorado I had already corresponded with quite a number of mothers there. In fact, I still have a close friend out here who was one of those women who had written to La Leche League for information about breastfeeding even before we arrived in Colorado.

MAC: So, how would you say La Leche League was received in Colorado?

MAK: Oh, we were received wonderfully. When we got out here I contacted a number of people, both interested mothers and some health care professionals. One of the first doctors that I contacted was Dr. Robert Bradley, obstetrician. You probably remember, Mary Ann, that he was known as one of the foremost proponents of husband-coached childbirth. I remember that Dr. Bradley said,

"I welcome you with open arms!" Yes, he was very happy to learn that La Leche League would be starting Groups in Colorado.

MAC: *Did you notice any different needs among the mothers in Colorado as compared to the mothers you had met at Chicago-area meetings?*

MAK: No, not really. When I read over some of our old meeting notes, the questions and concerns that came up were pretty much the same variety that we had already become accustomed to in the Chicago area.

I did find, however, that there seemed to be more doctors out here who were supportive of what we were trying to do than there were in Chicago. In all of metropolitan Chicago there were only two or three doctors who were supportive of what we were trying to do—Greg White and Herb Ratner, Dr. Kimball, and maybe one or two others.

But out here in Colorado I felt that there was a somewhat more receptive climate. In addition to Dr. Bradley, I remember Dr. Joe Butterfield, a pediatrician, as being very supportive, very welcoming. Dr. Butterfield was one of the first doctors to implement the concept of what we now call "rooming-in"—having the newborn baby stay with its mother.

In addition to Dr. Bradley and Dr. Butterfield, there was also Dr. Fritz Meyer—also very much in our corner and Dr. Max Bartlett. So we really had quite a lot of support from the medical and health care communities out here.

MAC: *Wasn't Dr. Joe Butterfield the one who asked you to give a talk at the Children's Hospital in Denver not long after you arrived in town?*

MAK: Yes, Dr. Butterfield asked me to go over to the Newborn Center at Children's Hospital to talk to mothers of premature babies about breastfeeding. He wanted me to encourage them to try to breastfeed because he knew that, if they were successfully able to breastfeed, it would be the best possible thing both for the "premies" and for the mothers.

At that time, Dr. Butterfield had a young medical resident working with him—a woman, Dr. Marianne Neifert. She had written some guidelines for successful breastfeeding of premature babies. The guidelines that she had put together were the best that I had seen on the subject up until that time, and for quite a while thereafter.

So it was an exciting time to be part of La Leche League of Colorado.

Marian Tompson

MAC: *Marian, how did you fit in all the extra work, typing all the letters, taking all the phone calls, helping start up a new organization and, at the same time, taking care of your family?*

MT: It worked out because first of all, I had the right husband for it. He wasn't a man who would get upset if something wasn't done when he got home. I always managed to have dinner ready when he walked in the door, but it was my decision.

And, I don't know, I worked around it. I think part of it was that I liked what I was doing. There were times in my life in La Leche League where I did resent the amount of work that I was doing.

I remember one time that I got all of you Founders together and I was going to take a leave of absence, but somehow that never worked out. Yes, there were times when it sometimes seemed a bit overwhelming.

But, for the most part, La Leche League grew slowly. I mean, there was a lot of extra work, but you were doing it at home. I always say that a woman who can work at home is really the most liberated woman because she can decide what she is going to do and when she is going to do it.

So maybe I didn't have a house that looked gorgeous or exciting because I didn't put all that time into thinking about decorating or doing a lot of those kinds of things, but for me those things were never that important to me.

MAC: *At first, Leaders who were starting LLL in other areas sometimes had questions about why LLL did things a certain way. One issue was childbirth. What do you remember about that?*

MT: Yes. I remember that Mary White and I flew to Northern California with our babies and each with an older daughter to babysit. In Northern California they were very upset about having childbirth be part of the Series Meetings. We wanted to go out there and explain to them, face to face, why it was part of the philosophy.

We talked about the advantages of having a baby without being drugged. Most women were drugged because they didn't know any better and they didn't have anyone to help them through the situation.

Most of the mothers who wanted to become LLL Leaders had never had an unmedicated birth. We used to ask them things like—it sounds so strange now—would you have an unmedicated birth with your next baby? How could anybody know what they would do with their next baby?

We used to put birth stories in our newsletter in the beginning. When we looked at the stories of our LLL mothers' births, and compared them with the stories from childbirth organizations, I always felt that we had a better record as far as unmedicated births went. With a lot of the other organizations, the mothers said they wanted unmedicated births, but their doctors wouldn't go along with it. In the end, the doctors would always insist on giving them something.

In our organization, on the other hand, the mothers just became so convinced that this was really so important for the baby that they would do everything they could so as not to have anesthetic of any kind. And so I think that's the reason why, at least in the early years, our statistics for the percentage of La Leche League mothers having unmedicated births were much better than those of childbirth organizations.

MAC: And what was the outcome of your trip to California?

MT: Oh, I guess it turned out okay. They stayed in La Leche League and we kept talking abut childbirth! There were two issues, actually. There was the non-medicated childbirth issue, and then there was the issue of the Leader who would go out to speak at high schools or other outside organizations. Some of the Leaders felt that these Leaders were not being good mothers if they spoke outside of La Leche League because they were leaving their families. We were addressing both issues at that time.

MAC: You were also busy taking phone calls from anxious mothers in the early days.

MT: Yes, Edwina and I were the ones listed on our first brochures, so we got a lot of phone calls.

MAC: So how did you educate yourselves to help these mothers?

MT: Well, in the beginning most of the calls were just simple breastfeeding calls, not from mothers in particular crisis situations. Mothers in unusual situations wouldn't even consider breastfeeding their babies in those days. So most of the calls were just sort of normal questions.

Nowadays, we have such a different population in terms of the calls we receive. We get women calling who are really convinced that they want to breastfeed even though they might have a premature baby, or have triplets, or have a baby who doesn't seem to be doing well because of low birth weight or a medical problem. So we have mothers who really need a special kind of help.

We had those kinds of calls in the early days, too, but not a lot of them. Most of the calls were about simple things, like reassuring women that their milk was the best milk for their baby, or that the baby would determine how much milk they had by how often they nursed. Or that it's perfectly normal for a baby to wake up at night, or to cry when you put him down. That doesn't necessarily mean that a baby is hungry. Babies need to be held. Just simple, basic mothering ideas like that.

We as a culture had gotten so far away from understanding what babyhood was all about. And that was the thing—as soon as you'd explain it, mothers would recognize what you were saying right away. When we would say, "You don't have to let the baby cry, you can pick him up," mothers would be so relieved because they really didn't want to have that baby crying. But people had been telling them that the baby had to learn to get along without their mothers holding them.

Chapter 7—SPREADING THE WORD

Each time La Leche League's address appeared in a newspaper, magazine, or other printed material, an upsurge of mail was sure to follow. It came to 3332 Rose Street, the home of the Froehlichs, which for years functioned as a clearinghouse for La Leche League. Edwina dealt with the letters regarding organizational matters and for the most part distributed the rest, the questions and concerns from mothers, to the other Founders and the three Chicago Leaders. Many of the mothers who wrote to us were desperate for help, having failed for one reason or another in their attempts to breastfeed, often with more than one child. Those answering the letters often found themselves staying up late at night to get a reply sent out. Further, they were becoming increasingly frustrated, since they were writing the same information over and over again. "Nurse often—supply follows demand" became a mantra. In an effort to save time, they had composed answers to the most common questions, which they could draw on. Even so, Mary Ann Kerwin recalls that she was devoting every spare minute of her day to answering mail. Years later, she could still vividly remember how the mothers' pleas for help had touched her heart.

Once again, a change was in order, and a call went out for a meeting at Edwina's. Going to Edwina's often involved forays into the latest findings in nutrition and picking up the specially milled wheat germ flour that Edwina purchased in large quantities and made available to others.

And there was always time for "family talk." On this particular morning, the group took time out to examine the array of unusual and beautiful toys lining the mantle in the living room that the Froehlich grandparents had brought back for their dear grandsons from their travels abroad. But, the stacks of letters demanded attention.

They were piled on the large dining room table, along with Edwina's sturdy typewriter. The room was pleasant, with light coming in from four windows on one side. The Founders took their place at the table, getting up occasionally to check on a child, but always coming back to the pressing question of how to simplify answering the mail.

The idea of having pre-written answers to specific questions seemed logical and workable. The wording that each of the letterwriters had developed for her own use was ready and waiting to be used. Since they covered the most commonly asked questions, they could call it a "Course by Mail" and send the sections out as needed. The outline would follow the topics of the Series Meetings.

But how could they know which section—or sections—a mother really needed? The various parts built on each other. The course must be complete, or as complete as they could make it, and include both the how-to of breastfeeding and whys and wherefores of mothering.

In the end, they had talked themselves into producing the first manual. Mary, Marian, and Edwina did the major part of the writing, with the others poring over their work and adding or suggesting changes. The title, THE WOMANLY ART OF BREASTFEEDING originated with Dr. White. The first printing came off the press in September 1958. Two years later, a Spanish translation was available.

The money earned from the Dr. Dick-Read lecture covered the cost of the first printing, but not the assembling, of the thirty-three page manual. Bundles containing 1000 sheets of each page were delivered to Edwina's house, where they were laid out in order around the big table. A crew of assemblers followed each other around the table, taking a sheet from each bundle, to form a completed manual, which was then fastened into a two-prong folder. Each copy sold for two dollars, which included the cost of the postage for mailing.

As relieved as the letterwriters were to have more complete information to send to mothers, they still felt the need to include a personal note. A typical message was "Do not get discouraged and lose confidence in your ability to breastfeed. Hundreds of modern mothers have succeeded, and you will too. When in doubt, call or write me and let me help you over the hump." A mother who later became an LLL Leader, Paula Pettengill, ordered a manual when expecting her third child. A letterwriter had quickly scrawled the message, "Avoid supplements like the plague!" It kept her going.

While a "Course by Mail," as it was originally planned, never got off the ground, the idea didn't totally die. It resurfaced in the form of single-topic Information Sheets, which cover a particular subject and supplement the more general information in the manual. As La Leche League grew, so, too, did the number of Information Sheets. They are ample evidence of LLL's ever-expanding pool of information.

Sales of THE WOMANLY ART OF BREASTFEEDING were brisk. What had been born of necessity with no thought to bringing in money, was doing just that, modestly but steadily. It is hard to imagine how La Leche League would have evolved without its flagship, THE WOMANLY ART OF BREASTFEEDING.

Not surprisingly, their small booklet-manual was no sooner completed than the Founders wanted to make it bigger and better, a real book, bound, and with illustrations. The task called for outside expertise. The Whites were acquainted with an experienced editor, Mary Carson, who had worked with them in producing *Emergency Childbirth*, a manual that Dr. White had written for use by emergency

The Founders gathered together in 1996 to review the various editions of
THE WOMANLY ART OF BREASTFEEDING *in English and other languages.*

rescue personnel. Mary Carson, her husband, Gordon, and their two children also lived in Franklin Park, making it convenient for Mary to take on the job of editing the book.

The writing was slow going for the Founders. Mary White and Marian did much of the work, with others contributing a chapter or a section, giving the book its trademark, eclectic style. All critiqued the work and added suggestions along the way. It was May 1963 when the beautiful, new, blue-covered second edition of THE WOMANLY ART OF BREASTFEEDING made its debut, in both hardcover and soft cover editions. It had been almost five years since the first edition made its appearance and a whopping 17,000 copies of the loose-leaf manual had been sold. Dr. Ratner wrote the Foreword for the new edition, which in itself has become a classic. Whimsical line drawings by Joy Sidor enlivened the pages of print.

An even longer period was to pass before the next edition came out in 1981. Mary Ann Cahill was the principal writer, with the others again critiquing the material. Margins on its 368 pages are tight, so packed is it with information, and there are photos, black and white, depicting mothers and babies from different places and cultures. Some early misconceptions are corrected, the age when babies are likely to wean, for instance. Earlier editions give this time at about a year old, based on what the Founders knew at the time. When they met Ashley Montagu, author and anthropologist, and asked him how long children in more natural societies tend to breastfeed, they were in for a surprise. Dr. Montagu told of children age five, six, and even seven years old still taking their mother's breast.

Succeeding, updated editions of THE WOMANLY ART OF BREASTFEEDING have since been coming off the press regularly. The blue-covered edition sold 1,172,200 copies and the current, 1997 edition, is the sixth revision. THE WOMANLY ART OF BREASTFEEDING has been translated into nine languages. All seven of the Founders are considered the authors of the book, but no specific author is listed, a cause for some confusion among librarians. The Founders have never claimed royalty; all proceeds go to support La Leche League.

But even before there was a book, there was the *La Leche League News*. La Leche League was only in its second year when the decision was made to produce a newsletter devoted to stories about breastfeeding. For mothers living at a distance, it became a lifeline. Marian took on the task of pulling together the bimonthly, mimeographed paper as its first editor. The initial issue, 200 copies, came out in May 1958. Mary White helped Marian staple them and the Tompson children readied them for mailing. The price of a subscription—one dollar.

Mary Ann Cahill followed as the second editor, and about that time, La Leche League News took on a new and more professional look, due to the work of a couple from Vermont, Floyd and Meredith Arnold. In the early sixties, the readers were encouraged to submit drawings for a logo for La Leche League. It was to be of a mother breastfeeding her baby and have universal appeal. As closely as anyone remembers, the winning design was submitted by Madge Bennett of Illinois. Her delicate outline adorned La Leche League materials until 1983, when a professional graphics firm developed the present logo.

Early issues were frequently late due to a bout of illness in the family or, on a happier note, the birth of a new baby, or perhaps holidays or any number of other reasons. The editor, whoever she was, took comfort in practicing "Family First."

A major development came about in 1984, when the name was changed to NEW BEGINNINGS and the old newsletter took on a more professional magazine look. Then in 1992, it became an inviting, full-sized magazine, complete with a four-color cover and advertisements. What didn't change was the focus, which continues to feature stories of breastfeeding families, wonderfully inspiring and encouraging stories. The little *News* has come a long way.

It was only a matter of time until a communique was designated specifically for Leaders. Edwina was working at the office in Franklin Park and doing her best to keep Leaders informed, when it became obvious that the Leaders needed a newsletter, or something like it, of their own. Edwina called Mary Ann Cahill, who came up with the name LEAVEN, inspired by the many batches of bread that LLL mothers were turning out for their families. From its beginnings as four 8½ x 11 pages of solid type, LEAVEN, too, has graduated to a magazine format. Sections of it now travel to Leaders in distant parts of the world, where they are translated and combined with material that is pertinent to their own culture and customs. Since 1977, Leaders have also had a treasure trove of information and ideas in THE LEADER'S HANDBOOK, everything from planning and leading meetings to helping other mothers become LLL Leaders. It's a world away from 1956, when the first tentative steps were taken to form La Leche League, but the spirit, the philosophy, the commitment are the same and as shiny bright as ever.

Marian Tompson, Edwina Froehlich, Betty Wagner, and Mary Ann Cahill at an LLLI Conference in the late 1960s, with the logo used at that time to designate LLLI.

Marian Tompson

MT: I remember being surprised at all the mail we were getting, and having problems dealing with that. I used to feel guilty not writing to my relatives—instead I was answering all these LLL letters.

And sometimes I used to get a little angry because my desk was in the bedroom, and the first thing I would see in the morning and the last thing at night was all this work that had to be done. I really debated about buying a screen to put in front of the desk so that I wouldn't have to look at all those letters every time I came into the room. But I never felt that I could spend the money to buy a screen.

MAC: *As we grew and more people heard about us and we got more letters, we decided to do something about it.*

MT: We decided to do a "course-by-mail." We were going to send out a chapter at a time. Then we wouldn't have to answer all those letters. So we put together those first 33 pages with clips. Our children all helped to collate, walking around the table, and we sent it out.

As we heard from more mothers, we kept hearing about a variety of breastfeeding experiences. So, after about three years, we realized that we should enlarge this booklet and put everything we knew about breastfeeding into it.

And at the same time, we brought out a newsletter because we realized that many women had nobody nearby to learn from. And so while some of the Founders were getting together that first manual, I was putting together the first newsletter.

MAC: You were the first editor of the newsletter.

MT: Yes. And I was so naive. With the first issue, I never even put a date on it. Never even thought of that! But the idea was to give women some source of current information. And in that very first issue, we talked about a mother who was going back to work and whose doctor told her she couldn't breastfeed. We were so proud of ourselves, that we helped her breastfeed that baby.

The second edition of the manual, of course, was the one we worked on together and we met almost weekly. I remember people coming to my house, and the children would play in the swimming pool, and we would put all our notes together.

Then Carol Huotari, who was a 16-year-old living down the street, would come to my house and she would sit at the dining room table at my little portable typewriter and she would type up all our notes. Little did we know that she would grow up, get married, become an LLL Leader, and work in the La Leche League office as the Manager of the Center for Breastfeeding Information.

Of course, we sent the chapters to the doctors if there were medical things in them. I think it took us three or four years and a lot of babies (!) before that book came out. But that was another example of the serendipity that seemed to be part of our La Leche League life in those years.

I remember that we didn't know how we were going to pay for having it printed. Then came Mary Carson, who helped us with the editing and indexing. She and I worked on the captions for the illustrations. I remember being pregnant and nauseated. It was so hard to concentrate.

Mary suggested a printer in Danville, Illinois. I asked him how many books we would have to print to get the best price, and he said 10,000, which was like saying a million! I asked him if we could pay him so much a month, and he said that would be all right.

Unbeknownst to us at that time, Karen Pryor had a book coming out called *Nursing Your Baby* and *Reader's Digest* had taken the chapter that she had written about us, called "They Teach the Joys of Breastfeeding." That article came out the very same month our book came out. In two months those 10,000 copies of the book were gone. We were on to our second printing!

In the beginning in *LLL News* we listed all the Leaders and their babies as they were born. We told about everybody's baby. We talked about personal experiences. I remember when Edwina was nursing Peter at 18 months. That was a big thing. Edwina wrote a rather lengthy article about it. In the very first issue we talked about the discussion we had with Dr. Ratner and how we realized we were really teaching more than facts about breastfeeding.

Mary White

MAC: In the early years, Mary, you and Greg played an important role with all of our publications, especially in regard to the factual accuracy of the information that we were presenting. We have never been proven wrong on any of the medical or breast-feeding information that we presented. This was certainly true of the first manual.

MW: Of course, most of the Founders had a hand in writing the first manual. We all contributed from our own experiences and backgrounds. We did have Greg, Herb, and other doctors check it out for medical accuracy. So we weren't just "winging it" scientifically speaking.

MAC: Do you remember what place LLL philosophy had in that first manual? Would you say that it was a prominent role, or did that come later?"

MW: Oh, La Leche League philosophy was at the heart of our manual right from the beginning

Edwina Froehlich

MAC: One of the big undertakings for the Founders was putting together a manual, getting it down in writing so that mothers had a core of information.

EF: Yes, we had many sessions together, talking about how we were going to do this. We conceived of it as a "course-by-mail." Our idea was to start educating the mother about breastfeeding before she has the baby, so that she doesn't make so many mistakes. Mistakes can be so hard to correct, like a golfer who teaches himself the wrong kind of swing, and then it takes hours and hours of practice to undo what he has learned. Better to learn it right the first time.

So, that was the theory behind the course-by-mail. The mother would subscribe to it early in her pregnancy and receive it once a month. As I recall, we were going to have some information on childbirth in there, too.

But pretty quick we could see that there were a lot of problems with this course-by-mail idea. For starters, we had a lot of mothers coming to us who had already had the baby. The course-by-mail would have a limited amount of information on a specific topic each month, but what if that month's edition didn't address her particular problem? She couldn't very well wait till next month. And then too, what about a mother who might deliver prematurely, before she had finished the course?

We soon realized that the course-by-mail wasn't a very good idea, that what we really had to do was to get all of this information down between two covers—to put together a "how-to" manual.

Nobody pushed harder than I did to promote the idea of putting together a book on breastfeeding. You see, I was the secretary so I was the one who got all the mail. And while I did have help answering the mail, still, I was the one who did the bulk of it. I just wanted to be able to write a nice short letter saying, "Here's all the information you need. Get back to me after you've read it all, if you still have any questions."

We didn't have much money for printing. Mary White said she knew somebody who was a printer. She said she would talk to him and see if he could give us a break on the price. I remember that Marian and Betty and I were very worried about the money. We said, "What if we can't sell more than a few books?" But Mary kept reassuring us.

Anyway, with Mary's reassurance we stopped worrying about the money and moved ahead with the project. It was mostly the four of us, Mary Ann Cahill, Mary White, Marian Tompson, and myself who did most of the actual writing.

We lived very close together. We could run over to each other's homes after the kids were in bed. And we could talk to each other on the phone without it costing us extra. And we did talk—for hours on end. We each took a section, as I recall. I had the section on nutrition.

So that's kind of the way it worked out. Our first manual was put together in a hurry. With the second edition Herb Ratner went over it with a fine tooth comb and made a lot of improvements. Marian was the one who worked with him on that edition. But the writing was a group effort. It was teamwork that got the job done.

Mary Ann Kerwin

MAC: *Soon after LLL got underway, you moved to Denver. Did you take LLL with you?*

MAK: Yes. Almost as soon as we got unpacked, I was hosting the first La Leche League meeting in Colorado We got there in January and I think we had our first meeting in February.

MAC: *Ahh!*

MAK: It had become so much a part of my life that I just assumed that was the thing to do. Of course, we were one of the first Groups outside the Chicago area.

MAC: *That's great!*

MAK: Yes, we were one of the very first outside of Chicago, one of the early ones. And it flourished. I did write up the history of Colorado groups for one of the Western Area Conferences, for our 30th or 35th anniversary.

MAC: Did you see any different needs there in Colorado compared to what you had seen in the Chicago area?

MAK: No—it was pretty much the same. And, as I re-read our old minutes, what we were primarily doing was offering information and encouragement to mothers who wanted to breastfeed their babies. And it was the same thing there. I did find that there seemed to be more doctors in Colorado who were supportive of breast-feeding and natural childbirth than there had been in Chicago.

THE WOMANLY ART OF BREASTFEEDING came out in 1958. What I recall about that is that we were so tired of writing all those letters. I don't think any of us was even using a typewriter, were we? Perhaps Edwina? Mary White?

MAC: Edwina, yes. She was the secretary, and, Mary, too.

MAK: Yes, but I didn't. Today we have computers. But back then we were writing longhand. It's my recollection that we were paying our own postage. I'm not sure, but I think we were.

So I answered letters—we all did—and it was very rewarding. But it was also very time-consuming. I remember getting together with the other Founders, and we were all highly motivated to get something mimeographed that we could send out. Then we could add short notes to the mimeographed material. We would always write a note or a short letter. But the idea was that most of the information that we used to write out longhand would now be part of the mimeographed material.

MAC: So you're talking about the mimeographed material.

MAK: Yes, I mean the mimeographed material. See, I brought a copy with me.

MAC: Oh, my gosh!

MAK: Anyway, that is my recollection of the origin of the manual—that even before we put together THE WOMANLY ART OF BREASTFEEDING, we had begun to put together some loose-leaf sheets of information on certain things.

MAC: That was the beginning, yes.

MAK: Anyway, THE WOMANLY ART OF BREASTFEEDING really saved a lot of hours and helped us a lot. And it seems to me that we were doing so well selling the loose-leaf notebook form that we pretty quickly proceeded toward publishing the blue book. At least, that's my recollection.

Viola Lennon

MAC: What do you remember abut the "Course by Mail" idea?

VL: I remember we looked at a marriage course from Canada that had everything on cards and we discussed that kind of presentation for a while. Then we decided "No." We did some outlines. I remember going through this kind of thing.

MAC: Was this for the meetings or for information to send out to mothers who wrote?

VL: Both. Did we send out cards to people who wrote to us? I don't think I have much information on that. But I remember the cards. This was all part of the process of doing the first WOMANLY ART OF BREASTFEEDING.

MAC: And of course, the first one was the loose-leaf.

VL: I don't think it was even loose-leaf. I think it had a sort of funny binding on it. I have a copy of it somewhere. It looked to me like a high school chemistry manual. It was that size. Very dull-looking.

MAC: Eventually, of course, we developed the blue book.

VL: Right. That was dull-looking, too. But right from the beginning the information was pretty solid. And we didn't have to worry too much about looks. The mothers were desperate for information. But now, as we move into the 21st century, you are competing with some very good-looking publications. So we have to keep up with the times.

MAC: Do you have any recollections about the production of our "little blue book"?

VL: I remember sitting down for long sessions as we started to compose the mimeographed booklet, and then the blue book. We were beginning to accumulate pretty good experience in terms of breastfeeding. So I thought that the production of the blue book was a step forward.

MAC: Did you get many calls from mothers in the early days?

VL: Yes, lots of calls from mothers, many calls. Mothers were being referred to us by their friends and by their doctors.

MAC: Do you recall the kind of calls you were getting?

VL: This has always been interesting to me. The kinds of calls I was getting and the questions I was answering in those days are exactly the same kind of calls I'm answering today. And now the calls are coming from my children and their friends. They want to know, "How long should I nurse?" "Do I nurse on both sides?"

"What do you do with a baby that's nursing every fifteen or twenty minutes or so?" So you have to tell them that this is probably a growth spurt—and so on. In other words, exactly the same kinds of calls that we got in the early days of La Leche League.

I don't spend that much time trying to talk people into breastfeeding. My children do all that. And they are good role models. But for the most part, you don't have to work on people's conviction that breastfeeding is best. They just need to be told what to do, rather than having to talk them into breastfeeding. You have to teach them or show them how to solve their specific problem. Usually the problems are not really serious.

I always tell the new mother to put The Womanly Art of Breastfeeding on her nightstand and never remove it. That's important.

Lately I have heard lots of compliments about The Breastfeeding Answer Book. Several of my daughter's friends have bought The Breastfeeding Answer Book not because she told them to, but because the kinds of information they want is easy to find there.

The Womanly Art of Breastfeeding is more the saga of how to breastfeed and why, while. The Breastfeeding Answer Book has the answers to specific questions.

Chapter 8—GROWTH SPURTS

Letters by the thousands, a veritable avalanche, became the straw that almost broke the back of Edwina's mailman. He went so far as to suggest that she and the organization she represented open their own post office. The letters descended over a course of several months following an article that appeared in the May 1963 issue of *Reader's Digest*, and they put considerable strain on an already stressed LLL operation.

The *Reader's Digest* article, "They Teach the Joys of Breastfeeding," had been excerpted from the book *Nursing Your Baby* by Karen Pryor. Karen had visited us in Franklin Park some time earlier to find out what she could about breastfeeding and La Leche League. From the start, the Founders had adopted a policy of sharing information freely, welcoming even those who were planning to publish breastfeeding material on their own. They reasoned that the more information—good information—that was made available, the better. As for LLL, the resulting exposure from the English, Spanish, and French editions of the *Reader's Digest* was more than ample reward.

The deluge of mail also confirmed a decision that had been made some months earlier, namely to relocate the La Leche League office. For years the Froehlichs' dining room table had served as Edwina's work desk as well as eating space for the family. A four-drawer file cabinet and stacks of boxes of LLL materials had taken over the back bedroom. Boxes were literally crammed to the ceiling. At the same time, the three Froehlich boys, ages six, ten, and twelve and all destined to become champion wrestlers in high school and college, were sharing a single bedroom. That arrangement, too, was bursting at the seams.

A solution presented itself when Edwina made a visit to the podiatrist in town and, along with having a corn removed, learned of a small, one-room office that was for rent in the building. It was an easy walk from Edwina's house and, after a little on-the-spot negotiating, the owner agreed to rent it for $50 a month and no lease. Edwina was ecstatic. A call to Marian produced a cautionary, "Where will we get the money?" Marian was known for being ultra-conservative about spending.

Looking for a more encouraging answer, Edwina called Betty, who was considered more daring and, more importantly, was the treasurer. "If we have to do it," Betty responded, "we have to do it. Go back and tell the man you'll take it."

Things were coming together. Several months prior, again in desperation, Edwina had hired a typist to help with the mail. She had been coming to Edwina's house three mornings a week. Now both women worked in the office for those hours, which was perfect, since they could then be home with their children at lunchtime. The plan was for Laverne Spadaro to continue in the job until the mail was under control. She remained for 20 years, a valued LLLI employee who worked in a number of positions.

Mothers who previously would not have considered breastfeeding their babies were now encouraged to try and were contacting La Leche League for help. Such was the case of a mother who called Marian for help with relactating. Few people had ever heard of a mother bringing back her milk months after having "dried up." They couldn't even imagine why she'd want to. Lorraine Bormet knew exactly why she wanted to breastfeed her fifth child.

David was three months old and suffering from almost constant tummy aches and diarrhea. None of the many formulas that had been tried agreed with him. His parents were desperate when the family doctor advised them to try feeding him mother's milk. A call to Dr. Kimball and the milk bank at Evanston Hospital led to their contacting La Leche League in Franklin Park, and an anxious but hopeful Lorraine went on to talk to Marian almost daily for weeks. The outcome was that at age four-and-a-half months, David was healthy, happy, and completely nourished at his mother's breast. A newspaper article reporting on this story brought even more publicity to the burgeoning LLL.

Soon another mother, Marcia Cohen, undertook to do the same for her son, Mark, who had also reacted badly to multiple formulas and was, in his mother's words, "just a very, very sick baby." Marcia and her baby also triumphed, with Mark nursing until he was 13 months old. To help Mark get started, Marcia used the "medicine dropper technique" that became a standard for coaxing babies to continue at their mother's breast even when her milk supply is low.

La Leche League was adding to its store of information on unusual situations and attracting other people who were equally interested in solving problems. Eventually, the medicine dropper technique was developed into the Lact-Aid® system for supplementing by an adoptive mother who wanted to feed her baby at the breast.

Inverted nipples—nipples that retract inward and make it difficult for the baby to get started at the breast—were another difficulty that discouraged many mothers from breastfeeding. Mary White found a product from England, the Woolwich Breast Shield, that can be worn under a mother's bra during pregnancy to gently draw out the nipple. In 1959 when La Leche League placed its first order, it was the only source for this remarkable little item in the United States. The shields sold for $2.75 a pair. With this step, La Leche League began providing more than just written information to help mothers realize their dream of breastfeeding their babies.

Karen Pryor spoke at several LLL Conferences;
she is shown here with Betty Wagner.

The nursing mother who needed a medication was especially vulnerable, since she was invariably told to wean her baby. As for the doctors, it was a defensive move, due to the fact that very little information was available to them. The same applied to the treatment of certain kinds of jaundice in newborn babies. Mothers were being told to stop breastfeeding until the jaundice cleared, advice that other doctors, mainly those more experienced with breastfeeding, had found was not warranted. In fact La Leche League doctors were finding few reasons to suggest weaning when treating an illness or prescribing a medication for a breastfeeding mother.

It was a thorny issue, and the Board and Founders struggled with it. They had always shied away from giving medical advice, preferring instead to simply pass on the best information available and encourage the parents to consult their doctor and then decide for themselves. The challenge now was to find a way to make what the LLL doctors had learned more readily available to others. Doctor and Mary White reviewed all the research on medications and how they reacted in the nursing mother and child. Working with Dr. Mark Thoman, they were able to get this information published in the *Journal of Veterinary and Human Toxicology*. The Whites' pioneering work in reviewing research and responding to questions about a variety of medical issues that relate to breastfeeding has since been expanded and compiled by Nancy Mohrbacher and Julie Stock into THE BREASTFEEDING ANSWER BOOK. Today's LLL Leader or anyone else who is interested in helping mothers can look up questions and answers covering a multitude of breastfeeding situations and draw on 45 years of experience in keeping babies healthy and breastfeeding.

By the early 1960s, the work going on in Franklin Park comprised much more than serving as a support group for the local community. La Leche League had been established in countries outside the USA, the first in French-speaking Canada, then in English-speaking Canada, and in Mexico, Puerto Rico, the Virgin Islands, and New Zealand. For the Founders, it became a question of distinguishing local

LLL Group activity from the broader work directed from the little office on Franklin Avenue. A name change seemed in order, and papers were filed with the state of Illinois to change the corporate name from La Leche League of Franklin Park to La Leche League International. The new designation begged for new recognition, and in 1961 an official LLLI logo was selected. Mary Ann Cahill, who was then editor of the *La Leche League News*, remembers superimposing the final choice, a line drawing of a mother and baby, on a map of the world lifted from the family encyclopedia and using it in the News.

It was a hectic, exciting time, and the seven Founders couldn't imagine adding one more thing to their already busy schedules. But they did.

MAC: Do you remember the responses we got at first to the idea of forming a breast-feeding organization?

MW: I still remember getting a letter from a woman who had read Karen Pryor's article. That article was one of the first ways in which word about La Leche League and what we were doing was made known nationally.

Anyway, this woman wrote to us, and she was kind of indignant. She said, "Why do you have to have an organization to tell mothers how to nurse their babies? That's silly. All mothers know how to nurse their babies." And I thought, "Oh, lady, if only you were right!"

Granted, this idea of having an organization to promote breastfeeding did seem kind of far-fetched. But we got such a tremendous response from everybody who read that article that we knew we had touched something in mothers. Their response to that article was, "Oh yes! This is something I've always wanted to do."

So I think the desire to breastfeed was always there, along with the conviction that "breast is best." We certainly didn't have to use a hard sell on anybody. We weren't promoting a product that people had to be convinced about. But very few young mothers knew anything about the "how to."

Women had forgotten the wisdom of previous generations. By the time LLL came along, new mothers did not have the support of family or friends, let alone doctors, nurses, and hospitals. Mothers who tried to breastfeed on their own in the early 1950s were almost destined to fail—it took a very unusual woman to succeed at breastfeeding with all the social pressures that were lined up against her at that time.

MAC: Mary, please talk about the evolution of LLL's response to some of the medical issues that affect breastfeeding.

MW: Sure. Well, from the beginning we had very good medical advice. With the help of our medical advisors we put together a list of all the drugs a mother could or should not take when she was breastfeeding. All the references were there. We answered all the standard questions: What about aspirin? What about this or that antibiotic? And so on.

Mark Thoman published the list in the *Journal of Veterinary and Human Toxicology*. We used that list for a long time as a guide and reference list. Then, after a few years had gone by, some people felt it wasn't as up to date as it should be. Questions about new medications were always being asked. So they went on and got more references, and did a lot of writing, and brought the list up to date. Now a similar list is published every few years by the American Academy of Pediatrics. But we were among the first to put something like this together.

Incidentally, none of our references has ever been disproved. You can still go back and look at that first toxicology journal and look up a reference for this or that drug, and if it is in there, you will find that our original recommendations still stand, they still hold up. Nobody has said, "Oops, La Leche League told me that that drug was okay and now it's been proven that it isn't okay." That hasn't happened.

Mary Ann Kerwin

MAC: *Mary Ann, do you remember when we first rented an office for La Leche League?*

MAK: I think we felt that we needed an office because doing all that La Leche League work out of our homes had become impractical—there was simply too much paperwork, too many phone calls, and so on, for us to continue conducting LLL's business from our homes. I believe that we financed the move through sales of THE WOMANLY ART OF BREASTFEEDING. And then, once we had moved LLL into a regular office, we began to pay salaries to the staff, whereas when we were working on LLL projects at home, almost all work was done on a volunteer basis.

And then Karen Pryor's article on La Leche League was published in 1963— "They Teach the Joys of Breastfeeding." When that article came out, it was featured on the cover of *Reader's Digest*, and it was a big boost to us as an organization. Karen Pryor was a very well-respected scientist. So to have her endorse what we were doing gave us a lot of confidence. It also gave La Leche League a lot of credibility with the general public.

Marian Tompson

MAC: *Marian, how did you fit in all the extra work involved in helping to start a new organization while, at the same time, managing to take care of your family?*

MT: It worked out because first of all, I had the right husband for it. He wasn't a man who would get upset if something wasn't done when he got home. It would have been much more difficult if I had had a husband who was demanding and expected me to live a different way.

Tom not only gave me moral support, but he was also willing to pitch in and help in practical ways, too. For instance, the first time we put out the blue manual, he drove to Danville and brought a load of books back in our car. We put the books in our garage. Our car sat outside that winter because we had to have a place to store the books. Tom was just totally behind what I was doing because he knew how important it was for mothers to have the right information.

Tom said to me once—and I was so surprised because I had really been a very obedient child—he said, "I could tell when I married you that you were a person who needed a lot of freedom." So he just decided to be there for me, and to give me the freedom to do what I wanted or needed to do.

MAC: Going back to 1963 when the decision was made to rent an office and give Edwina back the bedroom she desperately needed for her boys. Did you start to work in the office then, Marian?

MT: No. When we moved into that office, I was expecting our seventh child, and it wasn't until Philip was in second grade that I got pulled into the office one afternoon a week in the beginning. I really didn't want to go into the office because it wasn't my image of myself. I was a mother, not a career person. Even though I lived just five minutes from what was then our office on Minneapolis Avenue in Franklin Park, I really had to be convinced that it was more helpful, better, to be in the office than to work at home. And, of course, it was more helpful to be in the office, and have everything there that you would need, including a better typewriter. But I really didn't want to go in to the office at all.

Edwina Froehlich

MAC: For years the "LLL office" had been in your home. Then office space was found in Franklin Park. Tell us about your joining the staff at this office.

EF: When I started at the office, Peter was either in kindergarten or first grade. It worked out well for me because I could be home when the children came home. What I brought to the office were some very useful office skills. I had worked as a stenographer and secretary for some 13 years. I was very familiar with typing and shorthand and filing. In addition, I was good at writing my own letters, or writing a letter for the boss if he wanted me to. I could put things into words; I liked to work with words. That sort of thing was a natural for me, as natural as the business end was for Betty. She didn't like writing letters and I didn't like the business end—keeping track of money and selling things.

MAC: How many people worked at the office when you started?

EF: It was just Betty and I and Laverne Spadaro. Laverne was there usually for a couple of hours a day. Laverne was strictly a typist. I would dictate the letters and she'd type them up. Laverne was not one to initiate things and we did not need her for that. She was a wonderful typist. This was before word processors or anything like that, so it took a lot of time to get things typed.

We didn't even have copy machines when we first started, so everything was done with carbons. Laverne was invaluable because she was really an expert typist. She was a very good secretary.

I could do the organizing. I could set up files and I could take care of the letter writing. I was good on the telephone, counseling, or whatever kind of phone call it was unless it was strictly business-related—that Betty would take care of. It worked out well.

MAC: Were we then developing Groups outside of the Franklin Park/Chicago area?

EF: Groups were beginning to start then. We weren't initiating these Groups. They were the ones getting in touch with us. Groups were popping up all over. It seems to me that shortly after we got into that first office the *Reader's Digest* article came out and brought us such a deluge of mail. I remember Betty and I agreeing that it was fortunate that we were all set up with an office and ready to handle that deluge when it came, because prior to that I had been answering a lot of the mail at home.

MAC: And how did Marian Tompson fit into this set-up?

EF: Marian was president. She was exceptionally good at dealing with doctors and professionals. Marian could absorb a lot of information, including technical and medical information. The kind of thing I found hard to keep in my head. She could absorb it and give it back at a moment's notice. It would just roll off her tongue.

I was much more in charge of the Leaders who were dealing with mothers, while Marian was in charge of talking to doctors and other professional contacts. We didn't have it strictly catalogued like that, but in general that's the way the work was divided up.

After a while, I gave myself the title of executive secretary. At that time, an executive secretary was one who was involved with the letters, the correspondence, but she also was more than the boss's secretary. She had certain administrative jobs that she was responsible for. Betty would put me in charge of certain things and I could make certain decisions. Always it was regarding Leaders and Groups. I never really made decisions that I hadn't first discussed with Betty. We worked well together—it just was always very easy. We'd talk something over and decide and that was that.

MAC: What kinds of decisions were made at Board Meetings at that point?

EF: I remember that we talked a lot about money at the Board Meetings. How we would get money for this, that, or the other thing, or how the money was to be spent.

True, we were always discussing philosophy, and we were very concerned about the process for bringing in new Leaders, how that all functioned. Also, we would talk a lot about the Groups in other countries, how we could keep in touch with them.

MAC: Do you remember if we worked within a budget?

EF: Nobody really had a budget. If you wanted to spend money, you asked Betty, and Betty would look and see if there was money and she'd say, "Yes, you can" or "No, you can't" and that's the way it was.

It was kind of a new idea to us when somebody suggested that we should have a budget. A budget sounded like a good idea, but Betty was saying, "Where is the money going to come from for this 'budget'?" She always worried about the money and she didn't want to plan things unless she knew there would be money to pay for it!

Chapter 9—GATHERING TOGETHER

An offhand remark by Tom Kerwin rekindled an idea that had been in the air for some time but had seemed too outlandish to even think about, considering all that was going on. Tom proposed holding a convention, a meeting for all who were interested in breastfeeding. His comment, made one evening at a meeting at the Kerwins' home, might have been quickly dismissed as being overly ambitious or too radical had it not been for the letters that were coming from mothers living at a distance. Their number was far from an avalanche, but it was steady, and the message was always the same, "How I wish I could meet you."

And then there was Mary Jane Brizzolara, who was in charge of preparing interested mothers to become Leaders. On more than one occasion she had worried about the difficulty of conveying the spirit of La Leche League as well as the know-how of breastfeeding solely through letters. Even after they were helping mothers, new Leaders were looking for more—more information, more opportunities to learn from other nursing mothers, and more ways to be reinvigorated and recommitted.

The more the Founders thought about it, the better the idea sounded. They would be able to meet many of the women with whom they had been corresponding, and everyone would have the opportunity to hear the doctors and other professionals who supported breastfeeding. Knowledgeable, supportive doctors were still rare in many communities in the early 1960s.

On the other hand, such an undertaking involved a tremendous amount of work and planning. And who had ever heard of mothers and their babies leaving their families and traveling on their own to attend a convention?

Once again, need dictated action. In 1962 the decision was made to hold the first La Leche League Convention (the title "conference" wasn't adopted until some years later). The dates were June 22, 23, and 24, 1964, and the place was the Knickerbocker, a small, medium priced hotel just off Michigan Avenue in Chicago's downtown area. LLL Leader Nell Ryan, poised, low-key, and competent, was appointed Convention Chairman.

The back of the ballroom was reserved for babies and children at LLLI's first convention in 1964.

Nell and her committee soon found that they were negotiating uncharted territory, as was also, in many ways, the hotel. This was not the typical professional group or businessmen's meeting. Forget about setting up bars for drinks in the rooms. Rather, could they set up several dozen cribs for the babies? Yes, the manager assured them. Would there be places to change babies and dispose of diapers—many diapers? Again yes, that, too, could be worked out.

In response to the hotel's request for an estimate of the number of women who might be attending, the figure 50 was thrown out, then increased to 75, and finally doubled to 150. In the back of everyone's mind was the terrible thought, "What if the mothers don't come? What if it's too difficult to get away, or they don't have the money to attend? What if only a few people show up?"

Despite the concerns, plans moved forward, with calls and letters going to supportive doctors and others asking them to speak, pro bono of course. There simply was no money to pay anyone. At the same time, an all-out effort was put into sending out notices of the upcoming convention, and a great deal of thought went into making the program and other arrangements mother/baby friendly. The first Rock and Rest Room was designed, giving mothers a chance to slip away from a crowded meeting room and relax with their babies. Donations of thousands of disposable diapers were secured to simplify baby care. Such innovations soon became standard for La Leche League Conferences and many persist to the present day.

It was an event waiting to happen. Mothers came by the hundreds, 425 to be exact, with 100 babies and unlimited enthusiasm. The more typical patrons at the hotel were amazed and generally pleased by the influx of so many little ones, though somewhat taken aback by the prominent signs in washrooms warning against flushing diapers down the toilets. The hotel staff took it all in stride, even to the fact that they received fewer gratuities. It was still a world in which women traveled for the most part with a male companion, who assumed the responsibility for tipping, and the mothers fell short in that regard. By the next Conference, word had gone out and, along with toys to keep a little one occupied, mothers also tucked some bills into their pockets to give to the caring staff who helped make their stay pleasant.

The purpose that the Founders had in mind was clearly stated in the Program Book: "We welcome you, baby on one shoulder and name tag on the other, to La Leche League International's first convention, confident that through your participation we will hasten the day when every mother can be assured of whatever help she may need to succeed in the womanly art of breastfeeding."

No one was disappointed with the sessions; those attending could not get enough of them. Dr. Herbert Ratner set the stage with his powerful keynote address in which he stressed the importance of a mother's role and the impact it has on families, society, and a woman's own sense of worth. For the most part, the sessions were held in the main ballroom, with an open space in the back of the room given over to mothers with babies. Many babies were sleeping or playing on blankets on the floor, others were being pushed to and fro in strollers, often by an older brother or sister who had come along to help. At later conferences, the use of strollers was restricted due to congestion and concern for safety. Throughout the big room, a constant hum of baby noises held sway. Neither the speakers nor the audience seemed to mind, certainly not the mothers, who delighted in being with other breastfeeding mothers.

A sampling of session titles gives a clue to the interests at the time: "Starting of Solids" with panelists E. Robbins Kimball, MD, pediatrician, Illinois; Jody Nathanson, LLL Leader, California; Niles Newton, PhD, behavioral scientist, Illinois; and Gregory J. White, MD, family practitioner, Illinois. "Childbirth" with Robert Bradley, MD, obstetrician, Colorado; Margaret Gamper, RN, childbirth educator, Illinois; Helen Wessel, president of ICEA (International Childbirth Education Association). "A Psychiatrist and Pediatrician Look at Modern Baby and Child Care" with Marvin Schwarz, MD, and Robert Mendelsohn, MD, both from Illinois. A session titled "Medical Problems" included breast infections, allergies, premies, prescription drugs, and smoking. At one point in this session, Marian Tompson, the moderator, apologized for a delay in introducing the panelists. She explained that she had been preoccupied "running after my crawling infant," her son Philip, eight months old.

For the Founders, it was a special time to be together. Mary Ann and Tom Kerwin and family had moved to Colorado in 1960. Since that time they had celebrated the birth of Gregory Joseph and daughters Mary and Anne Marie. With eight-month-old Anne Marie in her arms, Mary Ann was eager to greet old friends.

At the end of the convention, those who came to listen and those who spoke were proud, excited, reinvigorated, and eager for more. The decision was quickly made to hold a second convention in two years time in neighboring Indiana. Betty Ann Countryman, backed by her husband, Dr. Frank Countryman, and Dave Bosworth, husband of an Indianapolis breastfeeding mother, agreed to chair the event to be held in Indianapolis. Registration fee was $31.75 and included two lunches. Hotel rooms listed at $7.50 for a single room, $11 for a room with a double bed, and $13.50 for a room with twin beds.

Again, the response exceeded expectations. In truth it can be said that each of the International Conferences to date have been a triumph in its own right, although a few stand out for an extraordinary event. Those who attended the 4th International Conference at the LaSalle Hotel in Chicago in 1971 still talk about the appearance of Princess Grace of Monaco, honored guest and speaker at the banquet. She attracted considerable coverage for La Leche League in the Chicago media, making every breastfeeding mother in the city stand a little taller knowing that someone so lovely and accomplished shared their vision of womanliness. Years before, when it had been announced that the princess was pregnant, an LLL mother had sent the Princess a copy of THE WOMANLY ART OF BREASTFEEDING. The princess went on to nurse all of her children, and a lasting relationship developed between her and La Leche League. At the Conference banquet, Her Serene Highness repeatedly used the word "nurture" endearing her to her audience. Her statement of how, when her children were babies, "State waited on mother," became a rallying cry for countless La Leche League mothers who often had to defend their decision to breastfeed their babies.

Ten years later in 1981, the star of the 25th Anniversary Conference, also held in Chicago, was a book, THE WOMANLY ART OF BREASTFEEDING, newly updated and expanded. After 28 printings of over a million copies, the beloved "blue manual" was being retired. The year also marked the 25th anniversary of the founding of La Leche League, and attendance at the conference was a record high. The celebration was further heightened by the fact that major pediatric associations in the US and Canada had come out with strong statements promoting breastfeeding as the preferred method of feeding the baby. Twenty-five years of hard work were paying off; the rest of the world was catching up with what LLL had been saying all that time. Sales of the new book were phenomenal, and a contract was signed with a large publisher, New American Library, to distribute the book in bookstores.

Conferences became a regular part of the LLLI program, attracting large numbers of mothers, babies, entire families, and professional people. Hope Melnick of Illinois was the LLLI Conference planner for more than two decades. Carol Kolar continues the tradition, as a certified meeting planner and Director of the LLLI Education Department.

Conferences are a popular way to bring people together in La Leche League Areas and Regions as well, educating, invigorating, and inspiring new generations of mothers. In each local area, volunteer power, teams of highly capable and dedicated LLL women and men, make them happen.

It was a volunteer, Vera Turton, an LLL Leader from Skokie, Illinois, who first proposed holding an educational meeting on breastfeeding for physicians. Like so many others in 1971, Vera was well aware of how little doctors were taught on the subject. She suggested that a program be offered for continuing medical education credits, a means by which doctors keep up to date in their profession.

The committee for the first Seminar for Physicians included Marian Tompson and Drs. Niles Newton, Ratner, White, and Mendelsohn. The doctors concentrated on information that they had found useful in practice, and Marian's contribution was from the mother's perspective. Dr. Ratner was the first moderator.

*Princess Grace of Monaco was an honored guest at
LLLI's Conference in 1971.*

The accrediting body at the time for such programs, the American Medical Association (AMA),
agreed to come out and survey the meeting.
Approximately thirty doctors attended the first seminar in 1973. One of the doctors conducting the survey told the committee that even if LLLI was not
accredited to offer these meetings for continuing
education credit, they should continue giving the
seminars, since there was no other place for doctors
to get information on breastfeeding.

The AMA did grant accreditation, although it
expressed concern for La Leche League's ability to present an annual meeting, one
of the requirements, because of budget limitations. Most heartening to the plan-
ners were the favorable evaluations from those who had attended. Doctors quickly
put what they learned into practice and were rewarded with marked improvements
in breastfeeding outcome. Attendance at the seminar grew over the years, reaching
more than a hundred, and accreditation was regularly extended. The faculty like-
wise grew, attracting physicians from various places in the world, among them Dr.
Derrick Jelliffe, who had lived in Africa for some time and was head of the Division
of Population, Family, and International Health at the University of California, Los
Angeles; Dr. Lawrence Gartner, pediatrician and associate professor at Albert
Einstein College of Medicine in New York, Dr. Paul Gyorgy, professor emeritus of
pediatrics at the University of Pennsylvania, renowned for his research on human
milk. Old favorites continued to add substance to the sessions—Dr. James Good of
Ohio, Dr. E. Robbins Kimball of Illinois, Dr. Richard Applebaum, Florida.

The LLLI Seminar for Physicians is currently an annual three-day meeting and
is presented by LLLI and co-sponsored by the American Academy of Pediatrics
and the American College of Obstetricians and Gynecologists, with the American
Academy of Family Physicians participating as a cooperating organization. The

Accreditation Council for Continuing Medical Education recently issued a very favorable review of LLLI's continuing education programs.

Viola Lennon

MAC: *What are your recollections of that first convention?*

VL: I think it was the first time that I had been away from home for any significant period of time since the children were born. I remember arriving late due to something happening at home. I don't remember now what happened.

However, I do remember being very pleased with the convention itself. I was amazed at how many people had come. Once again, the natural need for an organization like LLL was starting to become evident.

Mary Ann Kerwin

MAC: *What did you think about our first convention at the Knickerbocker Hotel in Chicago?*

MAK: That was a big, wonderful, exciting time. You know, I felt we were always doing things that were a little risky, kind of extending ourselves, almost like jumping off a cliff. We were anxious, yet we were solidly together on these things.

I remember that we were very eager to get together and meet these people who had been starting LLL Groups all over. Our only contact had been by phone and letters—mainly letters. So we just thought, "Wouldn't it be nice to meet everybody?" And maybe we thought that they wanted to meet us, too.

But we had not expected such a good turnout. I'm not sure, but I think the turnout was about 300 or so. I do know that it was more than we had expected.

MAC: *What was your impression of that convention?*

MAK: My impression was surprise that so many people attended. I had the same wonderful feeling I had when we met each other for that first time at Mary's house; I was so happy to know that there were other people who thought like I did.

MAC: *Any thoughts on how we financed that first convention?*

MAK: I don't remember any of the specifics of how we financed that convention. I remember that we were trying to be very careful with money. I don't think any of us felt that we had an unlimited budget. So we were keeping it pretty modest. But somehow we believed that people would come, and they did come.

MAC: What do you recall about the 1971 convention when Princess Grace of Monaco spoke?

MAK: Of course, Princess Grace was the highlight of our 1971 Fourth International Convention in Chicago. For many years, we had been seeing and hearing about this stunningly beautiful, talented actress. Then we followed her storybook marriage to a prince and the births of their three children. When we discovered that Princess Grace breastfed her babies we were ecstatic! The fact that Princess Grace was eager and willing to openly become connected with LLL gave us a tremendous boost.

The night of the famous banquet at which Princess Grace spoke so graciously and eloquently was extra special for everyone, including me. I had brought my one-year-old nursing baby, Mike, and my ten-year-old daughter, Mary, with me. While Mary, Mike, and I were getting ready for the banquet, someone asked me if I would mind sitting at the head table because there was an extra place. Without a moment's hesitation, I eagerly accepted. I could hardly believe my good luck. I sat at the head table with my baby and with Mary close by to assist me as needed. Mary was old enough to be as thrilled as I was.

As we listened to Princess Grace speak from the heart about breastfeeding, mothering, and about her children, we felt empowered. To have someone of her stature celebrate with us the joys and benefits of breastfeeding and mothering was like a dream come true. This indeed was one of my most unforgettable experiences!

After the banquet, a special reception followed during which the Princess greeted everyone personally. As I stood in line, I happened to look down at my feet. I was shocked to see that I had on one white shoe and one black shoe. With all the excitement, I had not noticed my mistake until then. Fortunately I had on a floor length dress. When my turn came to speak to the Princess, I asked her to look down at my shoes. She laughed. I said to her that she could see that I was not a bit excited about meeting her. She seemed to enjoy the fact that I was so transfixed by being with her. Another special remembrance was the way she greeted my children as warmly and personably as she greeted me.

Princess Grace undoubtedly captured the hearts of each and every one of the thousands of mothers, fathers, children, and babies she spent time with during those few precious days of 1971.

I remember we published some of the points she made in her banquet speech and mothers loved hearing these things coming from a celebrity. She said: "As women, it is one of our greatest prides that we have in our bodies, to give to our newborn children, every element that an infant needs for perfect health and growth....The frantic life of today has swept up women to the point where, either because of difficulties imposed by overcrowding, the necessity to hold down jobs, or even their own lack of inclination, they feel that there is not time for this vital, natural function....I have many duties and obligations of State along with my husband, but my family comes first. At the beginning, when they needed me and I, them, there were no compromises; State had to wait upon mother. And if, in my free time I had to work a little harder to make it up, that work became a pleasure for the sake of the newborn....It would seem to me that the closeness to the child resulting from breastfeeding is somehow an extension and affirmation of the very love that had resulted in the child's being there."

Edwina Froehlich

MAC: *Edwina, what do you remember about Princess Grace's visit to our 1971 convention?*

EF: Princess Grace's visit was certainly a coup. A Leader from New Jersey, Doris Haire, was the one who originally wrote to Princess Grace, on her own. It was a total surprise to us. The Leader sent Princess Grace a copy of THE WOMANLY ART OF BREASTFEEDING and invited her to become an honorary member of LLL.

Our first thought was, "My gosh, nobody gave this Leader permission to do that; what if the Princess is offended?" But Princess Grace accepted and became an honorary member of LLL. We knew that Princess Grace often came to visit her family in the United States during the summer. So we thought, wouldn't it be great if her visit coincided with our convention, which was scheduled for the next summer. I wrote a letter to Princess Grace on behalf of LLL, inviting her to attend the convention and speak at our banquet. I wrote this letter about a year and a half in advance of our conference.

Well, the answer came back—not a rejection, but simply a note saying that Princess Grace did not have her schedule made out that far in advance. So we sent a couple of reminders as the months went by, and each time there was a very courteous reply saying that they didn't know her schedule yet. We decided that she was worth waiting for, even if it did make it a bit difficult trying to plan the conference and not knowing who the banquet speaker would be until almost the last minute.

But we decided that we would just bide our time. And by golly, it was very exciting when she finally replied that she would indeed accept our invitation. That, of course, was a momentous occasion. It was at the LaSalle Hotel in Chicago. What a crowd we had at the banquet that night!

Yes, the Princess Grace banquet was certainly a gala occasion. Marian had a private interview with the Princess in Princess Grace's suite. Then Vi escorted her down to the banquet room.

I remember my husband, John, saying for weeks in advance of the event that he wasn't particularly interested in meeting Princess Grace. He said, "You women can go crazy over something like that, but what the heck, it doesn't mean anything to me. What do I care about celebrities? To me, she's just an ordinary person," and on and on like that.

Before we went into the banquet, there was a receiving line. I was standing next to Marian, and she was standing next to Princess Grace. As people came along, Marian would turn to the Princess and introduce them.

I had told John that he could meet the Princess, but he said, "That'll be the day!" So you can imagine my surprise when I looked down the receiving line and, lo and behold, I see my husband. I thought, "Oh dear, what is John going to say to the Princess when he meets her? What will he call her?"

But when he was introduced to the Princess, he said, very properly, "Your Serene Highness" and he bent over and kissed her hand.

He has never been able to deny that—that he was there and that he greeted the Princess so gallantly, because we have the photograph. I made sure we got a picture of that!

In retrospect, all I can say is what a wonderful, exciting evening it was—it represented the culmination and the highlight of all of our efforts to build up La Leche League, and make it better known so that more women would breastfeed their babies. For years after that event, people who were not in any way connected with La Leche League would say, "Oh, that's the organization that Princess Grace started" or "La Leche League—that's Princess Grace's group." Yes, it was a night to remember.

Mary White

MAC: *Do you have any recollections of the Princess, Mary?*

MW: Princess Grace—A lovely, warm, gracious lady in every sense of the word—so generous in giving her time to us all and seeming to enjoy it, too! In addition to speaking at the banquet and holding a press conference, she walked around the conference talking to the mothers and holding the babies. Everyone loved it!

Marian Tompson

MAC: *Marian, what do you recall about Princess Grace? I know you spent some time alone with her before she spoke at the banquet. What did you two talk about?*

MT: I was just very impressed with her friendliness, her lack of formality when we were together. I remember it was Doris Haire from New Jersey who sent her a copy of THE WOMANLY ART OF BREASTFEEDING and invited her to become an honorary member. We were stunned when Princess Grace accepted!

We corresponded for several years and yes, we did have time together before she spoke. She was a very caring mother and she was concerned as to what effect it would have on her children growing up in Monaco. And, she also had her babies at home—in the palace! She told me it was hard to remember how to speak in French when she wanted to say something to her doctors while she was in labor.

I was amused at her informality when we were alone in her suite, putting strawberries and ice cubes in our drinks with her hands. When we walked through a doorway she would often urge me to go ahead of her. The US Government had sent Treasury Agents to protect her because she was a Head of State. We didn't have to look at a schedule to know where to go; we just followed the Treasury Agents.

We could have had double the registrants for that conference if we had the room in the hotel!

Whenever she was interviewed after that, whether it was in *Vogue* magazine or *Life* or some other publication, she would bring up La Leche League and talk about what we were all about. She really did a lot to put breastfeeding and La Leche League on the map.

MAC: In 1964 we had our first La Leche League convention at the Knickerbocker Hotel. What do you remember about that?

MT: The first convention came about simply as a response to requests from many of our Leaders. They said, please give us an opportunity to come together. We had no idea how many people would come.

We asked Nell Ryan to take care of it. I know she went down to the Knickerbocker Hotel and they asked how many people we were expecting, and she said, oh, maybe about a hundred or so. As it turned out, 425 came. I was so impressed—I wondered how they had found out about us back then. I still meet people who say they were at that first convention.

The big conversation at that meeting, the big buzz, was about withholding solids until four to six months of age. At the time, Philip was my baby. He was eight months old. The other Founders didn't want to speak from the platform, so I ended up doing that. I was like a one-arm paperhanger, trying to talk and introduce people while holding this wriggly eight-month-old. I remember standing at the podium introducing someone as I watched Philip crawling down the aisle away from me. Later I was able to bring one of my daughters to take care of him when he wasn't in my arms.

As far as the people who were there, I just remember the "old-timers" we had there. Dr. Potts—Dr. Willis Potts was a featured speaker. He was famous for his "blue-baby" surgery on babies with heart problems. Charlotte Aiken and her husband, who were experts on nutrition and healthy eating habits. A lot of people heard about La Leche League for the first time by reading their periodical, *Child-Family Digest*.

Betty Wagner

MAC: Betty, what do you remember about LLL Conferences over the years?

BW: The conferences were a wonderful way to get everyone together and renew friendships. They always triggered a period of growth in the organization. I think people went home feeling renewed and inspired.

Over the years many volunteers worked on the Conference Committees to make them special. Faye Young and her Pizzazz Team always added the fun things that everyone enjoyed. Faye was from St. Louis, Missouri, but she worked as LLLI's Public Relations Director for more than 20 years.

A committee of volunteers and staff members work for many months to plan each LLLI Conference.

And, Hope Melnick was invaluable as our Conference Director from the early 1970s until 1992. She worked with a committee of volunteers from the local area where the conference was held, so this committee changed for every conference. It was a huge job!

For the 1971 conference, we did not find out that Princess Grace was going to speak until April or May. So the hotel had already been booked, but lots more people wanted to attend once they heard she was coming. The hotel added a second room for those who wanted to attend the banquet and her speech was shown in that room on a large screen via closed-circuit television.

Chapter 10 — SETTLING IN

Life went from busy to busier in the late 1960s and throughout the 1970s. Events outside of family and LLL work often faded in importance, though no one could miss the astonishment following the first space travel by a Russian cosmonaut in 1965 and a few years later, the excitement of an American astronaut walking on the moon. Through it all, babies were born and life celebrated. The deep sadness of death was felt as well when, in 1968, the Whites lost their oldest daughter, Margaret, "Peggy," to cancer at the age of 18. Two years later, when Mary was sure she was in menopause, she found that she was pregnant instead. In a matter of a few short months, all rejoiced at the birth of Elizabeth Margaret, the Whites' eleventh child.

Even beyond LLL circles, breastfeeding and La Leche League were attracting considerable attention. Breastfeeding was no longer a word to be shunned. Marian, as President, had become a much sought-after speaker, traveling all over the world to speak on breastfeeding and appearing regularly on TV programs such as the nationally syndicated Phil Donahue Show. Breastfeeding mothers and their families loved the attention, and requests for information deluged the office. In no time it seemed, La Leche League had once again outgrown its quarters and had to be relocated.

The new facility at 9616 Minneapolis Avenue on the other side of Franklin Avenue was bigger and, equally important, on the ground floor. Betty, working full-time, and Edwina, part-time, would no longer have to worry about hauling heavy boxes of books up a steep flight of stairs. LLL books, reprints, and other paraphernalia that had been taking up the whole of the Tompson's garage and a good part of their bedroom could be transferred to the new office/shipping room. Over a thousand books were being shipped out each month, and the files of Leaders and members and *News* subscribers names were bulging.

But it was only a matter of a few years before the organization again outgrew its space. The landlord, recognizing a good tenant, offered to extend the second story of the building and convert it into offices. Eventually LLL occupied both

Mary White, Mary Carson, Edwina Froehlich, and Betty Wagner
review copy for an issue of LLL News.

floors of the building. What seemed wonderfully spacious at first was soon crammed with desks and workers. Storage became a perennial problem, and archival records were placed in the basement or in a storeroom of the tavern next door. A major flood destroyed boxes of papers, books, financial records, and heaven only knows what else. Much of LLL's history was lost.

In addition to her duties as Executive Secretary, Edwina dealt mainly with Leader and Leader Applicant matters. She worked closely with two young Leaders in the Franklin Park area—Marybeth Doucette, responsible for New Groups and Judy Torgus, who handled Leader and Group concerns through a network of State Coordinators. Eventually they appointed committees of Leaders from the surrounding area who, in turn, had people reporting to them from La Leche League in various parts of the world. These jobs required extensive correspondence and problem solving. All of the women volunteered their time and worked out of their homes, traveling periodically to Franklin Park for meetings. They became known as the LLLI Committee.

Betty thrived on organizational matters and handled the business side of LLL operations. Besides being Treasurer of the organization, she carried titles ranging from Business Manager to, years later, Executive Director.

Marian was establishing herself as La Leche League's spokesperson and was traveling widely both within and outside the USA. In an issue of the La Leche League News in 1976, Marian wrote, " This summer I was invited to France to give a talk at an international symposium on non-cancerous breast diseases in Strasbourg. The physicians planning the conference felt the preventive aspects of breastfeeding important enough to warrant a half-day session just on breastfeeding. The trip also gave me the opportunity to visit with LLL families in France, Monaco, Switzerland, and England."

It was a heady time for everyone, with requests for a speaker coming on a regular basis from professionals and other organizations, as well as LLL Groups. Following each overseas trip, the entire staff gathered to hear an account of the people met and the places visited. There was also a steady stream of visitors to Franklin Park, some of whom were LLL Leaders who wanted to take care of "business," and others who just wanted to visit the headquarters of the organization that meant so much to them.

Mary Carson, who had done so much to pull together the 1963 edition of THE WOMANLY ART OF BREASTFEEDING, came aboard as head of the newly formed Publications Department. Years later, Judy Torgus took over the position and is now the Executive Editor and Director of Publications. The Publications Department has grown to where it produces a wide assortment of LLLI books, pamphlets, and other materials that can be ordered from its forty-five page catalog by phone, fax, mail, email, and on the World Wide Web.

With the expansion to Minneapolis Avenue, the decision was made to establish a Reference Library. Its modest beginning was a response to the need to organize information and collect relevant data from the scientific literature. Carolyn Hayes, a quiet, competent young woman, was hired as the first Reference Librarian. She quickly set about gathering studies on breastfeeding and creating paper files of pertinent information. When an inquiry came for specialized information or a breastfeeding issue was in the news, such as contaminants in mother's milk, Carolyn drew on the expertise of LLLI's medical advisors. For LLLI, it was a matter of standing behind its information and staying credible.

And then there was one of those blending of ideas that have enriched La Leche League over the years. Betty Ann Countryman had proposed a new category of Leaders to serve as a bridge between LLL, a lay organization, and the professional health community—doctors, nurses, hospitals. Appropriately, it was named the Professional Liaison, or PL, Department. La Leche League people had realized for some time that many of the misunderstandings between the two groups were the result of misinformation or a total lack of information, and a specially trained Leader could help remedy this situation. Once in place, the PL program evolved to meet a second need, that of being a resource for information of a more technical nature—an extension of the Reference Library—to the Leaders in an Area.

As the public's interest in breastfeeding increased, so also did the work and scope of the Reference Library. Gwen Gotsch and later Julie Stock and then Betty Crase assumed the role of Librarian and each refined the operation, adding to the documentation, cross-referencing information, and filling an increasing number of requests for information.

BREASTFEEDING ABSTRACTS, a quarterly journal that reviews scientific research, was developed with professionals in mind. Surprisingly—or perhaps not so surprising—a good number of PL Leaders also subscribe to it. Kathleen Auerbach, Beth Guss, and Cindy Smith were editors over the years. At present, Becky Hugh holds that title. Gwen Gotsch has continued as a resource to BREASTFEEDING ABSTRACTS over the years.

It was only a matter of time until "Reference Library" no longer reflected the extent of what the staff was doing. The new name, the Center for Breastfeeding Information, or CBI, points to its broader, more comprehensive purpose. Carol Huotari now manages the CBI and the full database is available online at the LLLI Web site. Many caring people have generously supported the CBI over the years, with the Niles and Michael Newton family, in particular, adding to its stature. For La Leche League followers everywhere, it is a matter of credibility. La Leche

Various Board Members, Founders, and others visited the mountains after the 1968 Conference which was held in Denver.

League does not take lightly its designation as an authority on breastfeeding—some say the world's foremost authority.

Once the Whites had moved to their large, frame house across the street from the Trailside Nature Museum in River Forest, Mary started an LLL Group there. She also served on LLLI's Editorial Review Boards and otherwise functioned as the unofficial ""keeper of truth," carefully going over the copy for the Area inserts that would be going into the News. Misleading or incorrect statements were scrupulously edited, another way of preserving the LLL's credibility. Along the way, Mary's red pen became famous throughout La Leche League. In 1964, recognizing the confusion in the rapidly growing organization over goals and procedures, she composed the Statement of Policy. It stood for years as a beacon light. Appropriate sections were later incorporated in LLLI's Bylaws.

Viola surprised everyone, including the doctor, with the birth of twins, the only multiple births among the Founders. She went on to breastfeed them with aplomb and in time began an LLL Group on the far northwest side of Chicago where she lived. In 1972, she took on the position of Board Chairman. Prior to that, Marian had led Board meetings since LLLI's founding. At first they were informal planning sessions, which then mushroomed into weekly gatherings with everyone involved with every decision.

The Founders were joined by other Leaders who took on various roles as part of what was then called the Executive Board. Some of those early Executive Board members included Rosemary Fahey, Nell Ryan, Judy Torgus, Marybeth Doucette, Betty Ann Countryman, Madge Bennett, Florence Carlson, and Diane Kramer. As the organization grew, the Executive Board, including the Founders, examined and re-defined various aspects of LLLI philosophy as well as planning procedures and policies. Lively debates often ensued. Vi was not opposed to using her gavel at those meetings!

The day after the Cahills moved into their home in Libertyville, a milkman and a nursing mother were knocking on the door. The milkman had heard of a family with quite a few children moving into town and was hoping for their business. The nursing mother, Paula Pettengill, had gotten Mary Ann's name from Franklin Park in answer to her inquiry for help. Paula and Mary Ann collaborated on starting an LLL Group, with Paula eventually becoming a Leader. Women from neighboring towns followed suit, creating a strong LLL and close friendships.

In Colorado, Mary Ann Kerwin became a Founder twice over, starting an LLL Group in Denver that moved out, sending shoots to neighboring communities and eventually taking root in the surrounding states. Mary Ann tracked down interested medical personnel and enlisted their help. A number of them became advisors to LLLI as well and further extended LLL's base of support. Once the Board Meetings in Franklin Park were spaced farther apart, she faithfully came in for them. It meant flying in, and once the meeting was over, heading back home to her young family. It also meant keeping up from a distance with the issues facing LLLI.

Throughout this period of time, breastfeeding rates were climbing, slowly at first, but steadily, and the number of Leaders was increasing by leaps and bounds. As for the Founders, spirits were high and the future looked bright. No one imagined the challenges that were waiting just around the corner.

Marian Tompson

MAC: You were our spokesperson, Marian, and consequently you had to travel a lot.

MT: Yes. It wasn't that I necessarily wanted to be the spokesperson. I never got excited about being the spokesperson. It was really just that I had the situation that made it possible. The other Founders, for whatever reason, found it difficult to get away.

I could never have left town to go on trips except that Tom was always excited about it. He'd say, "Marian, I could never afford to take you to those places. This is wonderful."

When I would travel somewhere, Tom would put a big map on the dining room wall and he and the children would put pins in it at the places where I went, and that made it an exciting thing and a learning experience for the children in geography.

When I would get to wherever I was going I would call home, feeling very lonesome, and he'd say, "Everything's fine. Have a good time. Don't worry about a thing." I used to joke that the house could be burning down and he'd still say, "Everything's fine. Don't worry about a thing." He was just looking out for my best interest.

I always told the children that they came first, that if they felt sick and I was supposed to go out of town, I wouldn't go. They almost couldn't believe it. Sometimes I would even call from the airport and say, "Are you sure?" And I meant it, I really meant it. I knew there would be people who would be disappointed on the other end, but you have to set your priorities, and my family always came first.

Marian Tompson with her mother, Marie Leonard.

And my mother lived nearby and she was always willing to help. She was always there to do anything she could to help me, and to do anything she could for La Leche League, too. In fact, she later became one of our regular employees at the LLLI office. She worked there for many years.

So I think with both my mother and my husband, their attitude and support made a big difference in what I was able to do for La Leche League. Their help was really what made it all possible for me.

MAC: As far as La Leche League was concerned, wouldn't you agree, Marian, that we did stick our necks out in some of the positions that we took, especially in the early days?

MT: Oh, yes. For instance, breastfeeding right after birth. That was very controversial. We heard stories from mothers about doctors saying, "If you are a 'good girl' during delivery, I'll let you nurse right on the delivery table." That kind of patronizing attitude was fairly typical of the medical profession in talking to their maternity patients in the 1950s.

MAC: Yes, that kind of talk sounds strange to modern ears. And yet that's often the way doctors and nurses talked to their patients.

MT: Yes. But it wasn't just health care professionals who expressed themselves that way—it was pretty much the norm throughout American society at that time. In fact, I can recall an incident from a La Leche League gathering that will illustrate my point.

Back in October of 1957 La Leche League arranged to have Dr. Grantly Dick-Read come to Franklin Park to give a talk on natural childbirth. This was a very controversial concept at that time.

In any case, it was decided that, as the designated President of La Leche League, I was the logical person to introduce the good doctor to the audience. Well, when the big night arrived, and we got to Leyden High School, there were hundreds and hundreds of people trying to get into the auditorium to hear Dr. Dick-Read speak. Every one of the 1250 seats was taken, and many people were turned away. Later someone told me that we had people from Indiana, Michigan, and Wisconsin there, as well as from Illinois.

We realized that we had a blockbuster event on our hands. I was going over in my mind what I wanted to say when I introduced Dr. Dick-Read. Just then, the husband of one of the Founders approached me and said, "You know, Marian, this Dr. Dick-Read fellow is a really important man. I'm not sure you should introduce him. You should get one of the men to introduce him."

Well, even in those "unliberated" days that amazed me—that he would think that I should step aside and let a man introduce Dr. Grantly Dick-Read because he was "too important" to be introduced by a woman!

But I stood my ground and I did the introduction and everything was fine. And in all fairness, I have to say that the same husband who suggested that I should step aside and let a man do the introduction, came up to me afterwards and said that I had done a good job.

Nevertheless, it was kind of amazing that he would even think to ask me to step aside, especially since we were dealing with a topic that pertained specifically to women. But that's just the way it was in those days.

MAC: I guess you could say that, whether we realized it or not, we in La Leche League were forerunners of the modern "women's lib" movement. Because it was very important to us to have as much control as possible over important decisions in our lives, such as how we gave birth and how we nourished our babies.

MT: Absolutely. We wanted to play an active role in the birth process and in the way our babies' emotional and nutritional needs were met. We weren't content to just "do what we were told," or to be "good girls."

We insisted on having a say in these decisions that so deeply and personally affected us as women, and affected our babies and families.

Viola Lennon

MAC: As I recall, our Board meetings helped us explore various aspects of LLL philosophy. Do you remember how those discussions went?

VL: Well, discipline was one issue we discussed a lot. As I look back, I see that in my own family when I was growing up, my parents actually used very little discipline, if by discipline you mean punishment. My father, in particular, was very easy-going, not harsh or strict with us at all. So I had a good background in this area. Nevertheless, I still had to get rid of some ideas that I had picked up along the way, ideas that were just part of the surrounding culture.

Becoming involved with La Leche League gave me a vision of what a human person is. For me, breastfeeding led to what I call "discovery," both self-discovery and a greater appreciation of the full humanity of this baby, this child, this little person who has been entrusted to your care.

If La Leche League had been solely about the "how-to's" of breastfeeding, I don't think that I would have even bothered to go to that very first meeting way back when. But La Leche League has always been about more than the techniques involved with breastfeeding. Essentially it is about mothering, how to be the best and most effective mother and parent that you can become. That's what got me involved in the beginning, and that's why I have stayed involved with La Leche League for all these many years.

MAC: *Talk a little about those years when you reviewed all of the Area inserts. That was a lot of work.*

MW: Yes, it was, but you know, that was a wonderful job as LLL Groups spread to other parts of the US and other countries, we wanted to keep the personal touch of mentioning things like new babies and so on, but this wasn't possible in the main newsletter. So each state or country was encouraged to prepare an "Insert" with local information. All of the submissions were to be sent to LLLI to be checked. It was my job to read all these, which I thoroughly enjoyed, because most of them were wonderful.

They were really marvelous stories about mothers and babies and all that good stuff. Once in a while you would run into something that might have been a little controversial, but I would just tell them to please take that out.

MAC: *So you had the "red pen."*

MW: Yes, they used to call me "the red pen."

MAC: *As I recall there was some controversy surrounding mentioning religious traditions and experiences in the newsletter or the Area inserts.*

MW: Some of the Board members and others at LLLI would get a copy of all the area inserts. A problem came up in regard to the Christmas—oops! pardon me—the November/December issue. That issue would frequently have lovely mothering stories that revolved around the theme of the Christmas holiday.

But some people decided that there was too much talk about religion in the *LLL News*. I still think it's because they were sitting down and reading 20 or 30 inserts all at one time. If you stop to think about it, people in New York are not reading the insert from, say, Ohio, and people in California are not reading the insert for North Carolina. So the average reader doesn't get this overdose of Christmas stories.

So the Board made a policy that we had to stop talking about religion in the LLL newsletters. That guideline included even general references to God. We weren't even supposed to mention the word "Christmas." Instead, you had to talk about "the holidays."

La Leche League is nonsectarian which means we don't endorse any specific religion. When I would go to Area Conferences, I would make that clear. We have no religious affiliation whatsoever. We don't question women who come to the meetings as to whether they are Jewish, or Muslim or Catholic or Quaker, or whatever. However, I would say that La Leche League is not a godless organization.

MAC: And were there other areas of controversy that you recall?

MW: Yes, of course there were problems from time to time. We on the editorial board get the stories for NEW BEGINNINGS sent to us in the mail. We read them over, and then we come together for a meeting. Well, at one point we had a story written by a father, and how he was left to care for their baby because his wife chose to go back to work. This was an extremely high-need baby. The baby screamed and cried a great deal. This was a baby that needed a lot of mothering, cuddling, nursing, and closeness. To make a long story short, it looked to me as though this was a baby that was missing its mother.

The father wrote a very clever story. It was written, naturally enough, from the father's point of view. He told about how hard he had to work to take care of that baby. Nevertheless, the message comes through that this was an extremely unhappy baby.

I raised a hullabaloo about publishing that story. We ended up taking the story to the LLL Board and they agreed with me. They said that this story had no place appearing in NEW BEGINNINGS because it would look as though La Leche League was recommending this sort of arrangement.

You may not believe it, but I get awfully tired of fighting some of these battles over things that should be so clear. You've got to know what you believe in–there should be agreement on what the organization stands for. There's room for a lot of difference of opinion along the way. But you've got to have something to hang your hat on. Everyone has to know what your principles are first—everything else flows from that.

Mary Ann Kerwin

MAC: After you moved to Colorado, how did you stay involved with the rest of us back in Franklin Park, Illinois?

MAK: Through Betty Wagner. Betty was the one who really kept in touch with me. We mainly kept in touch by mail. In those days, everybody communicated through the mail. Betty was the one who kept me informed, and encouraged me to come back to Illinois for the Board meetings. I would take the "red-eye" flight from Denver to Chicago at like four o'clock in the morning, attend the meeting, and then fly back to Denver that evening. It was rather exhausting, but I had lots of young children at home in those days, so I didn't want to be away any longer than I had to be.

MAC: Once you got a Group or two up and running in Denver, do you remember much about how you managed the Groups out there. Because at first you were La Leche League's only Leader out that way, our only contact west of the Mississippi?

MAK: Yes, I was the only Leader in Colorado, and in fact, in all the Western states for a while. I just remember spending a lot of time on the phone in the early days of the Denver La Leche League. When we still lived in Chicago, I seem to remember spending a lot of time answering letters with questions about breastfeeding. But when I got to Denver, I was the only one who could take the calls from anyone in Colorado or all the Western states. So I spent a lot of time on the phone.

As new Groups sprouted throughout the USA, a system had to be devised for keeping track of them. Those in a particular state or perhaps several States, were identified by the name of the state or states, and the person who kept in touch with the Groups was called the State Coordinator. When LLL Groups were established outside the US, in a province or district, for instance, the early decision-makers realized that "State" would not do. The term "Area" was adopted, and the State Coordinator became the Area Coordinator. With growth, Areas were combined into Regions, with a number of Regions making up a Division, the largest denomination. In time, a separate category, Affiliate, was established to accommodate La Leche League in an entire country, for instance. Matters of currency, culture, and constitutional requirements often called for different approaches. An LLLI Affiliate is autonomous in many respects, yet remains united in philosophy. But that came much later.

Chapter 11 — Bumps in the Road

Two events that would drastically disturb the peace were waiting on the horizon. Both evoked strong emotions, and both saw Founders taking opposite sides of the question. The first occurred in 1973 as the result of a ruling of the United States Supreme Court that directly involved women and babies—giving women the right to choose abortion.

The 1970s were anything but settled in the US. American troops were fighting a distant war in Vietnam, and masses of college students on the homefront were protesting US involvement in the conflict. Adding to the turmoil was another protest, a new "ism"—feminism. A popular song caught the mood—"The times they are a' changing." Long-held ways of thinking and doing things were being swept aside.

Early feminists regarded women's traditional roles of mother and homemaker as restrictive and confining. For too long, they insisted, women were defined by their reproductive nature and, to add insult to injury, were primed from childhood to put the needs of others before their own. Men, on the other hand, were expected to be their "own person," develop their talents, and make something of themselves in the world. The same "rights" were due women, including the right to control when and whether to have a child.

In January of 1973, the US Supreme Court ruled abortion to be a fundamental right, thereby nullifying the state laws that had restricted it. Proponents hailed the decision as a victory for a woman's right to privacy and right to choose. Opponents countered that more than a woman's rights were at stake, that abortion ends a baby's life.

The issue dominated the news and, as could be expected, spilled over into La Leche League. The LLLI Board of Directors at the time consisted of 10 members, the seven Founders and three long-time La Leche League Leaders. When the Board was asked to issue a statement on the matter, it was soon evident that members were split in their responses. The Board discussions continued for many months. Finally, a vote was taken with six of the Board members, including four Founders, voting against taking a stand either for or against abortion. They feared La Leche League would be caught up in an ongoing and disruptive debate. The business of La Leche League, they stressed, is breastfeeding, and anything that distracts from that goal must be avoided.

The remaining four held that it was unthinkable to remain silent. They pointed out that everything La Leche League stands for, its purpose and philosophy, is directed to supporting mothers in their mothering. Breastfeeding is a sustained and rewarding means to that end, yet not the whole picture.

After this Board decision was taken, an uneasy truce settled in until some months later when the situation came to a head at the 1971 LLL International Conference in Chicago. At the closing session, unauthorized written material about the abortion issue was found on the chairs, and, when it was her turn to speak, Mary White made a plea for La Leche League to take a stand in support of all mothers and their unborn babies. She received a standing ovation, though not everyone was pleased. The Board of Directors again met, and this time passed a motion stating that any LLL member who brought up the subject of abortion at an LLL function would summarily be dismissed from La Leche League.

The minority was stunned but fell in line. Abortion became a mute subject, but the age of innocence was over. The old ease with which the Founders had discussed issues was replaced by a sense of wariness. Yet no one gave up; no one dropped out. The cause was much too dear to their hearts and much work remained to be done.

Among the busiest was Marian Tompson, LLLI President. Speaking engagements multiplied, and LLL mothers relished having the young, well-spoken president of their organization represent them. Things couldn't have been better. Then again, maybe they could.

As several outside consultants had pointed out in the past, LLLI had created a number of titles that could make it difficult to know who was responsible for what. While Marian as president was doing a good job representing La Leche League to the outside world, she was only peripherally involved in the other functions that are normally associated with being president. At the LLLI office, Betty Wagner managed the day-to-day operations, yet was often unsure as to where her authority started and stopped. And then there was the Chairman of the Board who, at the time, simply formed the agenda and chaired Board Meetings and had no other leadership role, again an unorthodox arrangement. She did not follow the generally accepted practice of serving as a spokesperson for the organization. What could be done? How to untangle the knot?

Once again, the matter was taken up by the Board of Directors. This time, too, the vote was split, but in the end the decision was made to eliminate the position of president. Marian was invited to continue to work for La Leche League, though not as president. After 25 years, Marian stepped back and found other employment. She continued as a member of the LLLI Board of Directors, was frequently asked to speak at LLL Conferences, and assumed responsibility for various projects over the years. Without a "designated spokesperson," LLLI lost some momentum, though eventually others stepped forward and assumed the role. In

A picnic was held in Wilder Park to celebrate La Leche League's 25th Anniversary in 1981.

the meantime, new, less easily managed forces were gathering that would have an impact on La Leche League's future.

Throughout the late 1970s and early 1980s, new and exciting information, much of it from the scientific community, was coming out about breastfeeding. La Leche League responded with a completely updated edition of THE WOMANLY ART OF BREASTFEEDING, that made its debut at the 1981 Conference in Chicago. Sales of the new book were gratifyingly brisk. For the first time in LLL history, money was more plentiful than usual. The good times, though, were not to last.

When sales first began to drop in 1983, the shortfall was thought to be a temporary blip such as ones that had been experienced off and on in the past. At such times, plans such as bringing field directors in for a meeting would be cancelled, and all new ventures put on hold. Staff became old hands at switching gears. And somehow, they always came through the hard times. Somehow, Betty Wagner always managed to push, pull, prod, pray, and make ends meet.

This time around, though, more was going on than a temporary slow down. La Leche League was no longer the only act in town. Others had taken note of its successful publications, and multiple authors were rushing their own breastfeeding books to market. Sales that La Leche League would have formerly enjoyed were going elsewhere. And compounding the situation, the USA was experiencing a serious economic downturn, making revenues from other sources harder to come by. A deadening cycle began to build. LLLI, which had always enjoyed excellent credit, could no longer generate the funds needed to keep going day-to-day. An infusion of cash was desperately needed.

Everybody rallied. The future of the organization was at stake. An inspired Vi Lennon called on the president of the Rockford Institute, John Howard, a man with years of experience in the not-for-profit world and someone who held La

Leche League in high regard. His advice was for LLL to appeal for help directly from its Leaders and Groups. Straightforward, a plan was put in action and, in late summer 1984, the Second Founding was launched.

It was a wonderful, heartwarming, and never-to-be-forgotten chapter in LLLI history. The sketch of a large, brightly lit candle surrounded by long tapers taking up the flame adorned the cover of the next issue of LEAVEN, announcing the appeal. Financial reports filled its pages, explaining the situation in detail so Leaders could fully understand the need. LLL Leaders and Groups throughout the world quickly took up the cause and, with energy and imagination, held countless fundraising events. Enough money was raised to clear up old debts and give LLLI the where-withal to move forward. It was a switch in roles of sort; with the offspring assisting the parent. But no one could imagine doing otherwise. No one wanted a world without La Leche League. Tremendous strides had been made in giving mothers the help they needed to be the mothers they wanted to be. But there were still whole populations of mothers to reach and new ways of reaching them.

In between the trials and triumphs of keeping an organization on course, the seven Founders experienced the ups and downs of family life. Children went off to school, graduated, married, and started families of their own. Celebrations were interspersed with the sad times. Wayne Wagner was making plans to open a new business when he died in 1979 in an auto accident. His widow, Colleen, has remained close to the Wagner family through the years. Young, vibrant Charlotte Lennon, one of the twins, was killed in 1981 in an auto accident. Bob Wagner, Betty's husband, died in 1975, and Mary Ann Cahill's husband, Chuck was buried three years later. In 1981, "Tommy" Tompson was struck and killed by a car near his home while out for a walk. Friends came together, wept and supported each other. Somehow, the work went on.

Betty Wagner

MAC: *In regard to abortion, if I remember correctly Betty, you felt that the abortion question was not and should not be an issue that LLL should take a position on . You thought that some people see it one way, and somebody else sees it another way. But that in any case, it was not an issue that directly connected with the goals and mission of La Leche League.*

BW: Absolutely. That's not an issue that we, as an organization whose mission is to promote breastfeeding, should have to deal with or be concerned with. It is a personal issue with a lot of people, a strong personal issue. But it is not an issue that can or should have an impact directly on La Leche League.

Basically, I just didn't want that issue to separate and divide our organization. Unfortunately, it did divide us, at least for a while.

MAC: *You mean, not all of the Founders had the same viewpoint on this issue?*

Betty Wagner at her desk in the Franklin Park LLLI office in 1985.

BW: Yes, and I am sure that we don't all agree to this day.

MAC: I don't know if it would have made much difference, but personally, I would have felt better if we had come out and said that, as an organization that is concerned about doing what is best for mothers and their babies, we don't think that abortion is in their own best interest.

That was as far as I wanted to go. I wouldn't have wanted to have us arguing about it on a continuous basis. I just wanted to say, "Abortion is not a good thing for either mothers or babies."

BW: Yes, but you see, even saying that much does pull us into that discussion, and then there's no getting away from it. Even saying something as simple as, "It's not in your best interest" does draw us into that discussion. And that could alienate some of the women who would otherwise be coming to us for help with breast-feeding.

I mean, I am against abortion myself, but I think that to take a stand on that question as an organization, to say that the organization believes one thing or another, divides the organization. I believed that at that time and I still do. I guess that was one of those "bumps in the road."

MAC: Yes, I think you could say that abortion was one of those "bumps in the road." It certainly was.

Let's talk about another time when feelings ran high and Founders disagreed. We had no mechanism for changeover. We never held elections. We didn't rotate positions. Do you think that might have contributed to our problem when the questions came up about the presidency?

BW: Yes, that could have contributed to our problems at that time, although we did have elections. It's just that we kept re-electing the same people over and over again.

MAC: I think you're right, Betty. We did have elections, but... .

BW: But there were some on the Board who were feeling that they weren't being given a chance to share in the decision-making.

In any case, it's too bad it had to occur. It's too bad that it did occur. It caused a lot of hard feelings and unhappiness.

MAC: Yes. And then you were put in the position of Executive Director.

BW: I already was in that position. I became Executive Director in 1972. Over the years, I've had many titles.

MAC: Right, right. But in regard to the title of president, you say that you didn't see a conflict between what you were doing and what Marian was doing?

BW: Well, my concern was with the role of the Chairman of the Board. I felt that whoever held that position should be getting some of those assignments, some of the opportunities and invitations to travel and speak. But the Chairman wasn't getting those opportunities—they were all going to Marian.

Everyone seemed to want Marian to talk to their Group. She was so good at that—and she still is. She was better than any of the rest of the Founders. So you could see why outside people wanted to have Marian come talk to their Group.

MAC: We came out with the new edition of THE WOMANLY ART OF BREASTFEEDING in 1981 and we were sailing high. Breastfeeding was being recognized in all the medical journals, hospitals, and among more and more young mothers as the right thing to do for your baby.

So how would you explain the sudden downward shift, when things began to fall apart financially, and how that led to the Second Founding?

BW: Well, yes, we did have a lot of money coming in at certain times. And as soon as the money came in, we would spend it. We offered a lot of credit to our Groups and Leaders so our books were being shipped out to them but payments weren't coming in.

At that time we had a business manager who had been hired because we felt that we needed financial direction. A business manager is definitely an asset, but I think that this particular business manager led us down the garden path. He let us get into debt without a lot of warning that we were getting into trouble.

And I blame the audit company, too. They kept saying, "You're fine. You're fine." They kept saying that we were fine until we didn't have any money! So then we had to start calling people and saying, "Hey, we don't have any money." And they got really worried. And that's when our business manager quit.

Betty Wagner with Faye Young

MAC: *Yes, I remember that. But while this problem was developing, didn't he give you any financial statements—something that would show that we were headed for trouble?"*

BW: Yes, he gave me financial statements—I've still got some of them in a file at home. I was always very much aware of Accounts Receivable and Accounts Payable, and I always wanted Accounts Receivable to be much higher than Accounts Payable. And I really think that, at the time of the Second Founding, Accounts Receivable was still higher than Accounts Payable.

The problem was, however, that we weren't getting any money in. No one was paying us so we couldn't pay our bills. Suddenly it just seemed as if there were no orders or payments coming in, no cash coming in. In my opinion, it was a cash flow problem. We had to cut our staff—people were laid off who had worked there for years. We discontinued services we had been providing to Leaders and members. The remaining employees took pay cuts and days off without pay. Of course, this led to others leaving because they needed a full paycheck to support their families. Then at one point, we actually closed our doors for a week or two. But even then, some employees showed up to work, without being paid, to keep things going. I remember that Faye Young made up some signs to keep our spirits up. She had these cartoon characters she drew and she sent us signs that we posted all around the building to encourage everyone to "keep going."

MAC: *And you kept things going with only a skeleton crew?*

BW: Yes. And sometimes there was nobody. Sometimes I was in there alone. But then, gradually, we did begin getting orders and payments in again.

MAC: *That was always important to you—to get the orders out.*

BW: Well, that's where the money comes from.

Those who worked at the LLLI office in Franklin Park enjoyed the homey atmosphere as well as the special events over the years.

MAC: So you would go into the office and others also came to help.

BW: Yes. Everybody would pitch in. I mean, this was the way we worked. Everybody worked together.

We had a wonderful staff. We had wonderful, cooperative, helpful people. And they all did pitch in and help. And we got things turned around. It was a good group.

MAC: Yes, it certainly was.

BW: Do you remember, Mary Ann, all the wonderful letters we got from our Groups and Leaders during the Second Founding? Everybody was so happy to help. And so, eventually, with help from a lot of our friends, we got over the hump and got back to doing what we do best—helping mothers nurse their babies.

MAC: And then we had some good years.

BW: We did. We hired Sandy Tauber, who did know what she was doing, and she got us back on the right track. We sometimes had disagreements, but overall, I thought she handled the money well.

Later there were some disagreements in regard to the Funding Development Department. You were working in that Department at the time, right?

MAC: Yes, we always felt we were a little bit the stepchild around there.

BW: I felt you weren't bringing enough money in.

MAC: Well, yes. But we always felt, which comes first? There's always more that could be done.

BW: Right. But I think it did get better. I think we were much more cautious about spending and we were wanting that bottom line to be positive all the time. I think we did build up a fund balance so that, when I left, I think there was $800,000 in that fund.

MAC: Yes, I think it was about that much.

BW: We were cautious. I think that Conferences helped, not only to bring us together and to unify the organization, but I think that they also brought in extra money that was helpful and useful.

MAC: Yes, definitely useful.

Viola Lennon

MAC: What are your thoughts on the abortion issue, Vi?

VL: Abortion is an ongoing and disruptive debate. La Leche League always held a singular focus and this had proven very successful. I believe abortion was a political issue then and still is now.

MAC: What else do you remember about the abortion issue?

VL: The main thing I remember is that feelings ran terribly high. I think this was one of the most difficult times in La Leche League. We had some terribly strong feelings on both sides of the issue. We tried like mad to work it out and we heard from all kinds of people, pro and con, on this issue.

We debated back and forth—shall we take a stand or not take a stand on this volatile issue? This whole question came pretty close to breaking up La Leche League, particularly splitting the Founders.

Finally we voted and our position became "No involvement." LLL took no position on the question of abortion. I think that was the right decision. But there are several Founders who are still upset about the decision.

MAC: Let's move on with the reformation of the governing Board. We alluded to this earlier when we talked about Garrett Gruner. While you were Chairman of the Board, I think we worked with Garrett Gruner, husband of a Leader, who had some background with nonprofit Boards. Pick it up from there, Vi.

VL: All right. I remember all of those things very clearly and very well. Poor Garrett had a job to do, particularly on this lady. Now I agreed that the Board should be in charge of policy. I wasn't quite sure I knew exactly was included in the term "policy" but the general idea appealed to me—that there should be a Board that makes policy, and that the staff implements the policy. That was pretty clear to me.

But then Garrett introduced the idea that we should be using parliamentary procedure to formalize our Board Meetings. He had trouble with me there, because parliamentary procedure seemed like sort of a technical thing.

So we worked together day after day. He lived in Michigan but he came in often and he knew what he was doing and he started to form what turned out to be a very well-run Board. Our meetings were somewhat formal, and if you didn't know parliamentary procedure beware, because you wouldn't even be heard.

I think the first Board Meetings after these changes were interesting. I think they began to show us what a Board does and does not do. I am very grateful to Garrett for the amount of time he put in working with me and the Board in implementing these new procedures—and he did put in lots and lots of time.

MAC: When did you take over as Chairman of the Board, Vi?

VL: I'm going to say around 1975. I was the Board Chair for six years.

MAC: Regarding the process, how did you come to be Chairman?

VL: We had elections. Various people were elected to specific jobs.

As we recognized our role as developing policies, I remember a lot of discussion on, "What is a policy?" We started to define leadership—what it was, what you had to know to become a Leader, and we defined various job responsibilities.

We talked about our publications and our meetings. We began to put together a Policy Notebook that recorded all of our policies. That's about all I remember without going to my notes. Those were the basic topics that we talked about on the reconstituted Board.

MAC: Can you describe to me the Board's approach to finances?

VL: That's really hard for me to answer. In the mid 1970s, I think the Board's approach was not to think about it very much. We just sort of floated along, hoping for the best. As I've said before, I think we, the Founders, have always had a relaxed attitude toward money, and the necessity for it. And I think that part of the trouble we got into was because of that attitude.

When some say, "All you need to breastfeed is a woman with a breast and a baby." I always said that was not true. For starters, you have to feed the woman and, in most societies, you have to clothe her. And she needs at least a little tent to live in. I prefer something a little better but... .

The basic point is that you cannot live on this earth without money. And I don't think that, prior to the reorganization of the Board and especially prior to the Second Founding, we on the LLLI Board had really faced the importance of sound fiscal management.

MAC: Another issue that was difficult for us had to do with another consultant taking a look at our organization. This was when Bill Conrad, another consultant to nonprofit organizations, pointed out that we were not using the office of president in the usual sense of the word. Our president was our "ambassador to the world." Tell us what you recall about that whole issue.

VL: I think Bill Conrad knew more about how to run a not-for-profit organization than anybody I ever met. He told us it was unnecessary to have both a Chairman and a President. He tried to set us right, in that regard. As far as I am concerned, I think he did a good job. The elimination of the presidency was a painful experience and yet I think it had to be done.

MAC: What do you base that on?

VL: The history of other not-for–profits around the country. I mean, they have learned so much, and La Leche League needed to learn from their experiences.

You need a Board, and the Board needs to have a Chairperson. You also need an Executive Director—that is a paid position. The Executive Director handles the day-to-day management of the organization and reports to the Board. But you don't need a President—that position is redundant if the Chairman and the Executive Director are each doing their jobs.

Another complication we had was that some Founders who sat on the Board were also staff members. That was a conflict of interest because staff should never be sitting on the Board where they would have to make decisions about salaries and expenditures of money by the organization. So that was a problem that we had to get straightened out—and it took a while.

So sometimes we didn't like to listen to the experts, or depend on the experience of other not-for-profits. We liked to say, "We're unique." But everyone likes to think that their organization is unique. You still have to play by the rules when it comes to managing a not-for-profit organization.

So, yes, I would have to say that we have had some painful experiences, and this reorganization certainly was one of those situations. But, ultimately, I think it was the right decision.

Edwina Froehlich

MAC: *Tell us about what kind of job Marian did as President of LLL.*

EF: Marian was exceptionally good when it came to dealing with doctors and other VIPs. Marian was intelligent and could absorb a lot of information, including technical information—the kind of information that is so important in talking with experts in their fields.

For a while the organization functioned very well with this arrangement (Marian as president, Edwina as secretary, and Betty as treasurer). It wasn't until that friend of Marian's came in—what was his name? His wife was a Leader, and he just became very interested in our organization—he saw the importance of La Leche League. Anyway, he was the first one to begin telling us that he thought we needed better organization at the top.

MAC: *You mean Garrett Gruner.*

EF: Yes, Garrett Gruner. He thought that we needed to have somebody who would be in charge of the whole operation, who would take responsibility for being in charge of everything, business and leadership, everything.

That's not to say that she would do it all, but she would responsible for all of these things being in place and getting done. He described the job in detail. He said, "You need to get one of the Founders or somebody you know to take over this job." I said, "My goodness, that job sounds enormous. Who would want it?" And I remember being somewhat surprised when Betty Wagner said, "I would."

I thought, how wonderful that she would want it. It was more inclusive than what she had already been doing. And it was getting to be a little difficult because certain things, projects and programs and questions about what we were going to do would come up and it was a question of who was the person to make these decisions. We would talk about these things together, and we didn't always agree.

Well, when Betty agreed to take over that job he said her job title should be Executive Director. Marian was still president at that point. But if you keep someone on as president, it creates a problem as to who's really in charge. That was the whole idea, the whole reason, for creating the position of Executive Director—to have someone in a paid position who was in charge of day-to-day management of the organization.

That's where some conflicts arose. It was a sad and difficult time. Certainly nobody wanted not to have the full use of Marian's talents, which were very much needed. It was really just a question of who was going to be the one who makes the final decisions. Eventually we said it should be the Executive Director under the supervision of the Board. That was the decision that was made at that time.

MAC: *In the early days we had the LLLI Committee. Tell us something about that.*

EF: Yes, well the LLLI Committee was quite a large group working with the

Edwina shows the 1987 edition of THE WOMANLY ART OF BREASTFEEDING to mothers who were attending the local Franklin Park Group.

Edwina retired to spend more time with her husband, John, and their first grandchild, Leanne.

Leaders. There too, Garrett Gruner said that group was inappropriate for us—it was not good structure. He advised us that having these large group meetings was not an efficient way for us to be operating. He said important decisions should not be made by a committee. They should be made by the Executive Director.

MAC: So what happened to the LLLI Committee?

EF: Well, after listening to Garrett's advice, Betty approached the Board with a plan for restructuring and they agreed to eliminate the LLLI Committee. Of course, that was not well received. It was a difficult time. The women on that committee had put in lots of time, many hours, and they liked what they were doing. So the change was not easily received at all.

I'm not criticizing anyone one way or the other. But that too, was a difficult time. However, we did proceed, and Divisions were set up with people from each Division replacing the LLLI Committee in 1976. At that point, I was dealing directly with the Division Directors, keeping them informed, acting as their liaison, and so forth.

We didn't follow through 100 percent with representatives from other countries right away. But eventually we did more there, as well. We were slow with the Around the World (ATW) section, but we were doing the best we could with what we had here and it was almost organizationally premature for us to have an out of the USA division at all. We weren't quite ready for it, but the people in those various countries were eager to get involved and to have official representation, so that's what we tried to do.

MAC: We had an excellent year when we came out with our revised edition of THE WOMANLY ART OF BREASTFEEDING in 1981. You were still working at the office at that time, weren't you?

EF: Yes. I worked at the office until 1983. After that, I returned to leading a local LLL Group in Franklin Park for ten years. I loved working directly with mothers and babies again!

MAC: The revised edition of THE WOMANLY ART OF BREASTFEEDING *brought in much needed revenue at the time, but then there was the downturn that led to the Second Founding.*

EF: What we didn't have was the business sense to realize that we were getting in plenty of money because we had this new book on the market that was filling a tremendous need. We were the only ones who had anything like it, so it was widely accepted and sold beautifully. It brought in a lot of money.

But nobody on staff or on the Board looked at the bigger picture and said, "Okay, this new book will be bringing in money for a year or two, but then what?"

What we really needed was to come up with a new book every couple of years that would really sell. We needed more than one book. And in addition to a book, what else? The business vision was not sufficient.

MAC: We needed research and development.

EF: That's right. But we didn't have anybody aboard who had that kind of vision. So then we found ourselves calling for the Second Founding to shore up our finances. If I recall correctly, it was your idea, Mary Ann, to call it the Second Founding, wasn't it?

MAC: Yes. But it was Vi's idea to go to the Groups for help. She was advised to go that route by the Rockford Institute. She hoped that they'd give us some money, but they gave us advice instead. They told us, when you are in this kind of situation, you go to your membership for help.

EF: Yes, okay. I had forgotten how the Second Founding got started. So, of course, that was a tremendous thing.

MAC: I think that at that point, though, the Board became very conscious of money— how to bring it in, and how to use it wisely and prudently.

EF: The big thing the Board did concurrent with the Second Founding was to try to cut down on spending. But that was only one thing that had to be done. Unfortunately, when we stopped spending, we couldn't produce the publications that we needed to sell. Again, I'm not criticizing. But we didn't have the people on board who had the vision to see where you should cut down on spending and, conversely, where it would be detrimental to cut back on spending. As the old saying goes, sometimes you have to spend money to make money.

MAC: Edwina share your thoughts on the abortion issue, the first major split among the Founders.

EF: Well, first of all, let me make it very clear that I, speaking personally, had very strong feelings against abortion.

Nevertheless, I did not think that La Leche League should come out with a formal statement against abortion for two reasons. First of all, I did not think we could speak for all of our Leaders. The simple fact was that not all of our Leaders shared our feelings about abortion. I felt that if La Leche League came out with a statement on behalf of the organization condemning abortion, Leaders who had become Leaders in order to help mothers breastfeed their babies would be justified in feeling angry or resentful at having to defend or explain an LLL policy that they might not agree with.

So that was one reason why I did not support the idea of LLL taking an official position against abortion. The second reason was that that we were not sufficiently educated on the "ins and outs" of abortion. As one of the persons who would be answering those questions, I did not want that responsibility—I simply did not feel qualified to answer those questions. And I felt that these questions would be distracting me and the other staff members from our main purpose—to help mothers successfully breastfeed.

Of course, there were those who felt differently, who very passionately felt that LLL ought to take a stand against abortion. I remember one Leader in particular—she was from out of state. She approached me at a conference and said, "Edwina, I think you are so wrong in the position you have taken in regard to abortion and I feel so badly about that. How do you know that you made the right decision?"

I sympathized with her—I really did. And I told her, "I don't know for sure if I made the right decision. All I know is that I had to vote on this matter, and that I made my decision based on what I knew and felt at the time. And that was the decision that I made."

Mary Ann Kerwin

MAC: Mary Ann, what do you recall regarding the abortion controversy and the impact that it had on LLL?

MAK: Well, I was in Denver by that time—it was the early 1970s. I just remember that this became a real problem for La Leche League—whether or not we should make a statement about abortion. This issue caused great division among us, like no other issue before or since. It really almost broke us up.

Finally, a vote was taken. Those who were proponents of a statement against abortion lost—we decided not to take a stand against abortion as an organization. Somehow or other we managed to keep going. We went back to work.

MAC: And then there was the incident at the Conference. Let's see—had the vote been taken by that time or not?

MAK: At the Conference in 1971?

MAC: Yes. Do you remember—we were at the Conference and Mary White had information on abortion that she passed out to people.

Evidently a vote had been taken already by the Board to not make a statement on abortion. But that didn't stop Mary White. She went ahead and handed out information on abortion anyway. Then she addressed the whole Conference at the closing session. She reiterated the value of the child, and how we should cherish children. She received a standing ovation.

MAK: Yes, but there were also those who were up in arms because she had done that.

MAC: Yes, very much so. Now here I am telling the story, when it should be your story. But, to make a long story short, there had been a Board Meeting...

MAK: I just remember finally accepting the idea that we would not do anything about the abortion issue.

MAC: Yes, and that was when I felt faced with the question of whether I wanted to continue to be a part of La Leche League, or go elsewhere.

MAK: Yes, that's how I remember it too. But, you know, I had a brand new baby at that time. I may have missed that meeting. Maybe I just got lucky and missed that meeting when the vote was taken. Because, I know I would have remembered that.

MAC: Weren't you Board Chairman when the position of president of LLLI was eliminated?

MAK: Yes. Again, Bill Conrad thought that organizationally it was confusing to have a President and an Executive Director. I believe Marian was an employee at the time. So it was awkward for the Executive Director to have one of her employees be the president of the organization. That position just didn't fit into the new structure of the organization very smoothly. And then we also had the position of the Chairman of the Board, which was a volunteer position. It was difficult, no doubt about it.

MAC: Yes, it was a very difficult time. In retrospect, do you think that there is anything that could have been done differently?

MAK: Perhaps. I just don't know.

MAC: And as Chairman you had to handle that situation because it was a decision of the Board.

MAK: Yes, the Board took a vote on making those changes. But I don't think that it was a close vote. Do you remember? But still, it was difficult. Marian Tompson certainly had been the primary spokesperson for La Leche League for many, many years. And she had done a very good job in that position. She had represented us very well. But the Board voted, and the changes had to be made.

MAC: Yes, that was the Board's decision. But it was very difficult.

Marian Tompson

MAC: The question must be asked. How did giving up your position as president affect you, personally, Marian?

MT: It was a very painful episode that lasted a long time. But the pain did not come from losing my job. You know, I never asked to be president. As long as I held that job it was very important to me to do the best I could in representing LLL and Leaders to the world. But when I no longer had that responsibility, it was actually a relief.

The pain came from the way in which the change was accomplished and the willingness of some of the Founders to go along with a campaign that sought to remove the presidency by discrediting me personally. It might be portrayed as a structural change but for two long years I experienced it as a personal attack.

I was also concerned how this would affect our organization.

One of the Founders suggested I just resign as president and then they would not have to vote me out. So I wrote a letter to each Board Member, asking for an explanation of how LLL would be better off without a president, pointing out that the president didn't have to be me. If what they said made sense to me I would just resign because I wanted to do what was best for LLL. Not one Board Member answered.

And was LLL affected by this turn of events? Yes, I think it was. LLL lost some of its purity and openness in the eyes of some of our loyal supporters. This was evident to me during the Second Founding, when a number of Leaders and Groups refused to even consider giving us financial support.

But it is all water under the bridge now. I've been able to release my hurt feelings and I am not sure how much of this should go into the book. But you asked the question, and I had to answer honestly.

In a nutshell, losing my position as president actually relieved me of a lot of responsibility that I had willingly assumed trying to do my best representing LLL and its Leaders.

Mary White

MAC: *What do you remember about discontinuing the title of President?*

MW: We had people like Bill Conrad come along and tell us what a proper organization should be, and how we should run this or that committee, and telling us that Marian had been president much too long, and that we should have been rotating the presidency, and so on.

Personally, I thought that Marian was an excellent president. I thought she did a great job. She was a wonderful spokesperson for La Leche League, and still is, all over the world.

I didn't have any particular quarrel with her being president. I don't even remember how that all came about, but I sure wouldn't have wanted the job of Chairman of the Board at that time either.

MAC: *Let's talk a bit about finances. We had had great success with our publications They carried us for a long, long time. But then there was a difficult time in 1984 when we found ourselves facing the crisis that became known as the Second Founding.*

MW: Well, we suddenly found ourselves running out of money. Yes, that was a crisis. For whatever reason that it happened—and that gets pretty involved and complicated—I just hope that La Leche League doesn't lose its heart. It won't lose its heart as long as it's got mothers out there who care about the organization.

But I think you have to keep in touch with all the mothers out there in terms of what they are really interested in—breastfeeding and mothering—and not just in terms of asking them to help with La Leche League's finances. I think you get a lot more in the way of donations and contributions when people give from the heart. And people give from the heart because you have really helped them, because you have listened to their problems and so on.

But anyway, yes, we were running out of money, and so we had the Second Founding. Everybody was just marvelous and donated a lot of money and that really put us back on our feet, financially speaking.

MAC: *And finally, Mary, you were the one with the strongest views on the abortion issue. After all these years, how do you feel abut LLL's decision in 1971 not to take a stand on the issue?*

MW: Much to my everlasting disappointment, LLL to this day refuses to make a simple, pro-baby statement.

All we ever wanted was for LLL to say that we are here for the good of babies, all babies, and as such, we believe it's wrong to take the life of an innocent human being even before birth.

We didn't feel we needed to make a big issue of this. Just state it and that's all. It takes courage to go against popular opinion, but is that what we want? To be popular? And I still believe most of the mothers in LLL are opposed to abortion.

I think we're being two-faced to say we want to help mothers and babies, but at the same time, by our silence, to condone killing these little ones.

To "not take a stand" is taking a stand. It says we don't care. I think we should care.

MAC: I agree with you on this, Mary. I believe that La Leche League owed mothers as well as their unborn babies a simple statement assuring them that, in the long run, remaining true to the mother-baby bond is remaining true to their own nature. It is a choice for life and brings its own rewards. I felt it was not the time to look the other way and not be counted. As for fears that La Leche League would be drawn into the melee and take a more active role in the debate, many other organizations were already carrying those banners. La Leche League could have continued doing what it had always done, helping mothers have a good birth and supporting them, day after day, in breastfeeding and mothering their babies.

Chapter 12—MOVING AHEAD

Economic crises in Franklin Park and differences among the Founders were like storms in the upper stratosphere. The effect was intense, but for the most part, contained. At times, an aftermath of blustery winds blew through parts of La Leche League, though on the whole, Leaders in the field went about the business of helping mothers. At the Board level, Viola passed the gavel to Mary Ann Kerwin who, on assuming the role of Chairman of the Board, also found herself the main representative of La Leche League to the world at large. Increasingly, people in other countries were becoming alarmed at changes in infant feeding practices worldwide. The wanton promotion of formula by manufacturers, particularly in parts of the developing world, was responsible for a decrease in breastfeeding and a corresponding rise in infant mortality and morbidity. In protest, citizen groups launched a multi-national boycott against Nestle, the world's largest producer of artificial infant food, and a number of breastfeeding support groups sprung up in various parts of the world. When an alliance of such groups announced a meeting for all interested parties, the decision was made for Mary Ann Kerwin to attend. It was considered important that LLLI participate in such gatherings, both to contribute and to learn.

The learning process never ceases. While LLLI can boast that the basics of breastfeeding as first presented have stood the test of time, numerous refinements have been made along the way. One such had to do with weaning. As the Founders came to realize, weaning is more likely to be later, rather than earlier, if left up to the baby. As a result, a new culture developed at LLL Meetings. Whereas in years past, mothers often told of breastfeeding for only a short time, they were now announcing that the "baby" still taking the breast was a child of three, four, or more years old. And what would have seemed unbelievable years before had also come about—mothers were nursing more than one child at a time. It wasn't something that was planned. It came about simply enough when a new baby arrived, and the older sibling was not yet ready to give up the comfort of mother's breast.

The mother, being unwilling to end their loving relationship on a harsh note, accommodated the older child as well.

Long-term breastfeeding and tandem nursing are not without pros and cons. Again, all agree on the basic premise that weaning is best accomplished "gradually and with love." Yet emphasis differs on how to accomplish this, with some placing greater weight on what they perceive to be the child's need to nurse, and others assigning the mother a more active role. The mother, they contend, can lovingly guide the older child to a new plateau. The wise mother, of course, listens to both sides and considers what is best for her child, herself, and her family. The beauty of the situation is that there is always room to reconsider and adjust, to test and take small steps. Finding one's way takes time.

This was certainly true for La Leche League in yet another situation. At the same time that "La Leche League" was becoming a household word and the number of calls to LLL Leaders was skyrocketing, many of those calls were taking on a new dimension. While the mothers very much wanted to breastfeed, they also expected to be separated from their babies for extended periods of time. They were going back to work, often as early as six weeks after the baby's birth. Women were moving in two directions—they were mothers but they were also wage earners working outside the home, and a whole different set of circumstances applied. In addition to the usual help in getting breastfeeding off to a good start, they needed to know how to express and store their milk, how to get the baby to take a bottle, what they would have to do to keep up their milk supply. Above all, they wanted recognition for the fact that they, too, wanted their babies to have mother's milk. Some of the women who called were going back to work as a matter of choice, not need, but many others would have preferred to stay home. Regardless, all wanted their babies to have something of themselves, their milk with all of its benefits, especially when they were not there.

Leaders struggled with how to respond. In their own lives, they had embraced what La Leche League had been saying since its founding, namely, that babies need their mothers, not part-time, but on baby-time. To ignore this aspect of the beloved philosophy was unthinkable, an act of betrayal, some would say. More than ever, Leaders and mothers in general were looking to La Leche League for confirmation of their decision to stay home, a decision that was often bought at considerable monetary sacrifice to themselves and their families.

Much discussion ensued on all levels of the organization, and at the end of the day, a working arrangement emerged. It was not a case of either/or—of choosing between either stay-at-home mothers or mothers working outside the home. A mother is a mother is a mother. Working mothers were welcomed at LLL meetings, and information was assembled to meet their special needs. At the same time, the value of mother and baby togetherness remained intact. This is what we believe; this is what LLL Leaders are all about. Once again, the conviction came through—Breastfeeding is important, and so is mothering, and mothers need each other for support.

The euphoria felt by La Leche League in the early to mid 1980s, based as it was on greater recognition along with an ever expanding number of LLL Leaders, gradually settled into a comfortable glow and was eventually replaced by a new reality. Fewer mothers were applying for leadership, and those who were accredited remained active for a shorter length of time. They considered their contribution to La Leche League as corresponding to their children's early years, and once beyond that time, they moved on to other things. Also, families were having fewer children, and this, too, tended to limit a mother's commitment to La Leche League. But the dip in LLL leadership proved to be just that, a dip, and not the final outcome. The number of LLL Leaders began again to climb. Among the things that had not changed is the caliber of women working in LLL. They are intelligent and exceptionally dedicated, and the work they do is invaluable.

Mary Ann Kerwin

MAC: There have definitely been changes in the lives of the mothers coming to LLL for help over the years. What do you recall about those changes?

MAK: I think that women today are busier than we were in the 1950s and 1960s because many mothers today are employed outside the home. That's one reason why we have lost a lot of our Leaders—mothers today just don't have the time to lead LLL Groups. In the 1970s we had the most Leaders and Leader Applicants that we have ever had. But the number of women who wanted to become LLL Leaders declined rather sharply in the 1980s. Now in the 1990s, we seem to be growing again in regard to the number of Leaders and Leader Applicants we have.

But we still have a lot to accomplish. I think that our Leader Accreditation Department is making adjustments and trying to be sure that LLL is ready to help all mothers nurse their babies, both stay-at-home mothers and mothers who work outside the home.

MAC: When you say "help all mothers" do you mean through a different process of accrediting new Leaders, or what exactly?

MAK: Yes, I think our Leader Accreditation Department wants to be sure today's Leaders are ready and able to help all mothers, whether the mothers are at home full-time with their babies or employed outside the home. With the women who are employed outside their homes, the main thing that they are trying to help the Leaders deal with is how to handle separation issues—the time that a mother has to spend away from her baby.

MAC: So, in those cases, how do you see us remaining true to our philosophy that mother and baby should be together as much as possible?

MAK: Well, I see no reason why La Leche League can't help all women who want help with breastfeeding, no matter what their situation. Women often quit breastfeeding after they go back to work. In my opinion, there are two reasons for that: 1) Most of those mothers don't have enough information about how to manage working and breastfeeding, and 2) They don't get enough support from society.

They especially don't get support for breastfeeding from their employers. So it is hard.

La Leche League is set up to help mothers, all kinds of mothers, who sincerely want to breastfeed. I don't think there's any reason why we can't help employed mothers and I think that by and large we do. I think any Leader who doesn't is the exception.

MAC: Have the numbers of Leaders leveled off now?

MAK: Yes, it's leveled off a lot. The incidence of breastfeeding almost doubled from 1970 to 1975. I remember from having written it down and repeating it so often. We went from about 25 percent nationwide who were breastfeeding to 47 percent breastfeeding within five years.

We were accrediting Leaders—or certifying, I think we said at the time—at a phenomenal rate. At one point we were certifying Leaders at the rate of five a day! That was the biggest growth spurt we ever had. And by 1981, we had more than 12,500 Active Leaders—wow! And I don't know how many Groups.

MAC: What are your thoughts as to why we've slowed down in growth, though we have gained credibility?

MAK: I think it's pretty much tied into the changing culture where women are employed. In the 1950s, almost every mother was a stay-at-home mother. And now the majority, the clear majority, are not at home.

I think there are two factors that would account for the slow-down in growth in the number of LLL Groups and in Leader accreditation. We were perceived sometimes, and maybe rightly so, as not being supportive of employed mothers. I think that now we have learned how to help them and I think our Leaders, by and large, do encourage working mothers to breastfeed.

So I think the perception of us being only for stay-at-home mothers is part of the reason why LLL new group formation slowed down. I think that women are busier today because of working, and that's another reason why we have fewer Leaders. Mothers just don't have the time.

But I'm very pleased today (the late 1990s) that, in contrast to the 1980s, we are not continuing to drop in the number of Groups or Leaders. In the 1980s we began to see a decline in the percentage of breastfeeding mothers. But now we're back to where we were and the percentage of breastfeeding mothers doesn't seem to be dropping anymore.

We still have a lot to accomplish.

MAC: How do you see us remaining true to our mother/baby togetherness concept?"

MAK: Well, according to a very recent article in the LAD publication, what the Leaders are trying to do is help the mothers to evaluate the separation. They are looking at who is with the baby when the baby is not with mother. Is it the father, the grandmother, or is it a sitter? And they ask how the baby handles the separation. I think that's good as far as Leader Applicants are concerned.

MAC: Let's move on to when you took over as Chairman of the LLL Board.

MAK: Okay. That was a pretty exciting time. We were working with Bill Conrad and we had the Joyce Foundation grant. The Joyce Foundation felt that we needed to get our Board structure lined up to facilitate our work. So that's what we did. It was very exciting to develop the four primary committees as a way to handle the Board responsibilities. It just seemed like a very exciting time.

I was fortunate to be Chairman at that time. We were, however, making some big transitions. One of the reasons why the Joyce foundation gave us money was that they knew the Board and the staff were intertwined and they knew that wasn't good.

MAC: Why wasn't it good?

MAK: Because the staff viewpoint is different from the Board viewpoint. The Board should be engaged in policy-making and long range planning, that kind of thing, and the staff should be involved in implementation. But in LLLI, those two were intertwined. Board members should not also be staff members because that represents a conflict of interest.

The other thing was that we always had our financial concerns, and once again we were trying to get on a solid financial footing. After the reorganization, we had a Finance Committee and a Resource Development Committee to look into those things.

And we had major problems in the field, especially in the International Division which we called the Around the World Division. There was a lot of discontent in the field.

MAC: Could you be a little more specific about that?

MAK: Oh, some of the administrators were just not responsive to the Leaders in other countries. They were not responsive to their needs in many cases. And there were some requirements that were not necessarily appropriate for Leaders in other countries to follow.

What I found was that those people were not getting the answers that they needed and wanted. And I think that what was becoming clear is that the Leaders had to have more governance either by someone closer to them, or at least from someone with an international viewpoint.

MAC: You did some traveling as Board Chairman. Tell us about that.

MAK: Well, one trip in particular was to resolve some problems in Great Britain. La Leche League there was about to close down.

MAC: Leave the organization?

MAK: Yes, because there were so many Leaders who felt that LLLI was not attending to their needs, not communicating with them, not listening, not giving them what they needed. And they felt that some of the things that they were expected to do were inappropriate. Mainly, it had to do with wanting more autonomy. There was no problem with LLL philosophy. That was the link that kept the Leaders with us. They really believed in the philosophy.

MAC: So the problems were mainly procedural?

MAK: Yes, procedural, and other problems having to do with logistics. The situation in Great Britain is so different from the US. They just felt that they should be allowed to make their own decisions about procedural issues.

MAC: So it took people of good will on both sides.

MAK: Right. But autonomy was really an issue because they thought there was not an understanding of their culture and their circumstances.

MAC: So what was your solution to all of this, Mary Ann?

MAK: My solution was to go to Great Britain and see for myself what the situation was. I went around to various parts of the country and visited with the Leaders and listened to their concerns.

And then, one day we had a meeting in a central place—Birmingham, I think it was. At that meeting I got consensus from all those in attendance, a written consensus, as to what needed to be done. They all said, almost unanimously, that they wanted to have their own organization there, their own autonomy.

So I brought all of that feedback back to Betty Wagner, and to the Board of Directors. I brought all the individual notes and the summation back and the Board initiated a pilot program. I have to admit that we were guided a lot by Bill Conrad. He had some understanding of international work with organizations, and that helped a lot. So he helped facilitate this pilot program, and helped guide us in creating a new structure.

MAC: Was that the beginning of the Affiliate Program?

MAK: Yes. The pilot program in Great Britain brought about the establishment of Affiliates. They had their own autonomous structure, but were still part of La Leche League International. But LLL of Switzerland was the first country to sign an Affiliate Agreement with LLLI in 1987.

MAC: And all of this took place while you were Chairman of the LLLI Board?

MAK: Yes. I was Chairman of the Board from 1980 to 1983. After that, Betty Ann Countryman was Chairman, then Eleanor Randall was Chairman when Switzerland became an Affiliate. Later, Gail Berke and Brenda Toomey were Board Chairmen, then Paulina Allen de Smith, Cindy Smith, and now Ginger Sall.

Betty Wagner

MAC: Do you think having Founders on staff as paid employees somehow blurred the line between volunteers and paid employees?

BW: Yes, I agree. In fact, if you notice, in a lot of nonprofits the founders pretty soon are pushed aside because, I imagine, they have the same problem. They don't let other people, the new people, have their place in the sun.

MAC: Betty, you've probably heard it said that the Founders were more relaxed than many of the newer Leaders about following rules and so on. The Founders were not so much concerned about following the letter of the law, but rather the spirit.

BW: Yes, I think some of our administrators over the years may have been too strong, too rigid. I think perhaps there were too many layers of supervision; there may still be too many layers.

The sad thing is, these Leaders thought that they were doing what we wanted; they thought they were upholding LLL philosophy and LLL ideals. Whereas, in reality, the Founders overall were much more accepting of people's differences, and different ways of life. So we had to let the Leaders know this, and convince them to ease up a bit.

Mary White

MAC: One of the biggest decisions that women have to face today is when to go back to work. Would you agree, Mary, that the world is a different place today than it was when we were starting out as young mothers in the 1950s?

MW: Well, I would certainly agree that it is very hard for mothers to stay at home these days. Our whole economy seems to be geared to the two wage earner family. It's true that many times the father alone can't earn an income that is sufficient to adequately meet the needs of his family.

But when I talk to mothers at Area Conferences, there seem to be two distinct approaches to this dilemma. There is one group of mothers who can't wait to get back to work. And then there is another kind of mother, the one who doesn't really want to leave her baby. She does everything that she can possibly think of to put off going back to work. She makes the best arrangements she possibly can for her little one. She works part-time or she works from home, if possible. Or she will bring the baby with her in some cases, if that's feasible.

My heart goes out to these women. I know that they have no choice. They have to do this. I am perfectly willing to help all mothers continue breastfeeding when they go back to work. But, quite honestly, I don't have the same kind of sympathy for the ones who don't really need the money, who just have a different kind of lifestyle that they want to pursue.

I feel sad about that because their babies are being short-changed, their husbands are being short-changed, and the women themselves are being short-changed. They don't realize it, but they are not developing their potential as wives and mothers, or as women.

Often, with the birth of their second baby, many of these back-to-work mothers do decide to stay home for a while. They realize that this "two-career" family idea doesn't really work for them anymore.

MAC: There have been questions about whether LLL should accredit working mothers as Leaders. How do you feel about that, Mary?

MW: As for qualifying as a Leader a working mother with a nursing baby, this needs very careful evaluation. Each situation is different. If, for example, she were the only nursing mother for miles around, and was well-motivated as to mothering, you might want to consider it. Leaders should be examples for other mothers, you know. "Do as I say but not as I do" just doesn't work. A working mother is already a very busy mother. She has, of course, commitments to her family—husband and children, as well as the baby. Taking on the responsibilities of leadership in many cases could be too much. Leadership makes many demands on a mother's time and energy. She could end up getting burned out as a Leader, at her job, as a mother. A terrible price to pay. That's already happening to too many mothers. And the consequences of inadequate mothering are showing up in some very unhappy children and young people.

In fact, some very eminent authorities have been warning us for some time about this. For example, psychiatrist Arnold Raskovsky says, "In terms of family relationships, in terms of what the child grows up to be, everything that separates the mother from the child is risking the future."

The widely read and highly respected Dr. Robert Coles, Harvard child psychiatrist, says, "The first thing of significance in the parent-child relationship is the importance of parents being there for their children—morally, psychologically, spiritually, physically—to be attentive, to be responsive. One of the great tragedies now taking place in America is a kind of self-centeredness that has us putting ourselves and our careers ahead of our responsibilities as parents.... The ultimate question has to do with the values we have. If my values are to accumulate a lot of money and put my children as a secondary consideration, then that will show in the lives of those children. It's vital for parents to choose not only the amount of time they spend with their children, but, very important, the way they spend that time. To think that consumerism takes precedence over your responsibilities as a parent is to abdicate your moral obligations as a parent. That's the only way I know how to put it."

A great deal more has been said about this. But to add a truly inspiring person to the long list of those who understand what mothering is all about, here's what Mother Teresa had to say. Her message is so simple and so beautiful. In essence what she says is "Give, give of your love and of yourself. Give to those who need you the most.... For a laywoman, to be a wife and mother, to be a woman in the house, to share that womanhood, that gift of God, because no one can love as she loves. She is the heart of the family. And if we have trouble today it is because she is very little in the home." (What a wonderful mother she must have had!)

Edwina Froehlich

MAC: Nowadays, mothers are faced with different issues than we faced in the 1950s. How do you feel about that?

EF: Our message about the importance of breastfeeding was not always heard in the "bottle-crazed" culture of the 1950s, but we had no problem getting across the importance of being a stay-at-home mother. In fact, for the most part, it wasn't even an issue, because almost everyone who came to our meetings in those days was an "at-home mother." They didn't really even consider doing it any other way.

But today we are facing a rather different problem. Most new mothers today seem willing, even eager, to master the art of breastfeeding. Their interest in breastfeeding seems to be part of a larger trend in society to "do things naturally." Breastfeeding is seen both as a way of bonding with your baby and being responsible in regard to the environment.

At the same time however, the second wave of the feminist movement has told women that, to find true fulfillment, they must have a career. Full-time mothering is looked down upon as unnecessary and even demeaning. Women are still treated like second-class citizens if they do not have paid employment that takes them away from home. Full-time mothering is considered "boring" and young mothers are often told, directly and indirectly, that they are "wasting their education" and their professional training unless they go back to work, even when their babies are very young.

Now don't get me wrong. I am not one to knock the contributions of working women—I was a "working gal" for many, many years before I had my first baby. I worked as an executive secretary, and I was quite proud of the work I did, and I was proud of supporting myself.

Nevertheless, when I had my babies, I definitely wanted to stay home and take care of them. It never crossed my mind to go back to work when I had these new, young lives to care for.

So my final thoughts on the matter are that, there may be some ways that a young mother can work out of her home on a part-time basis. Or maybe she can bring the baby into the office while she works. We have certainly permitted and even encouraged that option at La Leche League's headquarters.

However, if a woman wants to be a mother-at-home, and to channel all of her energies and skills into that role, I certainly think that La Leche League needs to support her in that decision. Because today's mothers aren't getting that kind of support from almost any other part of society. They aren't hearing that full-time, at-home mothers are making a valued and vitally important contribution to society.

MAC: Well, Edwina, I certainly understand and agree with what you are saying about the importance of full-time, hands-on mothering. But, just to play "devil's advocate" for a minute, what would you say to young mothers who say that they just can't imagine being at home on a full-time basis? Some new mothers say that they would be "crawling the walls" if they had to stay home with an infant 24 hours a day, seven days a week. What would you say to those women, Edwina?

EF: Well, first of all, nowhere in LLLI publications or in LLLI philosophy do we say that a nursing mother has to be home 24 hours a day, seven days a week! Nursing mothers can take their babies with them and do lots of things! If mothers do leave their babies for short and sometimes longer periods of time, they can use a breast pump to express their own milk for their babysitter to give to the baby. They don't have to use formula.

We would hope this is not something that a new mother wants or needs to do on a regular basis. LLLI philosophy will always teach that the baby prefers having its own mother there to feed the baby from the breast, than for a "caregiver" to feed the baby with a bottle, even if that bottle does contain human milk.

At the same time, however, LLL has never said that we will not or cannot help the mother who finds that she needs to leave her baby for a period of time. It may take a bit of extra effort and planning to leave a supply of human milk for your baby, rather than just leaving a bottle of formula. But it can be done, and LLL will help you if you need to do that.

Viola Lennon

MAC: What do you remember discussing at Board meetings when you were Chairman?

VL: We started to formalize our accreditation process for becoming an LLL Leader. We tried to create a working definition of leadership—what it is, what you have to do to become a Leader. We talked about different jobs and what the specific duties of each job were. How you did your job was your business, but we spelled out what had to be accomplished. We began to form levels of responsibility—who reported to whom, and so on.

We discussed who has the final say-so in a particular department or on a particular project–that kind of thing. We talked about *LLL News*—what types of articles it should contain, who had editorial responsibility for that. Later we had a similar discussion in regard to LEAVEN.

There were also many lengthy discussions about concepts and LLL philosophy, and how best to communicate those basics. I remember a lot of discussion on, "What is a policy?"

MAC: What do you recall about finances?

VL: As long as there was enough money in the treasury to do what we wanted and needed to do, we didn't worry about it too much. It wasn't until Bill Conrad came along that we began to make changes in the way the finances were handled. Bill told us that responsibility for the finances, and setting financial policy, was the responsibility of the Board. He said that the Board should exercise more control over the finances and establish a budget.

MAC: What do you recall about accrediting Leaders?

VL: I think we've always had a little difficulty with the whole qualification process. How far do we go? Do we qualify a working mother under certain circumstances? I think we've made progress in this area. I'm not completely satisfied yet.

MAC: What is it that you still aren't satisfied with?

VL: I think we need to consider working mothers. What's the basic criteria for Leaders? You know I've traveled a lot in the last three years. I think it changes from region to region and area to area.

I'm not real good at helping a working mother because I never did it. I usually need to refer working mothers to somebody else. I tell them it would be much easier, not necessarily to be at home, but at least to be with the baby. If they can do it, I usually suggest they bring the baby with them. But that doesn't always work. Even at LLL headquarters we found that didn't always work. Still, I just think we should qualify working mothers as Leaders because I think we need them to help other working mothers in the future.

MAC: Do we need them as La Leche League Leaders or something else?

VL: That's a good question. I don't know.

MAC: There's the dichotomy—how do we remain true to our strong belief that mothers and babies belong together yet recognize that sometimes that doesn't work out?

VL: Right. I think it's like a lot of other things. That's the "ideal." But, let's face it. Do we all necessarily have to follow that ideal? I suspect not, because in every other area there aren't too many ideals that everybody follows every single time. I just feel insecure when I see mothers at home being critical of the working mother, and I still see that.

The pressures and stresses on today's mothers are far greater than they were 40 years ago. When women who became mothers gave up jobs in the 50s and 60s, this usually did not have a significant impact on the family finances as giving up second incomes does today. Further, men's jobs generally were more secure then.

Now, many mothers have to work because of their financial circumstances. Others may have established careers and are afraid to "fall behind" in their field of expertise. Also, because of widespread job insecurity among both men and women, many mothers are afraid to step out of the marketplace during their child rearing years in case the father's job is terminated or eliminated.

Chapter 13—New Approaches

As the 1980s dawned, far-reaching changes were occurring in the world. Personal computers were coming into their own and, unbelievably and peacefully, changing how people processed information and communicated with one another. About the same time, LLLI was testing the water with changes of its own. New programs were being launched to reach mothers who had heretofore been missed. Each innovation moved beyond the established way of doing things and broke new ground.

Increasing numbers of mothers in the USA were breastfeeding their babies, but mainly they were white and from a middle class background. For women in low-income minority communities, few inroads were being made in bringing the breastfeeding message to them. Mothers of color, especially, had little access to positive information on the value of breastfeeding. If anything, they were pulled in the opposite direction by the promise of free artificial infant food for their babies from large corporations and government agencies.

Yet the picture was not totally bleak. Here and there, enterprising LLL Leaders, to a large extent on their own but with La Leche League's blessing, had reached out to mothers in minority communities. In the Chicago area, two LLL Leaders were thinking seriously in terms of outreach to minority mothers. Marsha Hardin and Carolyn Tsikouris had gained a unique perspective on meeting mothers' needs in a variety of situations. Together they consulted with Betty Wagner, Executive Director, and Mary Lofton, who was then the Director of Leaders. Both endorsed the idea, and in short order, a petition to inaugurate a Community Outreach Program was presented to the Board of Directors, which unanimously approved the plan. Arrangements were set in motion to include an outreach session at the next LLLI Conference, which was scheduled for Kansas City, Missouri in 1983.

Scores of Leaders attended the session at the Conference, some of whom were already working in minority communities and a great many others who were interested in getting started. By the end of the session, the participants were deter-mined to stay in touch with each other, and a newsletter dedicated to the new out-reach effort was launched shortly thereafter.

Yet for all the good intentions, progress was slow. Many of the mechanisms that Leaders customarily used in making contacts in their own communities didn't apply when going into other communities. Distance was invariably a problem, with LLL Leaders living at one end of a town and minority families seemingly a world away. Opportunities to meet socially through church or children's schools were nonexistent and, even if contact could be made, the idea of a woman attending a meeting in a stranger's home was unacceptable in many minority cultures. Two years later, by the end of the LLLI Conference in Washington DC, the near-absence of mothers and babies of color among attendees said it all. It was time to look for a totally new strategy.

Marsha, Carolyn, and Mary Lofton headed back to the LLLI office to put their heads together and work out a whole new strategy. For Mary's part, she had been speaking at WIC clinics in Chicago on the importance of breastfeeding for a number of years. She knew the administrators and doctors, including the head of the Chicago Board of Health. And she knew, too, of mothers at the clinics who stood out for their desire and determination to breastfeed their babies. All indica-tions pointed to a peer-counselor type program, where mothers directly from a community would be able to help other local mothers. New criteria and training procedures would be needed, along with a training course of some kind to intro-duce the prospective counselors to La Leche League. The next LLLI Conference, scheduled to be held in Chicago, would be the perfect vehicle.

With a plan in place, work began on the details. Mary felt confident that WIC and the Chicago Board of Health would work with her on the project. "I'd been building a relationship with them for years," she remembers thinking. "Now was payback time!" With the names of likely candidates in hand, the planning commit-tee turned its attention to finding an outside source to underwrite the cost of the one-day program. A lineup of speakers had already been contacted and had accept-ed—the lovely Marcia McBroom Landiss, who had breastfed her own two boys and had been featured on a UNICEF breastfeeding poster; Dr. Eloise Skelton Forrest, a highly regarded black obstetrician with an enviable number of breast-feeding mothers in her predominantly black practice; and the renowned Dr. Leonardo Mata from Costa Rica, who enthralled his audiences with his down-to-earth explanation of breastfeeding's multi-level protection against infection.

Initially, the LLLI team hoped to find 50 women who qualified to attend. To everyone's delight and amazement, 100 applicants met the criteria. The team went scurrying for additional funding and was rewarded with a grant from the AHS foun-dation. At the final count, 70 scholarships were awarded, including some to WIC personnel, and funding was stretched to include dinner for those attending. On the big day, the proud and excited women took their places at the front of the main ballroom of the Chicago Hilton Hotel, where the Conference was taking place.

With enthusiasm high on all sides, Marsha and Carolyn announced the inaugu-ration of the LLLI Breastfeeding Peer Counselor Program to begin in October 1987 at the Daley Center in Chicago. Arrangements had already been made with

The Founders share a laugh at one of their recent get-togethers.

the Chicago Board of Health, and hours of work had been put into preparing the course curriculum. The Chicago program continued through 1990, and a number of the graduates went on to find paid employment in the health field. The program quickly moved beyond Illinois to Indiana, Ohio, and California. A Leader in Florida, Lou Boyles, began what has become one of the longest running Peer Counselor Programs in the USA. In Texas, WIC uses the LLLI program, complete with THE WOMANLY ART OF BREASTFEEDING as the textbook, to train its own Peer Counselors. In 1992, a call came from Sarah Gill of Great Britain, asking Mary Lofton to "please come and share your expertise." With funding available and a firm grasp of the Peer Counselor methodology, Sarah went on to develop a successful Peer Counselor Training Program that has spread all over Europe.

Back at the LLLI office, it soon became apparent that someone was needed full time to coordinate and manage the program. Marijane McEwan ably filled this position for a number of years. She was succeeded by Kathy Baker who, like so many of the women associated with La Leche League, had developed a variety of skills through volunteer work as an LLL Leader. This ability for LLLI to take on new challenges was soon put to the test in another part of the world, where the stakes were even higher.

An increasing number of babies in the developing parts of the world were becoming ill and even dying due to the use of artificial infant foods. Their unsuspecting families were grieving, and the mothers in particular were confused and hurting. Concerned people in both developed and developing countries rallied to protest the unchecked promotion of artificial infant foods by formula manufacturers and distributors. As heartening as this was, it was only half the battle in the fight to save babies. Desperately needed was support for the mothers in their efforts to give their little ones their own life-giving milk.

La Leche League responded with a peer counselor breastfeeding program that was to become the prototype of later such breastfeeding programs. It was LLLI's first experience working with a program that was funded through a government grant. The official name of the new project was Centro de Apoyo de Lactancia Materna or CALMA. The site was El Salvador. An American consultant who had contacts at the USAID Mission in that country was aware that funds were available to support breastfeeding and encouraged LLLI to apply for a grant.

A long-time LLL Leader from Indianapolis, Indiana and a member of LLLI's Board of Directors, Betty Ann Countryman, was chosen to spearhead the effort. She had long been interested in Latin America and was willing to devote the considerable amount of time necessary for such a project.

The new environment proved to be a challenge in a number of ways. For one thing, the country was embroiled in a civil war. Betty Ann says she never felt at risk personally, though the potential for danger came home on one occasion after she had walked alone to the American Embassy and personnel there insisted on sending her back in an armored car.

The grant was awarded, and work began immediately on forming a "Consego," or local Board of Directors. Almost simultaneously, office space had to be acquired, a staff hired, and appropriate materials produced in Spanish. Only then could the progress begin of training the new peer counselors. Procedures for measuring results, another important component, also had to be put in place. But just as the pieces all came together and CALMA lifted its wings to fly, trouble loomed.

The full impact of the threat became evident when the American consultant who had been on the scene early on openly moved to take over the operation together with the office manager, claiming that they would do a better job. In Betty Ann's words, "It was do or die for LLLI and the project." But LLLI was not about to give up. Betty Wagner and Betty Ann flew to El Salvador and spoke to the Consego and the staff, laying out La Leche League's position. As a result the office manager was dismissed and an early supporter, Dr. Cristina Villafuerta, took the helm.

Despite the setback, the project flourished. AID funding to LLLI for the CALMA project ended in 1985, but as Betty Ann says, "We went out in a blaze of glory." CALMA had been securely launched. Not only did it survive, the project garnered ongoing support from the community at large and established a second office. It also generated a side business for mothers making baby carriers. Eventually, a traditional La Leche League Group also took root in El Salvador. Just as telling, LLLI had gained a degree of sophistication and a healthy skepticism that it had not had before.

By the mid-1980s, word of breastfeeding's potential to save babies' lives had reached policymakers in Washington, DC. When notice came out of a new Child Survival project for Central America to be sponsored by USAID in Washington, it included a distinct component for breastfeeding support, a departure from past practices.

LLLI's Funding Development Department heard about the project from a devoted LLL couple, George and Becky Zocklein of Ohio, who had worked with government agencies for a number of years. The Zockleins generously offered to share their expertise with filling out the application and putting together the extensive proposal, which can be a formidable challenge in itself. Betty, as Executive Director, gave her blessing, and Viola, the Director of Funding Development and Mary Ann Cahill, her assistant, set to work. The deadline for applying was uncomfortably close.

In fairness, it must be said that neither party, La Leche League nor the government, knew exactly what to expect of the other. Certainly LLLI, despite the Zocklein's best efforts, was among the least sophisticated in formulating, filling out, and submitting the multiple forms, narratives, and budgets for a project of this magnitude. It was equally true that Child Survival had little idea of the complexities and scope of breastfeeding. Little was known of its full impact on a society or, for that matter, how to increase the number of mothers breastfeeding their babies.

. The decision was made to go ahead and apply. With help from LLL Leaders in Central America, plans were drawn up that would adapt LLLI's Breastfeeding Peer Counselor Program for use in three Latin American countries.

To everyone's delight, the proposal was accepted. True, it was for only two countries, Guatemala and Honduras, and the funding allotted was a third of what had been requested. Also, LLLI would have to contribute $75,000 as its match to the project. This sizable monetary obligation worried a number of Board Members, as they feared that other LLL programs could be shortchanged due to the additional burden.

Again, the Funding Development staff went to work, sending out special appeals and again, donors generously responded. One of the first contributions was for $10,000. The staff pressed on with renewed optimism and enthusiasm and eventually raised the needed funds.

The choice for overall manager of the project was Rebecca Magalhães, who had served with the Peace Corps in Brazil and had married and raised her family there. As an LLL Leader in Brazil, Rebecca had been involved in a local peer-counselor-type program. A move back to the States and the Franklin Park area put her in just the right place at the right time to take over the new project. In Guatemala, LLL Leader and Area Coordinator, Maryanne Stone-Jimenez stepped in as country manager for the project, while in Honduras, Judy Canahuati, long-time activist for breastfeeding and an LLL Area Coordinator, took over the reins. Again, in many ways, these women broke new ground.

LLLI's Child Survival Project lasted four years, ending in January 1993. As Rebecca points out, the first year or so was spent learning how to manage--how to conduct base-line surveys, work with consultants, develop strategies for getting into the community and establish mother-to-mother support groups, do evaluations and always, write reports. "There was a high learning curve," she explains. LLLI was growing and developing new ways to help breastfeeding mothers. At the same time, Child Survival was expanding its understanding of what breastfeeding is all about. Mother support groups that were headed by trained peer counselors, "monitora," became an accepted Child Survival strategy. Maternal nutrition also took on new meaning and prominence, to the benefit of all family members.

To better understand breastfeeding's child spacing attributes, LLLI worked with the Institute for Reproductive Health out of Georgetown University in Washington, DC on a study of LAM, the Lactation Amenorrhea Method of child spacing. The study was conducted in Guatemala from 1990 to 1995 through LLL Guatemala, with a similar endeavor taking place in Honduras through LLL Honduras. La Leche League's work with community breastfeeding counselors in Central America made it possible to bring a number of them to the 1995 LLLI Conference for further training. LLLI was also able to participate in a project to analyze the growth and sustainability of LLL Mother-to-Mother Support Programs in low income peri-urban areas of Guatemala City. At present, La Leche League is one of three partners in the LINKAGES Project, a worldwide, five-year program to promote improved breastfeeding, LAM, and a healthy maternal diet. These efforts, too, are funded by USAID.

LLLI's role expanded even further when it became an NGO (Non-governmental Organization) with the World Health Organization in 1993. In 1991, The Baby Friendly Hospital Initiative under UNICEF is pledged to "protect, support, and promote breastfeeding," in part by encouraging hospitals to put into effect the recommendations that La Leche League has been making since 1956.

In 1991, LLLI joined with other worldwide breastfeeding organizations to form The World Alliance for Breastfeeding Action (WABA).

Viola Lennon

MAC: Vi, do you remember working on the AID proposal?

VL: I certainly do. We had the help of George and Becky Zocklein, from Ohio, who had worked on government proposals in the past. But we had no idea how extensive the forms, budgets, and attachments would be. I remember we worked right down to the wire. The proposal was assembled, in triplicate, late on the last night. You were locking the office door as I set off in a newly falling December snow to deliver the bulky package to an overnight delivery service. The fierce storm that subsequently built and swept east probably saved our efforts. Chicago O'Hare and the Washington, DC airports were both closed down, and USAID extended the deadline.

MAC: I remember how worried we were about the funding for LLLI's "match." We put together this flyer showing a picture of a mother from the region. She was standing before a wooden shack with light shining between the boards in the wall and in the background, a rope held a few household items. The child she was holding was six or seven months old, totally breastfed. You could see from her smile how proud she was of her beautiful, healthy baby. That picture made it all worthwhile! No wonder the donors responded so generously!

Mary Ann Kerwin

MAC: LLLI was reaching out in new directions when you were Chairman of the LLLI Board. Do you recall traveling to other countries to discuss breastfeeding?

MAK: Well, let's see. Marian Tompson and I represented La Leche League at a conference in Jamaica. That conference focused on community-based breastfeeding support groups. So it was certainly appropriate for LLL to be at the table.

In fact, we co-sponsored the conference with UNICEF. The World Health Organization and the International Nutrition Association paid our way.

The Jamaican Conference consisted mainly of dialoguing with one another, touching base with the other organizations, and letting them know how our mother-to-mother support system works.

And then I also went to Australia to represent LLL. And the only group there that was really part of La Leche League was New Zealand, as I recall. All the others were breastfeeding support groups from various places—those groups were not part of La Leche League International.

The LLLI Board felt that it would be good to interact with them, to share what we had with them, and to find out what we could do to help them, or how they could help us. These groups came from southeast Asia primarily—Malaysia, the Philippines, countries in that area.

Then, on my way home from the Conference I stopped in New Zealand, mainly just to offer encouragement and support to our Leaders there. And I also stopped in Hawaii.

Another time I was invited to Indonesia to be on a panel with our good friend Dr. Derrick Jelliffe and his wife, Pat. I was on that panel largely through the auspices of Dr. Jelliffe. He was a great supporter of La Leche League because he was a very strong proponent of the concept of mother-to-mother support groups. And he had found that community-based groups were more likely to be persistent in advocating breastfeeding to new mothers than medical professionals were.

So that was the purpose of the Indonesian Conference—to promote the cause of mother-to-mother support groups. The Indonesian Conference consisted mainly of medical personnel, doctors, and nurses and so forth. And we were there representing the average breastfeeding mother.

MAC: Does anything stand out in your mind—cultural differences or other ways in which La Leche League learned from breastfeeding mothers in other countries?

MAK: Well, you know I have said that we learned from Indonesia how long it is "normal" to breastfeed. You may remember, Mary Ann, that when we started La Leche League in 1956 we had no idea how long babies should be breastfed.

MAC: Right! We thought nine months was the norm!

MAK: And by looking to other cultures we got some idea of how long to breast-feed—what is normal for most babies. In Indonesia we learned that most babies breastfeed longer than a year.

Unfortunately, just about the time of the Indonesian Conference in 1983, many Indonesian mothers were getting on the formula bandwagon—imitating the US and other Western countries. They were beginning to experience a decline in breastfeeding at that time.

So, when we traveled to Indonesia and other places in southeast Asia, the decline in breastfeeding was beginning to show. They were trying to reverse that decline because, for many babies over there, it was literally a matter of life and death. There were problems caused by the fact that many families had little or no access to refrigeration. Many babies were dying of gastroenteritis caused by formula that had gone bad.

There were also a lot of babies who were not getting an adequate number of calories due to mothers diluting formula since formula was so costly.

I guess all of this is building toward describing our association with UNICEF and the World Health Organization. And later the formation of The World Alliance for Breastfeeding Action (WABA)—all of that.

So yes, I certainly felt that we had a lot to learn from other cultures. At the same time, we were rekindling in them the importance, and in some cases, the absolute necessity, of breastfeeding. We were also sharing our experience in breast-feeding management and the benefits of mother-to-mother support groups. So it was definitely a two-way street.

MAC: How do you feel about LLL's approach to weaning nowadays?

MAK: It seems to me that some mothers and Leaders in LLL may miss the signs of readiness to wean. I still regret forcing my first baby to wean at nine months, and I encourage all mothers to breastfeed for more than a year. But from my experience and the experiences of the mothers we have helped breastfeed over the years, I believe most babies are ready to wean by the time they are two or three years old. Mary White talks about the many ways mothers demonstrate love and closeness to their older babies during and after weaning. Sometimes it appears that some in LLL think that the longer a baby breastfeeds the better adjusted the baby will be. LLL has never said this and never will. I am concerned when I hear that first time mothers or those who are pregnant with their first baby go to an LLL meeting and may be turned away. Recently I heard of a mother who proclaimed openly at an LLL meeting that her eight-year-old was still dealing with weaning. That can be very intimidating for a mother expecting her first baby or a new mother struggling through the first weeks of learning to breastfeed. I recall when I breastfed my first baby I thought I would be doing great if I could survive for three months. I think it's important for mothers of older babies who are breast-feeding to be discreet about it. Usually one can breastfeed an older baby without letting others know what is happening. Most mothers and babies develop their own code language for breastfeeding when the baby starts talking. Recently a jour-nalist with a local newspaper interviewed me on the telephone. She asked me if

LLL advocates nursing "children." I replied that LLL advocates nursing "babies." She said she had heard that LLL has been criticized for allowing older children to continue to nurse. I told the journalist LLL does not tell mothers when to wean but that we encourage mothers to watch for signs of readiness to wean. Weaning should happen when both the mother and baby seem ready. LLL does not encourage mothers to breastfeed indefinitely.

Chapter 14 —
MORE WAYS TO HELP MOTHERS

Another player arrived on the breastfeeding scene in the 1980s, the lactation consultant. She received payment for helping mothers with breastfeeding problems. In California, for instance, a number of lactation consultants were employed by clinics or hospitals. Some were doing excellent work, while others were of questionable ability. There was no way of knowing the level of competency, one from another, and the situation was ripe for poor standards and inappropriate licensing. In the midst of this new world, the local volunteer LLL Leaders were wondering how and where they fit in. Realistically, LLLI had two choices: stick to its basic program and ignore the new development, or play a role in shaping its future. The latter won the day, and work began on creating a first-class certification program for lactation consultants. It would draw from La Leche League but not become part of La Leche League. Forming it was a demanding task, since standards had to be ascertained, and regulatory boards satisfied. LLLI would be starting from scratch, having first to learn how to set up a testing program.

JoAnne Scott of Virginia, an LLL Leader with a talent for turning difficult situations into opportunities, was appointed chairman of the geographically diverse committee. Members brainstormed, mainly by letter. Should certification be for LLL Leaders only, or should it be open to other qualified persons as well? The task of producing a valid, reliable examination for certification, one that would be accepted by the National Commission for Health Certifying Agencies, proved more challenging. A conference on the topic was to be held in Washington, DC, just a short distance from where JoAnne lives. She said later that she probably would not have gone to the meeting had it been farther away, due to the extra cost. But she did attend and found a wealth of information on how testing is done.

As work progressed, the emphasis focused on credibility, something that all involved knew would have to be earned. Testing began nationwide in 1985, and in the spring of 1988, the newly formed organization was accredited, one of only three organizations to earn accreditation with its first application. By then it was known as the International Board of Lactation Consultant Examiners (IBCLC). In order to qualify as a certifying agency, it severed formal ties with LLLI and formed its own Bylaws and Board of Directors. LLLI remained an interested, caring supporter and loaned the fledging organization money to meet initial operating expenses.

In answer to the question of why, considering the excellent work that LLL Leaders do, there should be another category of breastfeeding help, JoAnne believes there is room for both Leaders and lactation consultants. She makes the distinction that an active, well-read Leader with five years experience is on a par with a certified lactation consultant, although a brand new Leader is not likely to be so well prepared. JoAnne points out that Leaders know about babies at different ages and stages, while in contrast, a hospital LC is an expert in an infant's first three days. Also, she believes that Leaders represent a greater variety of disciplines. Skilled Leaders know how to get to the base of a problem. They know how to help a mother feel that she's being heard, which is often the first step in discovering what's really bothering her. And Leaders have the advantage of one of La Leche League's greatest strengths, its system of Leaders supporting other Leaders.

The IBCLC exam is now offered in 35 countries each year, and has been translated into Arabic, Dutch, French, German, Italian, Portuguese, Spanish, and Korean. Icelandic and Japanese translations are planned for 2001, and Hebrew will be added in 2002. Over 16,000 people have been board certified, and over 10,000 are currently certified. Candidate numbers for 2001 are approximately 2,000. JoAnne Scott continues to serve IBCLC as its Executive Director.

In 1987, LLLI took another leap of faith into providing the kind of help mothers need. A formula company, no less, provided the impetus for LLLI to establish another innovative program to reach breastfeeding mothers—an 800 toll-free phone line. It wasn't as though LLLI hadn't already wanted, even longed for the opportunity to provide this kind of service to mothers. Finances had always been the major deterrent, and so when the formula company offered to fully fund a breastfeeding hot line with LLL Leaders taking the calls, the proposal was tempting. But shortly into the conversation, the full extent of the proposition became clear. Along with encouraging a mother in breastfeeding her baby, counselors would be expected to recommend the company's brand of formula when "something more" was needed. La Leche League declined the offer, but the fact that a formula company planned to sponsor a nationwide toll-free number for breastfeeding mothers could not be ignored. It was unthinkable that LLL would not also be a player. No other organization knew as much about breastfeeding, nor could any come close to offering mothers the kind of support that had become La Leche League's hallmark.

And so once again, the decision was made to take move forward and offer mothers a new convenient way to reach LLL and get the information and support they need. From there, choosing the phone number was easy—1-800-LALECHE. Funding was—and is—the greatest challenge to making it work. Beyond the initial installation charges for the phone, there are the monthly phone fees and also the

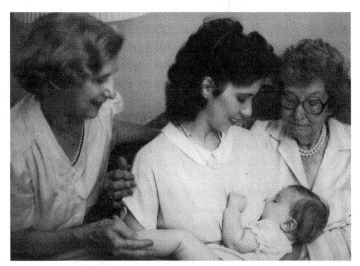

Betty Wagner shares a special moment with her daughter, Helen, nursing her daughter, Lauren, as Betty's mother, Valerie Redmond, looks on.

staffing costs for the 800 Line Leaders who take the calls. It would have been unrealistic to expect totally volunteer help for such an intensive responsibility, though volunteer Leaders to continue to provide telephone help to mothers all over the world.

Motherwear, a manufacturer and distributor of fashions for breastfeeding mothers, became one of the first major donors to the project. Judy Wright, the founder of the company, and her husband, Prakash, generously pledged a monthly sum to help cover basic costs to get the project underway. As funding from other sources has increased, the number of hours that the 800 Leader is available has also been expanded. Motherwear continued providing support for the 800-line for more than a decade.

When a mother calls, her immediate question is answered and she is referred to the LLL Group nearest to her. She also receives a free LLLI Catalogue, which in itself opens up a whole new world of breastfeeding and parenting information.

Betty Wagner

MAC: *Betty, you were the Executive Director when questions about lactation consultants started coming up. What do you remember about that?*

BW: We decided to investigate setting up a program to certify lactation consultants, and I asked Judy Good to head the search for a Leader to be in charge of the committee. Judy had been the Director of Leaders for the Eastern US and had her finger on the pulse of things. She knew the good work that JoAnne Scott was doing in Virginia and urged her to apply. JoAnne had worked with a hospital near her that was known for making breastfeeding difficult. She totally turned it around. JoAnne became chairman of that first committee and then went on to guide the IBCLC Board to what it is today. Of course, others helped, too.

Mary Ann Kerwin

MAC: Mary Ann, you had something to do with the original expansion of the certification program for lactation consultants into other countries, didn't you?

MAK: Yes. In 1983, I was in touch with Maureen Minchin, an Australian researcher, who told me they were having similar problems in her part of the world in regard to establishing standards for lactation consultants. So I referred Maureen to JoAnne Scott. Maureen convinced JoAnne that the exam should be international.

Chele Marmet, LLL Leader and founder of The Lactation Institute in California, was placed in charge of developing a series of workshops or seminars which would travel around the country, presenting pre-service and in-service education for lactation consultants and others with in depth interest and skills in lactation. These became the Lactation Specialist Workshops which are still offered by LLLI.

Kathleen Auerbach, living at that time in Chicago, was put in charge of developing a series of monographs directed to lactation consultants and other health professionals, which became LLLI's Lactation Consultant Series, still in print and periodically expanded.

Mary Ann Cahill

MAC: I remember when we first discussed the 800-Line. I had just gotten to work one morning when Betty motioned for me to come into her office. She said a formula company was talking about starting an 800 number to answer questions from breastfeeding mothers and they wanted LLLI to be involved. My first thought was "No way!" Both of us knew that it was a great idea, but it was something La Leche League should do. It was what we were all about! And besides, we felt we could do it better than anyone else! Finding the necessary money was the big concern, but once the decision was made, we forged ahead. The next appeal letter that went out talked about "being there" for mothers and, bless them, people responded—Leaders especially. As one wrote, "I've wanted something like this for such a long time. Of course we must 'be there' for mothers!" It was so good to hear, so reassuring, and so like La Leche League.

Chapter 15—TRANSITIONS: A CHANGING OF THE GUARD

Among LLL Leaders, certain stories are told and retold at Series Meetings because they quickly and neatly illustrate a point. One such story has to do with a mother and father joyfully introducing the new baby to the family, only to find that the "old" baby wants no part of the new arrangement. Dr. Ratner, who originated the story, brought understanding, if not an immediate cure for the difficulty, by looking at the scene through the eyes of the suddenly "big" sister or brother. Here is mother, he explained, entering the room with a perfect stranger in her arms and letting it be known that the stranger is here to stay. He would ask the mothers to consider how they would feel if their dear husband were to walk in the door with another woman on his arm and announce that now we will "share."

The analogy helped countless families put the experience of blending new and old into perspective. In retrospect, it could just as easily have been applied to the events that surrounded bringing in a new LLLI Executive Director in 1992.

Besides Betty, two other Founders were working at the LLLI office at the time, Viola and Mary Ann Cahill. Marian had already moved on to other employment and, to the surprise of many, Edwina had opted to retire in 1983. John was already retired and wanted Edwina at home with him, and both wanted to spend more time with their grandchildren. As Executive Director, Betty Wagner was well liked by the staff. A good listener and fair in her dealings with others, caring and unfailingly loyal, she represented La Leche League to all who knew her. Betty had let it be known that she would like to work until 1993 and then retire, but there were others, including members of the Board of Directors, who were eager for a change. After all, Founders had been in charge of LLLI for 35 years.

At a meeting of the Division Directors, Betty announced her intention to retire as Executive Director and told them she was willing to resign as soon as a suitable replacement could be found. So, the Board of Directors authorized the first-ever search for a new Executive Director. Founders participated in the interviews of the candidates. There was general agreement that the woman hired as Executive Director in early 1992, Mary Lawrence, had a creative bent and was well spoken. On the negative side, she was not an LLL Leader, though she had breastfed her children when they were infants. For many of the staff and key volunteers, it was a case of wait-and-see.

Early on, several decisions on Mary's part were to haunt her down the road. The first had to do with a request to reprint a pamphlet supporting mother-baby togetherness. Based on a technical problem, Mary ordered the pamphlet withdrawn. Word of this spread quickly, along with conjecture that this cornerstone of LLL philosophy was to be diluted.

The second incident was even more damaging. Mary Lawrence cancelled the LLLI Conference that was to take place the following year, in 1993, and she notified the Conference Director that her position had been cut from the budget. The move was supported by a majority of the LLLI Board but, to the volunteers and staff members who had already begun planning and working on the upcoming Conference, it was a devastating blow. From then on, the die was pretty much cast. A contingent of influential LLL people were openly suspicious of Mary, and she of them.

Despite the negative undercurrents, new ground was broken and some positive steps taken. Mary promoted the idea of broadening the representation on the LLLI Board of Directors. Hundreds of La Leche League Groups and Areas were flourishing in far-flung parts of the world, yet Board membership was mainly from the US, with one or two persons from Canada or Mexico. Cost had played a role in perpetuating this practice, since LLLI traditionally covered the cost of Board Members' transportation, as well as their housing and food during meetings. The rationale was that potential Board Members should not be limited by their ability to pay their own way. As worthy as this goal was, it favored those living in the USA, where Board meetings were held.

As it was, the composition of the Board had evolved over the years from when the seven Founders made all the decisions into a Board that was more inclusive and better organized. The solution to even greater representation came with the adoption of the Zone System that is now in effect. The "I" for International in LLLI has taken on new meaning.

Despite positive accomplishments, serious problems were looming. The gulf between the early dissenters and Mary Lawrence had widened, various changes were made that pleased some and angered others, and matters came to a head when Mary dismissed a long-time LLL Leader who was in charge of a major department. Reaction was sharply divided between those who supported Mary and those who opposed her. The upshot was that Mary Lawrence resigned near the end of 1993. To keep things going until a new Executive Director could be hired, the Board appointed a team consisting of Mary Ann Cahill as interim Executive Director and three Department Directors.

Pockets of discontent continued to smolder, and the way out of the morass was far from clear. With no time to learn on the job, Mary Ann placed a phone call to one of LLLI's Management advisors, Hugh Switzer. His response was immediate

The "old" building in Franklin Park; the New LLLI Building in Schaumburg.

and generous. He traveled from his home in Georgia to confer with the staff a number of times and was readily available by phone. Other members of the Management Council also stepped forward and helped provide much needed stability.

The next Executive Director, Lee Ann Deal, came aboard in June of 1994. As an LLL Leader, Lee Ann was more readily accepted, and much of the earlier turmoil subsided. But a year or so down the road, an old bugaboo, money problems, revisited, and Lee Ann, too, resigned. Paulina Allen de Smith, who was Chairman of the Board at the time, replaced Lee Ann in late 1996, filling the position of Executive Director as a volunteer for the first year. In 1997, she resigned from the Board of Directors and was hired officially as the LLLI Executive Director. With characteristic energy and imagination, Paulina pulled the staff together, set goals, and moved La Leche League ahead into the new millennium. Paulina served as LLLI's Executive Director until September of 2000.

Since 1963, when La Leche League moved into its first one-room office in Franklin Park, the organization had been paying rent. Over the years, several consultants had advised purchasing a headquarters building because there would be advantages to owning property rather than renting. By 1992, a decision was made to pursue this possibility.

The building at 9616 Minneapolis had already been renovated a number of times to accommodate the growing organization and options for expanding had run out. LLL had started by renting space on the Minneapolis side of the building. Then several more offices had been acquired on the main floor, running through to Franklin Avenue. Finally, the landlord raised the roof and put on a second level, which was totally occupied by LLL. The final arrangement wasn't fancy but whatever the Franklin Park office lacked in style and space it made up for in homey feelings that were evident everywhere you looked. The staff enjoyed working there and would have happily stayed except that aisles were dangerously crowded with boxes, desks were jammed into every available corner, rooms were overcrowded, and employees had trouble getting their jobs done. Something had to be done.

Members of the Capital Campaign Committee.

The search for a building began with the enthusiastic help of Dr. Hugh Riordan and a sizable donation from a long time supportive doctor. Knowing that a Capital Campaign would be a major undertaking, the Board hired a consulting firm, Campbell and Company, to get it underway. Pam Lungmus, a charming and experienced fundraiser, was our capable contact. A Capital Campaign steering committee was organized, headed by Marian Tompson, Eleanor Randall, and Cathy Marquis. With Joan Blick, our Funding Director on staff, the LLLI Capital Campaign was launched. In an orderly and speedy fashion, meetings with La Leche League Leaders were initiated across the country and many of the Founders and Board members introduced the Capital Campaign at Area Conferences both in the United States and Europe.

Near the very end, several generous La Leche League families agreed to match funds, which encouraged others to contribute. Foundations also supported the effort. Within the planned timeframe—three years—we were pleasantly surprised to have $1,500,000 pledged. Our goal was surpassed! With many capable and hard working people on this project, we were able to purchase our current building at 1400 North Meacham Road in Schaumburg, Illinois. La Leche League International has secured a wonderful home to continue to help and support mothers all around the world in a much more spacious and attractive environment.

In the entrance hall of our new building a beautiful golden sculpture of a tree is displayed. The leaves are engraved with the names of our generous donors. La Leche League International Founders, Leaders, members, friends, and foundations all participated in the Capital Campaign. This tree is a monument to mothering through breastfeeding and a symbol of motherhood, the most rewarding of feminine vocations, which reaches into eternity.

Edwina Froehlich

MAC: *Let's talk about the change from Betty Wagner, our long-time Executive Director, to Mary Lawrence being the Executive Director. What are your recollections of those events?*

EF: I don't know if we could have done anything that would have made it easier. It was a big change, not having a Founder in that role. Over the years we went through a lot of reorganizing with different consultants trying to help. Sometimes, members of the Board would feel that they should be making certain decisions as opposed to having them made by the Executive Director. They were probably decisions that Betty had been making for many years. At times, we (Betty, Edwina, and Marian) viewed some of these suggestions as kind of trying to push the Founders into the background, and put other, newer people in charge. How much of that was the intent, I don't know, but that's the way we viewed it.

One thing several consultants did tell us was that the Executive Director should be making management decisions, and she should be allowed to implement those decisions without constantly having to be worried about being "called on the carpet" for overstepping her authority.

But, if the Board finds that it consistently does not like the decisions that the Executive Director is making, then it is up to the Board to replace the Executive Director. But they should not be trying to micro-manage the day-to-day operations of the organization.

A lot of effort has been made in that direction (clarifying Board /Staff roles). Even after all this time, I would say that there are still times when there is some confusion about whether a particular decision can be made by the Executive Director and her staff, or whether that is a matter that must be brought before the Board. Overall, though, I would say that we are doing a lot better in that area at the present time than we did years ago.

MAC: *But getting back to Betty—she said that she wanted to retire when she was 70, but she ended up retiring before that. Could we have made the transition to a new Executive Director any easier?*

EF: You see, the difficulty was—and I remember you saying this, Mary Ann—that when a company is in trouble, the first person who gets blamed is the Executive Director. Even if the Executive Director isn't the one who caused the problem in the first place. But that's the way it's done—you go to the top of the organization, and then you take the blame.

So the Board wanted to make a change, and I think that some members of the Board felt that maybe we could get an Executive Director who could make better business decisions and bring in more money. I don't think that it was mismanagement of money that they were concerned about. It was the fact that there wasn't enough of it coming in.

*Everyone celebrated LLLI's 40th Anniversary and the successful completion of
the Capital Campaign at a Gala Anniversary dinner.*

There didn't seem to be any new ideas as to how to bring in more money. And
if anybody did come up with an idea, there was no one available to carry out that
idea. So the Board just felt that it was time to bring in somebody new, somebody
who could bring a new perspective to the situation.

Well, as it turned out, that's easier said than done. The LLL Leaders wanted
the new Executive Director to be a Leader. So the Personnel Committee advertised—some have said insufficiently, but I don't know about that.

In any case, the advertisement that was sent out listed all kinds of requirements
in regard to business and management skills, and also stated that the qualified
applicant should be a current or former LLL Leader.

I sat in on at least one of the interviews. And all I can say is that the person
who was finally hired—Mary Lawrence—was chosen because she gave all the
"right" answers during the interviews, and because she seemed to be full of ideas
as to how to raise money. She didn't have a lot of business experience and she was
never a Leader. She was hired mainly on the basis of the creative ideas that she suggested during the interview process. Nevertheless, those of us who recommended
her believed that she would be equal to the job. Unfortunately, that did not prove
to be the case.

*MAC: When Betty was Executive Director at LLLI, she was able to bring a business
sense to La Leche League, but was also able very readily to speak for LLL in any number of situations. In other words, she combined the business acumen and fundraising
skills with a bone-deep knowledge of LLL philosophy, and the ability to articulate that
philosophy. Is it impossible to find someone who combines both those skills these days?"*

EF: Well, it certainly would be great if we could always have someone at the head
of the organization who had both of those abilities (fundraising and a deep knowledge of LLL philosophy). It's true that every time we find ourselves in the position

of looking for a new Executive Director, our LLL Leaders tell us that they want a Leader at the head of the organization.

MAC: So what they are really saying is that they want someone who has spent many years as a full-time breastfeeding mother and LLL Leader, and at the same time, has the business experience and training to run a multi-million dollar organization.

EF: That's right. And that combination is not easy to find. So I think we simply have to face the fact that we need two people at the helm of our organization— one as a business person, and the other who speaks for LLL to the world, just as Marian did years ago. It's kind of going back to what we had before!

Betty Wagner

MAC: Betty, what do you remember about the Capital Campaign and moving into the new building?

BW: Well, the Capital Campaign got started while I was still the Executive Director. Hugh Riordan helped us get started and encouraged us to believe we could raise enough money. We hired an architect, Ken Hazlett, before we even started looking at buildings. He helped us identify what kind of facility we would need—how many square feet of office space, how much warehouse space, and so on. As it turned out, it was not that easy to find a building to fit our needs. The one we found needed a lot of remodeling to adapt it to our needs. But I was no longer the Executive Director when the decision was made to move into the building in 1994. We began with a rental agreement with an option to buy, and we were able to purchase the building in 1996 just in time to hold our Fortieth Anniversary celebration in our new home.

MAC: Betty, what was your reaction to the hiring of Mary Lawrence as Executive Director?

BW: In 1989 or 1990, I announced at a Board Meeting that I planned to retire when I reached 70. This was giving them ample time to seek a replacement. I remember one Board member saying "That gives us lots of time to search and there isn't any hurry trying to find Betty's replacement."

When they did start looking in earnest for a replacement, I was glad to help. However, when they interviewed Mary Lawrence, I was very upset. She had less schooling than I had, she had just filed bankruptcy with a previous business venture, and she had no experience with LLL. I wanted them to hire someone with more experience than I had, not less. But the Board firmly believed she was wonderful and would do a great job. So she was hired. Still I was willing to work with her and help her learn, but she soon let me know she didn't need my help. I continued to work at the office until the situation with Pam Ahearn. At that point I left the office position and only remained on the Founders' Advisory Council.

I wasn't unhappy that they were seeking a new Executive Director. I was just very unhappy they would hire someone who I felt wasn't better qualified.

Mary White

MAC: Talking about the organization . . . for so many years everything was very secure. We had Founders working at the office. A Founder, Betty Wagner, was in charge. But, like all good things, that time came to an end. Any thoughts on how we could have made that transition easier?

MW: Boy, that's a hard one. You're right, Mary Ann. When Betty was the Executive Director everything seemed to run pretty smoothly. Betty is a unique sort of person. She is very warm and understanding. People like her. She was willing to listen and give a little—a little here, a little there. And things got done because everybody responded to Betty. You can't replace someone like that, not really. Simply put, she was the right person for the job for many, many years.

But, as time went on, the focus became more and more on the business end of things. We kept hearing that we had to get someone in that spot who could bring a lot of money into the organization, someone who knew all the "ins" and "outs" of fundraising. So we got somebody like that and some people were disappointed because she wasn't an LLL Leader. "If only we'd gotten a Leader," we were told over and over again, "we wouldn't be having all these problems."

So then we hired another Executive Director and she was a Leader. And we thought, "Well, fine, that's going to satisfy everybody. She's a Leader, she'll understand." Unfortunately, this person, too, had some drawbacks.

So there we were, back at "Square One" again. Now, to my way of thinking, you have to get someone in that spot who is a "people person." I don't care if she was an LLL Leader or not. I don't care if it's a man or a woman. You want someone who is capable of running an organization, doing all the kinds of things that Executive Directors are supposed to do.

But you also have to have somebody who is going to be willing to relate to people, to listen to them. Even if you end up going off and making your own decision, you should consult with other people, listen to what they have to say.

MAC: How do you perceive La Leche League is doing out there at the grassroots level?

MW: Well, for the most part, I think they're doing a great job at the grassroots level. There are a lot of wonderful Leaders out there who are helping mothers in the way they need help the most.

Of course, you are always going to run into some problems here and there. One of my own daughters was disappointed with the LLL Group that she got involved in at one point, but she has since moved to another area, and maybe she will have a different experience this time.

Viola Lennon

MAC: *Vi, what do you recall about the Capital Campaign when we raised money to purchase the new building?*

VL: I was very enthusiastic about the Capital Campaign. I think I went to at least 12 Area Conferences in two years. Normally I would never do that many, but I wanted to introduce the Capital Campaign and point out the necessity of having a central headquarters, a central office, or whatever you want to call it. I knew that purchasing a building would give the organization credibility and stability.

MAC: *Vi, can you talk a little bit more about the Area Conferences that you attend—what does LLL look like and feel like out in the field these days?*

VL: Okay. For example, I went to an Area Conference in the spring of 1996 in Michigan and there wasn't much knowledge of the Capital Campaign, or the real need for the new building. I thought it was relevant to show the Leaders that this headquarters is for them as much as it is for office staff. We're all in this together.

We found a person to chair the Michigan Campaign. I had a lot of conversations with the husbands while I was up there. The men were very interested in what we do at the international office. What's there? What are the needs? Those kinds of questions. I had a great time, and I think this kind of interaction really pulled the Leaders into the Campaign.

And then, let's see, when I was down in Texas recently, they raised over $17,000 in two days. One of the reasons we were able to raise so much down there was because we had a matching grant from a Leader in Texas. Also, the medals sold very well there too—you know, the Board sold logo medals to raise money for the Campaign. What we tried to do was say, "Would you like to start your contribution to the building project by buying a medal?" This worked very well because then we would talk about the matching fund in Texas.

As usual, Texas spirit is good. Texas is very proud of being Texas. So when you asked for a pledge as a way of showing Texas spirit, you usually got one. I just thought it was a remarkable meeting. Also, just to mention something else that was interesting, that meeting was a combination of an Area Conference for LLL of Texas and a group of people from Texas WIC. The first session was just marvelous. It was led by an LLL Leader who's working for WIC. She did a remarkable job. The whole meeting was really excellent.

MAC: *Is La Leche League in Texas working on an ongoing basis with low income mothers?*

VL: Oh absolutely. As I said before, I asked to talk at the area council meeting and was granted permission, of course. And when I walked in I saw 50 people and I thought, "Oh, there must be a lot of visitors because this was a huge group. But no. There were four of us who were visitors and the rest were Texas people, lots of

Betty Crase, Director of the CBI, and Joan Blick,
Funding Development Director, hang a portrait of
Niles Newton on the wall of the CBI in the new
Schaumburg building.

whom were working with WIC. They were working in every kind of environment you could imagine. They are just the most enthusiastic group of Leaders you could imagine. All ages, I might add.

Doctor Ed Newton (the son of Niles Newton, an early LLL supporter) was there and I was talking at the same time as he was. He is very much the beloved doctor of Texas. People were telling me he did a very charming thing. He ended his presentation with a picture of his mother ,Niles, nursing him. That went over very well because Niles was very much loved and respected by Texans, and all LLL people, for that matter. So it was a very effective way to end his talk.

MAC: Any memories of the building we left behind in Franklin Park?

VL: When I left the old building I turned around and looked at the building and somebody walked out behind me and said, "You must be very sad today." I looked at her and said, "Not at all, I am so delighted to leave this building I can't tell you what it means to me! Now the ideas, the people I've met, the things that happened in that building will be memories I will treasure forever, but to leave that moldy old place is my joy and my delight." And then off I went, while everyone stared after me.

Marian Tompson

MAC: Marian, you came in to work at the LLLI office again near the end of the Capital Campaign. Tell us about that.

MT: Lee Ann Deal was Executive Director at the time. I was already working on the Capital Campaign as a volunteer along with Eleanor Randall and Cathy Marquis. But the Funding Director, Joan Blick, asked if I could come into the office a few days a week to bring the Campaign to an end. And it worked.

We were able to bring the Capital Campaign to a successful conclusion and buy the building outright, with no mortgage or payments. Near the end, when we didn't think we were going to make it, I got a phone call at home from a long-time LLL Leader. She and her husband had already given a generous gift to the Campaign and they wanted to give another, even larger gift. She wanted to discuss with me how to make the best use of this donation. I recalled other situations where our Leaders and members had responded well to a "matching funds" offer. This is what we decided to do. We got out the publicity about the matching funds offer, and the final amount we needed was raised in just a few weeks' time! It was very exciting to bring the campaign to a successful conclusion in time for LLLI's 40th anniversary.

Chapter 16—
OUR LIVES TODAY;
OUR HOPES FOR THE FUTURE

Over the years, one after another of the Founders became inactive on the Board of Directors. Mary Ann Kerwin represented the Founders' perspective the longest, staying an active Board member through 2001, a forty-five year record. Some time earlier, the Board had voted a provision into the Bylaws known as the Founder's Privilege, which recognizes the formation of the Founders Advisory Council, or FAC. It reads, "The purpose of the FAC is to advise the Board; provide historical perspective and inspiration; and represent LLLI to the public."

The Founders enjoy getting together and do so regularly, either as a group, or by mail, phone, or email. Edwina continues in the role of secretary, patiently sorting out each Founder's views for the record. It is rare when they do not arrive at a consensus.

Especially satisfying to them is knowing that their work continues. Mothers in the year 2001 struggle with many of the same worries and have as strong a need for support as did mothers when La Leche League began. This came home to Mary Ann Cahill recently when she spoke to her youngest daughter, Fran Brunow, who is an LLL Leader in the Colorado Springs area where she lives. Fran was describing an LLL meeting she attended one afternoon on "Overcoming Difficulties." The two regular Leaders for the Group, Amy Brown and Connie Whitttaker, were leading the meeting, which was in a home. Fourteen mothers other than the Leaders were present, along with 18 children, aged birth to six years. The older children played contentedly in the lower level of the house, while their mothers talked about their latest concerns.

Nursing in public concerned one young mother who was breastfeeding her first child, a ten-month-old. On a trip to the mall, a relative had admonished her

Edwina, Mary Ann Kerwin, Betty, and Marian always enjoy getting together with mothers and their babies.

not to nurse the baby, since the mall is too "dirty" and "people will be watching you." Another mother had weaned her first child at a year on the urging of her husband, who kept asking, "When is this going to end?" She came to the meeting with her second child, a six-month-old, looking for ideas on how to convince her husband of breastfeeding's continuing worth. She very much wanted to nurse this second child longer. Biting came up. The mother of an eleven-month-old told of how her baby was starting to bite and how she hesitated to talk about it to people outside of La Leche League, since they couldn't imagine a child with teeth still breastfeeding. With good humor, the other mothers by turns empathized with each mother and encouraged her in her desire to breastfeed her baby. The Leaders skillfully wove the suggestions given by the mothers with tried-and-true LLL practices and philosophy.

For Mary Ann, the scene as described made her realize how much has remained the same. She had only to close her eyes to imagine the meeting taking place in her own home when Frannie was a baby. The mothers' concerns and hopes for their babies were not all that different from those of a generation ago. Their need for support is also every bit as strong. One difference is that now breastfeeding is more often accepted, and La Leche League is a name known in many parts of the world.

Providence brought the first seven women together, and Providence will watch over the new Leaders. The philosophy that has so indelibly identified La Leche League is given to each generation to use and pass on, lest it be lost. When the Founders discovered glimpses of the philosophy back in the 1950s, they realized that nothing can replace mother-to-mother sharing. Nothing else is as authentic and enduring. With that in mind, the way ahead is clear and full of promise.

Marian Tompson

MAC: Marian, tell us what is going on in your life these days.

MT: I spend quite a bit of time going to LLL Conferences. I was recently at the "Stand for Children Conference" in Washington, DC, and before that I spoke in Peoria at the Illinois Breastfeeding Task Force. That invitation came about because the Illinois Task Force group in Peoria has a lot of LLL people in it—Leaders and lactation consultants. The head of the Task Force turned out to be Bonnie Cox, whom I remember as the LLL Leader who got fathers into the delivery room in Illinois. She was really one of the prime movers in getting the legislation passed that would allow fathers to be in delivery rooms in Illinois.

So I am quite busy and very happy with my life today.

MAC: What was the main issue that was discussed at the Task Force Workshop you attended?

MT: It was all about breastfeeding. I gave the keynote speech, and they brought Dr. Jack Newman down from Canada and he led a lot of the clinical workshops. And LLL Leaders and other people gave sessions on things from sucking problems to being a working mother while breastfeeding—a wide range of breastfeeding issues.

MAC: Do your children and grandchildren still live in the Chicago area?

MT: Yes, all of my grandchildren live within easy driving distance of Chicago. The farthest one lives in Oshkosh, Wisconsin but that's a drive you can easily do in three to four hours from here. My 20-year-old granddaughter is a junior at Northwestern University right here in Evanston, so she's very close by.

Marian Tompson's family today.

Marian Tompson with Rebecca Magalhães and Vicki Nizin at the Women's Conference in China.

MAC: *What is going on in your life?*

MT: I am still very much attached to LLL through the Founders Advisory Council and invitations to attend Area Conferences throughout the world; I also attend meetings of the Board of Directors. Attending Area Conferences give me reassurance that the work we are all doing is making this a more baby friendly and family friendly planet. In recent years I've also been privileged to participate in gatherings outside of LLL, like the UN Conference on Women in China; and a UN meeting to draw up guidelines on the use of chemicals that pollute the environment, in Bonn, Germany.

We never suspected 45 years ago that this kind of advocacy for breastfeeding and breastfeeding mothers and their babies would still be needed today. And yet it is.

Then there is my family, who along with my friends and LLL continue to lift my heart and keep my love juices flowing. Six of my seven children are married and they have brought fifteen grandchildren into my life.

MAC: *How's your family doing?*

MT: Melanie, Deb, Allison, Laurel, and Philip and their families live within an hour or two by car, so I get to seem them fairly often. Brian lives in Arizona and Sheila is in New Jersey. With three grandchildren graduating from high school this year, and a number of them appearing in school plays and musical presentations, we've had a lot of opportunities to get together. At Christmas, everyone comes home to my apartment for Christmas brunch and a turkey dinner later, for those not having to share the day with in-laws. The out of towners stay for as long as they can, bedding down all over my apartment, on the floor in sleeping bags, sleeper sofas, and a blow up mattress.

And last year on my dear, late mother's birthday, my first great-grandchild, Shiloh Destine was born to Deb's son, Mark, and his wife, Ronnah. It was a totally natural birth, which is getting to be unusual these days and yes, she is a happy, breastfed baby.

MAC: So how do you spend your days?

MT: Well outside of a few necessary part time jobs, most of my time, during the last three years has been spent examining the issue of breastfeeding and HIV/aids. When I first looked into this issue, it didn't take much reading and talking with others to realize that many of our assumptions were not backed up by hard scientific, evidence. In February of 2000 some of us who were interested in this matter began a private chatlist, AnotherLook, which now has over 50 subscribers from all over the world.

AnotherLook was recently incorporated as a not-for-profit corporation dedicated to gathering information, raising critical questions, and stimulating needed research in an objective search for meaningful information about breastfeeding in the presence of HIV/aids. Currently we are working with researchers at the University of Texas on a pilot project to determine if infectious HIV virus can be found in mother's milk.

We are looking for scientific proof that infectious human immunodeficiency virus is transmitted from mother to baby through breastfeeding and evidence to back up the claim that infants of HIV positive mothers will be healthier if they are not breastfed. At this time, there is no hard science to back up these assumptions.

MAC: What are your hopes for LLL in the future?

MT: That we will be here as long as we are needed and I can't see that need going away very soon. I would hate to live in a world that did not have the resources that LLL provides through its meetings, its phone service, and its conferences. Although there are many places to get breastfeeding information today, few acknowledge the role of breastfeeding within the context of the family, the culture, and the planet. A mother's decision to breastfeed her baby affects us all.

In fact, when we see that young mother, embarrassed maybe at finding herself having to nurse her baby in public, we should not only smile at her with approval, but we might thank her for making this a better world for the rest of us.

Being a Founder of La Leche League has put me in touch with the kind of people I need in my life to be the best that I can be. It's been a marvelous never-ending journey.

Edwina Froehlich

MAC: *Edwina, to what do you attribute the fact that the seven of us Founders have managed to stay involved and remain friends for more than 40 years, with all of its ups and downs?*

EF: Well, in answering that question I have to start from what I feel and assume that the other Founders will do the same.

What I have for each of the seven Founders is, #1, Respect with a capital "R." Respect for the kind of persons they are, and the special talents that each brought to this endeavor In many cases, their special talents are gifts that I don't possess myself. So I admire that in them, and I think that LLL benefited tremendously from that diversity of talents and gifts.

Today I still count each one as a friend, and I've come to understand what friendship really means over the years. We've had conflicts with each other at times, we've had some difficult times, but we all basically have respect for each other. You remain friends because, in one way or another, these particular people have had a positive impact on your life.

That's on the personal level. On the larger horizon, in regard to our work with La Leche League, is the fact that together we conceived and started this organization. For each one of us, our motive was pure. We really and truly wanted to help breastfeeding mothers and babies.

At times we have had very strong disagreements on issues. And at times we may have felt that a particular Founder was annoying, mainly because we weren't seeing eye-to-eye with her on a particular issue.

I think the thing that kept us together during the difficult times was that we all wanted La Leche League to achieve its purpose. So we would say to ourselves, "We are not going to let this kind of thing get in the way. This is a problem that we are going to have to live through, and work through, and resolve, so that we can continue to do what we originally set out to do—help mothers successfully breastfeed their babies."

MAC: *What do you see as important for the future of breastfeeding?*

EF: Tremendous growth in LLL Groups has taken place outside the Untied States in the past few years. As Western medical practices and infant formula have spread to the rest of the world, both natural childbirth and breastfeeding have almost been abandoned in many cultures and communities.

Fortunately, in many countries, there are now La Leche League Groups, ready, willing, and able to help the new mother. But sadly, only a small number get the help they need. On the other hand, in some of the less developed countries, sometimes with financial aid from UNICEF, the tables have been turned, and breastfeeding is once again becoming the cultural norm and formula-feeding has wisely been restricted.

Edwina Froehlich's family today.

The good health of all future generations demands that breastfeeding be given serious consideration by the professionals caring for new mothers. When health care professionals start to recommend breastfeeding and refer their patients to a knowledgeable resource person or a support group, breastfeeding will once again become the norm.

The duration of breastfeeding is short-lived but its benefits last a lifetime. As the late Dr. Grantly Dick-Read said, "The newborn has but three demands: one, warmth in the arms of the mother, two, food from her breast, three, security in the knowledge of her presence. Breastfeeding satisfies all three."

If it takes an organization to help mothers fill those three demands of their babies, so be it. La Leche League plans to hang around to do its part as long as the need remains.

MAC: Edwina, is there anything you've learned over the years that would be helpful to today's young mothers?

EF: In the very early years of LLL, one of the biggest worries of the mothers who came to our meetings was whether their children would grow to be independent, well balanced adults. They worried about giving all this devoted attention to the infant, always responding to his needs, and allowing the toddler to roam about investigating his environment, instead of putting him in the playpen where he would be under control. They wondered if this would result in a poorly behaved child who would not fit into society's expectations. Fathers especially worried that their sons would become "mama's boys" if they were so dependent on their mothers. Heaven forbid! Much of what we were recommending was the opposite of what doctors and male authors of child care books recommended.

We kept reassuring the mothers that our mothering approach would absolutely not be harmful in any way and could only result in good development for the child, despite what society was telling us at the time.

Our firstborn, Paul, was a very active child. He was big for his age and strong, and as such was the natural leader of his peer groups. When he was in kindergarten, his father and I attended our very first Parents Night when it was customary to hear from the teachers just how the child was doing in school. Paul was one of the youngest children in his class because he started school in September even though his birthday was in mid-November. You can imagine how proud we were to be told that Paul was the teacher's biggest helper. Many of the children would let their jackets drop to the floor instead of placing them on the hook provided. Paul would show them how to do it. Paul not only knew how to tie his own shoelaces but did it for others as well. I also remember the teacher saying when she told the children to line up, Paul responded immediately and then would help her get the rest in line. He was indeed very independent and very helpful. This was the child who seemed to be attached to me at the hip when he was a baby! My friends would ask me whether I ever put him down? Actually, I hardly ever did, because he much preferred being "up." I told this story over and over as living proof to the mothers that our mothering approach did work. Paul majored in political science and the first ten years after college he taught high school history. His real love is politics and after he resigned his teaching job, he became executive director for a volunteer organization with which he had been involved. Ultimately he was able to get into local politics and has twice been elected to township jobs. He loves it, is good at it, and people respect him.

David, our middle son, has a totally different personality. As a toddler, he too hung on my apron strings, but was much more docile which made it easier for us. He was very bright, however, with great ability to learn and absorb what he learned.

In high school, David followed in Paul's footsteps and wrestled for four years. That got him a scholarship to Northwestern University and he ended up winning All American Athlete in the final competition—which means he was fourth in the nation in competitive wrestling. For a number of years he has coached wrestling and other sports in high school and his wife and I have been most proud when parents tell her what a great influence Coach Froehlich has been on their son. He is now athletic director at the high school.

Two years after David was born I had a miscarriage. Two years later I conceived our third son, Peter. All the boys are tall, but Pete is the tallest. Again, from various people I was warned that I let the boy cling too much to me from infancy on. By that time, however, my confidence was at an all time high and I was no longer even slightly intimidated by such comments. He became independent early just as his brothers had—quite able to do all sorts of things for himself as well as to lend a hard to his buddies. He followed his brothers' footsteps and wrestled in high school and earned a scholarship to the University of Illinois in Champaign where his father and grandfather had attended. He is now a mortgage broker. He has a drawerful of cards and letters from grateful clients. He says it gives him great pleasure to be able to help the couples get started with their first house.

MAC: And what about your family today? Your grandchildren?

EF: All three boys got married—in proper sequence. First Paul married Marilyn, then David married Sharon, then Peter married Paula. Then in the same sequence (our boys have always been very competitive) they produced their first, second, and third child each. Paul now has Leanne in college, Kristin entering college in the fall, and Laura going into sixth grade. David's oldest, Steven, will be a senior in high school this fall, Michael will be in eighth grade, and Colleen in fifth grade. Peter's Katrina enters junior high school this fall, Jenna will be in fifth grade, and Christian will be in second grade. If you asked any one of those children to rate their dad as a father, I suspect they would each get at the very least a B+ from their children.

So those three boys have made me a happy grandmother of six girls and three boys. My husband, John, died in 1997 so I live alone now, and treasure every moment I can spend with my family.

So all you new mothers—don't be afraid to nurture devotedly. It pays off handsomely. Don't misunderstand—no one can promise us perfect children, after all they are the offspring of imperfect parents. But we can promise our mothering approach stands a better than average chance of helping children become well developed, well balanced adults who will be able to cope with whatever life dishes out.

Viola Lennon

MAC: Vi, tell us about your life today–where do you live, what keeps you busy these days?

VL: I live in a condominium now in Park Ridge, all by myself, very close to all of my children. I feel very blessed because all of the Lennons are in Chicago or close by and they are all buying property in the Chicago area which anchors them here even more.

My involvement with La Leche League is volunteer at this point. I've been working with Pam Oselka and Sue Christensen. to build up the Alumnae Association. We want to make it into a real alumnae association much like you would find at a college or university. We haven't quite achieved that yet, but we are working on it.. The alumnae newsletter, CONTINUUM, gets bigger and better with each issue, offering fascinating insights into the countless ways that LLL involvement has shaped women's lives.

MAC: Vi, what are your hopes and dreams for the future of La Leche League?

VL: I would like to see more and more involvement of La Leche League in every project and organization worldwide that has anything to do with breastfeeding. That's a pretty ambitious idea, I grant you, but I think that's where we belong and where we ought to be for the future. I still think we offer the best advice and expe-

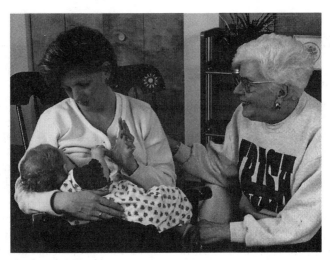

Vi Lennon looks on as her daughter Rebecca breastfeeds Emily.

rience on breastfeeding. But, once again, it takes money—money is always a consideration, whether we like it or not.

Another thing that I would like to see us do is to become much more statistical. We need numbers—how many people do we reach, how long do they breastfeed, what motivates a woman to start breastfeeding, or to continue breastfeeding—those kinds of things. This is something that never occurred to me until recently—that we should try to keep track of the statistics on those kinds of topics. Unfortunately, I am not sure that we have sufficient staff to be able to gather that kind of information.

MAC: Why do you think it is important to have statistical information on those kinds of topics?

VL: Because that's what you are asked for out in the world. That is what the press wants, that is what researchers want. And that's the kind of data you have to provide when you are writing a grant proposal. You've got to have the figures and the statistics, along with good ideas about breastfeeding.

Up until now we haven't put much time or money into that area. So now, we have to change, we have to learn how to keep track of that kind of information. We need to learn to use data processing programs to collect this kind of information, and then we need to find ways to distribute that information all over the place, so that people will really see and understand the impact that La Leche League is having on successful breastfeeding management.

Betty Wagner

MAC: Okay, Betty, tell us about your life now—what you are doing?

BW: Well, I'm retired. I live with my second husband, Paul Spandikow—we got married in 1993. My first husband, Bob Wagner, died in 1975. With my marriage to Paul I also acquired his seven children and 15 grandchildren, so that bumped my numbers up quite a bit.

Paul and I live most of the time in a little house in Tennessee, just four rooms and one bathroom. It's small but it's very easy to keep clean. There is a lake out in the back. Sometimes it's just a mud lake, but most of the time there's water in it. It's lovely because it's a nice, big lake and everybody in the family loves to come and swim and ski and jump off the dock into the water, and just generally have a good time. So we really enjoy that because between us we have so many children, grandchildren, and now great-grandchildren. So it's really great.

We also have a condominium in Illinois where we can come and visit our children who live in the Chicago area. So we really have the best of both worlds.

MAC: Tell us about your family, the Wagners.

BW: Well, I had seven children, all of whom married. I have 24 grandchildren and ten great-grandchildren. One of my children lives in Michigan, another lives in Atlanta, one lives in Virginia, and one lives in Florida. The rest are in the Chicagoland area. We see everybody regularly because they either come on down to Tennessee or we see them when we come up to Illinois.

*Edwina Froehlich was the Matron of Honor when
Betty married Paul Spandikow in 1993.*

MAC: *The number of girls and the number of boys?*

BW: Oh gee, that's always hard. I have mostly girls (as children and as grandchildren). Paul's grandchildren are pretty evenly divided between girls and boys.

MAC: *And what about your own children—how many boys and how many girls did you have?"*

BW: I had five girls and two boys. I lost a son, Wayne, at the age of 26. He died in an automobile accident. Paul also lost a son who was a little older than Wayne. Paul also lost a grandbaby at age eight months, and I lost a grandson, my daughter Mary's little boy, at the age of three. So Paul and I have a lot in common.

MAC: *So how did you and Paul meet?*

BW: We met at square dancing. It was at my club. You know square dancers all have clubs. Paul came to our club dance on a Sunday night. It was what we call a "student dance." He was just learning to square dance.

We happened to pull into the parking lot side by side and got out at the same time. Since he didn't know anything abut this club, I took him along and showed him where to go and how much to pay and got him all situated so he would be set to dance.

Then he and I danced the first tip together. We had a good time, and before the night was over, he asked if he could see me the next night, if he could take me out to dinner. I thought that would be nice so I said, "Sure, that would be fine."

So the next night when he came to pick me up, I had pictures of my children and my grandchildren out because I thought right away he should know that I have seven children and all of these grandchildren. So when he came, I started showing him all these pictures. He was very appreciative.

He was wearing a pin that said he belonged to St. Paul Church, which I thought was a plus. We went out to dinner and then he pulled out his photo album and showed me pictures of his seven children. I thought, "That's perfect. I don't have to worry about him not understanding how important my children are to me because obviously his family is important to him, too."

So it worked out very well. We met in November and got married the following November. We invited all the granddaughters and great-granddaughters to be flower girls. there were ten in all, and they looked so sweet in their long pink dresses with flowers in their hair. We had square dancing at our wedding and we have been square dancing ever since.

MAC: *Betty, what are your hopes for the future of La Leche League?*

BW: It's important for the Board to continue hiring the right person in the role of Executive Director—someone who knows LLL philosophy and is also a good business manager. That's my hope. I think that is the major thing the LLL Board has to do now and in the future.

Many LLL Founders and friends enjoyed being part of Betty and Paul's wedding.

You know, I had Edwina working with the Leaders for years, and you, Mary Ann, along with Vi in the Funding Department, and Marian as LLL President and spokesperson. Then later I had Sally Murphy and Judy Torgus and Mary Lofton. They were all Leaders who knew what the organization was all about. I always had a wonderful staff, great people to work with, people that you could really count on to do what they said they were going to do.

MAC: And you were always open to other people's ideas and were willing to listen.

BW: I was? That's good. I mean, it's nice to think that's how people remember me. But you know, I never worked alone—it was always a team effort. We had some great people working for LLL in those days. There were some long-time staff members who worked for La Leche League for years and years—Eileen Appler, Joyce Kashe and her sister, Jean Henkels, LaVerne Bollig, Doris Ditchkus, Bernie Heimos. And a few who worked in Franklin Park still work for LLLI out in Schaumburg—Mary Young, Fran Cassano, Diana Grinvalds, and Tony Yee. And some of the Leaders who worked for me are still there, too—Sally Murphy, Carol Kolar, Judy Torgus, Carol Esposito, Sharon Barsotti, Elaine Caper, Mary Lofton, and Carol Huotari. That's one thing I can say for sure, we had some really dedicated, hard-working, wonderful people. It was great.

Mary White

MAC: When La Leche League began, you had six young children, Mary. A lot has happened in your life since then! Can you bring us up to date on your family?

MW: Forty-five years after La Leche League was founded, in April 2001, our family has grown to eleven children, almost 54 grandchildren, and nine, going on eleven, great grandchildren. We truly are blessed to have such a great family, and we love each and every one of them dearly. (And, yes, I do know them all!) Our three boys, Joe, Bill, and Mike are all in family practice as was their father, until he retired in June of 2000. Joe and Bill are in the same office in Franklin Park. Mike has moved with his wife, Debbie, and family to Wisconsin, and his office is in Nequon, where the LLL families up there are keeping him busy.

Joe and Susan have seven children. Their oldest, Gregory, born seven months before our youngest, Elizabeth was born, is now married. He and Isabel have one son, and another baby due in a few months. Bill and Cathy also have seven. Their oldest, Paul, is in the Army Medical Corps and is in a surgical residency at Walter Reed Hospital in Washington, DC. He is to be married this summer. Their oldest daughter, Sara, is married and she and her husband, Brian Burch, have two-year-old twins, which came as a surprise to everyone up to the very time they were delivered by Sara's dad, Bill. Bridget and Martin are looking forward to a new baby in June.

Our oldest daughter, Peggy, died in 1968 of cancer. But in many ways, she is still with us, and a wonderful part of our family. (We have several granddaughters named after her.)

Next comes Katie, married to Kevin Thornton, one-time Publications Director at LLLI. The Thorntons have eight children and four grandchildren. Their oldest, Patrick, and his wife, Jessica, have three, and their oldest daughter, Clare, and her husband, Patrick McCormack, have a baby girl.

Our daughter, Anne, who until recently was in the banking field, is contemplating a change in careers. She has just returned from Bolivia where she was part of a medical mission group there. Last year it was Peru. Joe, Bill, and Anne all live fairly close to us. The Thorntons aren't very far away either, in Villa Park.

Which brings me to Seton Academy, a small Montessori school, also in Villa Park. Bill is president, and Katie is principal. Several of our children and a few friends founded the school about 25 years ago. It is a great school and thriving.

Jeannie and Jim Stirton live in Germantown, Wisconsin, close to Mike and Deb, as well as to Mary and Greg Dooley. The Stirtons have eight children, the last of whom was born after Jeannie's first grandson was born to their oldest, Broc, and his wife, Katie. Broc and Katie live in Austin, Texas and now have a second child, Mary Grace.

Getting back to Mike and Deb, who come next in line, they also have eight. So far, none married, but a great and busy bunch as are all the others. I guess you could say that Mike was our first LLL baby, as he was born in 1957 when LLL was just getting underway.

After Mike comes Mary, married to Greg Dooley, who, with their two little adopted ones, Liam, six years old, and Grace, almost four years old, also live in Wisconsin, just a couple of miles from Jeannie and Mike. Mary has spoken at several LLL Area Conferences, and does phone counseling to help adoptive mothers with breastfeeding. Mary completely nursed both her babies, with the help of a Lact-Aid nursing supplementer. She swears by it.

Hang on, we're almost to the end! Our two youngest, Molly and Liz, both moved out east, to Lancaster, Massachusetts, where their husbands are lawyers with the same law firm. Molly and J.J. Smillie have five children, and are expecting their

Mary and Greg White with their granddaughters Ciara Smillie and Maggie Dillon, who were born on the same day in 1999.

Mary's twin great-grandchildren, Bridget and Martin.

Mary White's family today.

sixth. Liz and her husband, Tom Dillon, just had their third baby, first boy, Sean Daniel. The youngest Smillie, Ciara, and Maggie Dillon were born on the same day two years ago. Made it nice for us to go out and lend a hand with both new mothers at the same time.

As for us "old folks," we're in the process of moving from our wonderful house in River Forest, Illinois where we've lived for 42 years, to something smaller. As I mentioned, Greg has retired, and all the children have flown the nest. (They do come back to visit, of course.) I manage to keep busy helping out at Seton Academy, where I drive the car pool once a week, as well as keep the books, and do the payroll and easy taxes. (Keeps me out of trouble.) I also do quite a bit of knitting, which I love (except in the hot weather).

Greg is home now, most of the time, although he enjoys dropping in at the hospitals where he is on the emeritus staff, just to say hello to his old friends. We hope to be able to spend more time at our place in Michigan where the children love to go and spend time in the summer, and on weekends during the year. Then, of course, there is the Annual White Family Oktoberfest, held in the Forest Preserves, and various family reunions, baptisms, weddings, christenings, and such, to get us all together. Birthdays, of course, pop up with increasing frequency.

Nearly all of our grandchildren and great-grandchildren were born at home, and of course, all were breastfed. The mothers of these children were and are all stay-at-home mothers. They made a lot of sacrifices to do that, but with careful managing, and buying food in quantity when it's on sale, and shopping at garage sales and resale shops, they did it. Of course, a great advantage of big families is the passing around of hand-me-downs. Everything from maternity dresses to children's clothes travel from family to family as it is needed. The old wicker bassinet my mother used for me when I was a baby 78 years ago, is still being used by our grandchildren.

A word to the wise, and those who want to preserve memories: take lots of pictures. We have heaps, and they're wonderful to behold.

As you can see, I love to talk about our family. It is truly my first love, starting, of course, with the wonderful man who made it all possible, my husband, Greg. So, God bless families, and long may they wave.

Mary Ann Kerwin

MAC: Mary Ann, what's happening today with the Kerwin family?

MAK: My life has changed dramatically since the busy days of what I call the "heavy-duty" stage of parenting, when often the days were long and the nights short. Throughout those years, I kept a favorite quote on my refrigerator, "Bloom where you are planted." I'm still living in Colorado but have moved just south of Denver to a town called Cherry Hills Village. Rearing eight of our nine children was a demanding but wonderful experience. After all these years, I remain convinced that parenting is the hardest, but most rewarding, job there is. It's worth every minute we put into it.

Mary Ann Kerwin's graduation from law school.

Our eight living children, five sons and three daughters, are now adults. They range in age from 45 down to 30 years old. Six live in Colorado. Seven are married now. I feel particularly fortunate because I can honestly say I really like and respect our two sons-in-law and five daughters-in-law. We have eleven grandchildren, all of whom have been breastfed even though two were born prematurely. I am inspired and humbled as I see our younger generation of parents in their parental roles. They are more at ease than I was in providing for the needs of their babies and children.

Our oldest, Tom, is a lawyer. He and his wife, Mary, have three children, Catriona (six), Mariana (four), and Declan (two). Ed, born in 1957, is a doctor— an allergist. Ed and his wife, Karen, have four children, Lewis (ten), Cecilia (eight), Clara (six), and Avery (four).

Greg, born in 1960, is also a lawyer. Greg is married to Donna. It was Greg who helped fill my empty arms after the death in 1959 of his older brother, Joe.

Our oldest daughter, Mary, born in 1961, is a mother and a family doctor. She is married to Dan Wilkerson, who is also a lawyer. Mary and Dan were married while she was in medical school. They now have two sons, Michael (14) and Ben (11), who happen to be our oldest grandchildren. Michael was born almost two months prematurely and he had hyaline membrane disease, jaundice, and a collapsed lung. Fortunately Mary was able to produce plenty of milk by using a double breast pump and her milk was given to Michael through a tube until he became strong enough to latch onto her breast. Mary was able to completely breastfeed Michael by the time he was about three weeks old. Ben was born only a month prematurely and was able to start breastfeeding the day he was born. Mary interrupted her medical studies when her sons were born but eventually she was able to finish medical school.

Anne, born in 1963 works in one of the most wonderful bookstores in the world, the Tattered Cover. She is everybody's favorite aunt. Anne loves to travel and periodically takes long trips to interesting places.

Katie, born in 1965, worked as a journalist for almost ten years before she married Cyrus McCrimmon, a Pulitzer-prize winning photographer. After Katie won the National spelling Bee in 1979, she became interested in journalism. For a number of years, she has been the ESPN commentator during the National Spelling Bee. Katie and Cyrus now have two sons, Sebastian (three) and Cormac (one). Katie had a difficult start with breastfeeding when Sebastian was born. But with great determination and excellent assistance, she succeeded. Cormac took to breastfeeding like a duck to water. Katie's sister, Mary, assisted with the births of both Sebastian and Cormac.

John, born in 1968, is now married to Lisa. He is pursuing a master's degree in computer science at the University of California at San Diego. Our youngest, Mike, born in 1970, just completed his doctorate in geology.

I became a lawyer 14 years ago. My primary practice has been in family law cases. I started law school in 1983, graduated in 1986, and then took the Colorado Bar Exam.

I decided to go to law school later in life. My husband almost died after surgery in 1982. I felt I had to get a job to help support our large family. At that time, our children were in graduate school, college, and high school. Dr. Niles Newton, who was serving on the LLLI Board of Directors at that time, suggested I consider law school. I had never thought of that even though my husband is a lawyer and two of our sons were then in law school. Because of Dr. Newton's belief in me and my great respect for her, I decided to apply to law school and was accepted. After I plunged in, I wondered sometimes if I was crazy to do this. It had been 30 years since I graduated from college. I felt as though I could literally feel my brain being stretched by this intense experience. My husband gave me lots of support and helped me as much as he could. However he had gone to law school 30 years before and there had been lots of changes during the interim. My children and I reversed roles. The two who were law students became my mentors. They also gave me the encouragement I needed to survive. Recently, I decided to become an inactive lawyer. As I prepare to turn 70 in 2001, I realize there are many personal matters I want to address which I have not been able to find time .to do. Nevertheless, I am still fascinated by legal issues. And with so many lawyers in our family, there is no shortage of opportunities to discuss legal matters!

I have continued to be very involved in LLLI. While I was an active member of the Board of Directors. I chaired, co-chaired, and served on a number of Board committees. Serving on the LLLI Board of Directors with so many superb women and a handful of men was in itself an ongoing education as well as an inspiration to me. Now, however, it is time for me to become an inactive member of the Board. I will change my status with confidence that LLLI is in very good hands.

MAC: What are your thoughts about the future of LLLI ?

MAK: I believe LLLI should continue to do what we do best, namely, give mother-to-mother support to breastfeeding mothers. The challenge is to find ways to reach out to mothers in all circumstances so that breastfeeding for a year or more becomes the norm. The number of breastfeeding mothers has increased substan-

Mary Ann Kerwin and her husband, Tom, with their grown-up children.

tially. For example, in Colorado, over 80 percent of new mothers now initiate breastfeeding. Unfortunately, by six months, only 39 percent are continuing to breastfeed. Far too many babies are not given the best start in life by being breast-fed for a year or more. The health and cognitive benefits have been clearly stated over and over again. LLLI is perfectly positioned to not only help mothers get started with breastfeeding but also to assist in increasing the duration of breast-feeding. LLLI has helped hundreds of thousands of mothers all over the world successfully breastfeed despite obstacles.

LLLI must continue to reach out to all breastfeeding mothers worldwide, listen to them, affirm them, embrace them. We must reach mothers of various economic and ethnic backgrounds. We must help mothers who work outside the home in addition to continuing to support those mothers who stay at home with their babies. Mother-to-mother support is needed as much or more than ever.

LLLI must continue to collaborate with doctors, nurses, hospitals, birthing centers, lactation programs, lactation consultants, and government agencies that offer breastfeeding support. Often health care providers are able to assist breast-feeding mothers and babies in ways LLLI cannot. In turn, health care providers must recognize that LLLI assists breastfeeding mothers and babies in ways they cannot, namely with our mother-to-mother support.

It seems clear that LLLI helped bring about the renaissance of breastfeeding all over the world. Dr. Jim Good, who with his wife Judy was one of our earliest supporters, entitled a talk he gave to physicians: "La Leche League to the Rescue!" In 1956, breastfeeding in the United States was a lost or dying art. I believe that never before in the history of the world had a resource as valuable as human milk been so widely discarded. Most US mothers (about 80 percent) were using infant formula. Only about 20 percent of mothers initiated breastfeeding. Subsequently, mothers in other countries including mothers in underdeveloped countries jumped on the formula bandwagon and abandoned breastfeeding. Eventually in 1974, the World Health Organization urged vigorous action to stress the importance of breastfeeding. LLLI was ready and eager to work with them. Then, in December 1979, the American Academy of Pediatrics in collaboration with the Canadian Paediatric Society issued "Breast-Feeding: A Commentary in Celebration of the International Year of the Child, 1979." The 1979 commentary was another milestone in the renaissance of breastfeeding.

I have been deeply involved with LLLI for almost two-thirds of my life. The tremendous worthiness of the cause of breastfeeding has kept me involved even when other demands on my time have made this involvement very difficult. The wonders of breastfeeding never cease to amaze me. It is not an exaggeration to say breastfeeding provides the perfect infant food and perfect method of infant feeding at minimal cost. With the passage of time, I am even more thrilled by the multiple benefits of breastfeeding. Some years ago, I was pleased to hear a member of the LLLI Health Advisory Council from Brazil, Dr. Jairo Osorno, refer to "the miracle of breastfeeding." Breastfeeding indeed is a miracle. Another favorite quote comes from HAC member, Ruth Lawrence, MD: "Breast Milk is A-Plus—Accessible, Acceptable, Affordable, Amazing!"

Another aspect that has kept me involved with LLLI is the wonderful people I have worked with, many of whom I consider good friends. This includes the other Founders, of course. To have had a support group of people, primarily women, who feel as strongly as I do about nurturing babies and in turn families has been extremely rewarding. I feel very fortunate to have worked with so many truly outstanding, inspiring people.

Finally, I remain involved with LLLI because there is still a tremendous need for LLLI. There are many factors today that challenge breastfeeding. I believe the primary factor is the fact that currently many mothers all over the world are employed outside the home or otherwise separated from their infants. This brings with it special challenges that must be overcome. LLLI has learned how to assist mothers who experience separation from their infants and is eminently suited to do so.

Periodically the Founders still get together to talk about LLLI. Being one of the seven Founders. has become a lifelong involvement even though initially I very casually said "yes" to Mary White's invitation to help start a breastfeeding organization. I certainly did not know then that LLLI would always be an important part of my life. I think all of the Founders feel this way-- that our getting together just kind of happened without much thought to the future. We simply said "yes" to an invitation. Perhaps we were the right people at the right time. We will never know if someone else might have done the same thing if we had not said "yes" when we did. Now that I have been involved for almost 45 years, I realize that LLLI will be a never-ending part of my life.

One of the key factors in helping LLLI move forward is the importance and emphasis the Founders placed on regularly communicating with each other. We found time to talk to and listen to each other (often late at night after our homes had quieted down!). As I look back at the ways we worked together for more than 40 years, clearly the seven us of worked as a team. We unknowingly were an example of the power of group dynamics. One of us would speak up and trigger the thoughts of the others. We energized, strengthened, and learned from each other. Frequently our discussions resulted in action. We were very results oriented. We had to make use of the limited amount of time we could extract from our family responsibilities which we always tried to keep primary. Without being consciously aware of this phenomenon, in retrospect I realize we all learned early the value of brainstorming. Further, we provided a mutual support group for each other not only regarding breastfeeding and mothering but also in regard to establishing one of the earliest mutual support groups in the US.

We learned individually and as a group to stretch beyond our boundaries and limitations. This was true both with our children and with LLLI. Working closely together we reinforced our mutual determination, optimism, self-discipline, sense of humor, courage, and perseverance. Then and now, we have retained our respect for each other even though we inevitably disagreed at times. During the course of these many years, we have developed a very deep friendship and kinship among ourselves. We are unquestionably united by a special bond. In retrospect, as I have said many times, LLLI is just the kind of organization I would have chosen had it not chosen me!

Mary Ann Cahill

MAC: It seems like only yesterday that my children were still all home and the noise of their comings and goings, of their growing up, filled the house. Now my home is quiet, especially so since I live on a country road just outside of town—McHenry, Illinois. Instead of a youngster bounding in from school and announcing in a loud voice, "Mom, I'm home," I now pick up messages on my answering machine. "Hi Mom, this is Charlie. Talk to you later." "This is Liz, Mom. Sorry I missed you." "Yo Mom. This is 'lil Robbie. Give me a call." They all call regularly and complain that I am the hardest member of the family to reach. (The busyness of my life surprises even me at times.)

Mary Ann Cahill's family.

Mary Ann Cahill's grandchildren.

My children are all grown now—my three sons, Bob, Tim, and Joe, and my six plus one daughters, Liz, Tee, Mary, Maggie, Charlie, Frannie, and Janet, our dear foster daughter/sister. They have long since spread their wings and scattered, east and west, to either coast and points in between, though three are within an hour's drive from me, for which I am grateful. There are 18 grandchildren and two great-grandchildren. One of the joys of my life has been watching my children parent their children, lavishing love and tenderness on the babies and patience and prayers on the teens. On occasion they have commented on examples of other, harsher parenting styles and found them wanting. Their reward is seeing their own children develop into kind and caring people. It is in their bones, to be passed on again.

But we are far from perfect. There have been some strong differences or what I would call misunderstandings between siblings, which saddened me, but there have also been reconciliations. And should one of the clan suffer an affront from the outside, the others rally to his or her defense. The love is evident, and when we get together, we have a wonderful time. My heart is full.

About La Leche League

La Leche League International offers many benefits to breastfeeding mothers and babies. Local La Leche League Groups meet monthly in communities all over the world, giving breastfeeding mothers the information they need and the opportunity to learn from one another. La Leche League Leaders, women who have nursed their own babies and who have met accreditation requirements, are only a phone call away. They provide accurate information on breastfeeding problems and can lend a sensitive ear to women with breastfeeding worries. You don't have to be a La Leche League member to contact a Leader or attend Group meetings. However, members receive added benefits. They receive LLLI's bimonthly magazine, NEW BEGINNINGS, which is filled with breastfeeding information, stories from nursing mothers, tips on discipline and common toddler problems, and news about breastfeeding from all over the world. Members also receive a 10% discount on purchases from LLLI's extensive Catalogue of carefully selected books, tapes, pamphlets, pumps, and other products for families. Members may also borrow books from local Group libraries. Membership is $30 a year in the USA and helps to support the work of local LLL Groups as well as LLL projects all over the world. You can pay your dues to the LLL Group in your area or directly to LLLI.

For more information on a Group and Leaders near you, call 1-800-LA LECHE. (In Canada, call 1-800-665-4324 or 613-448-1842.) You can also visit our award winning website at www.lalecheleague.org for more information about LLLI and resources for breastfeeding support. In addition to finding information on membership or a Group near you, you can also find links to Group pages in the USA and all around the world. You can learn about the history of La Leche League International, browse the LLLI Catalogue, or peruse a collection of articles and selected passages from LLLI publications. The website also offers information and schedules for online LLL meetings as well as information on upcoming educational opportunities offered by LLLI.